Say It Plain

Say It Plain

A Century of
Great African American Speeches

Edited by Catherine Ellis and Stephen Drury Smith

THE NEW PRESS

NEW YORK
LONDON

Requests for permission to reproduce selections from this book should be mailed to:
Permissions Department, The New Press, 38 Greene Street, New York, NY 10013

Published in the United States by The New Press, New York, 2005
Distributed by W. W. Norton & Company, Inc., New York

Pages 253–254 constitute an extension of this copyright page.

LIBRARY OF CONGRESS CATALOGING-IN-PUBLICATION DATA

Say it plain : a century of great African American speeches/
edited by Catherine Ellis and Stephen Drury Smith.
p.   cm.
Includes bibliographical references.
ISBN 1-56584-924-8 (hc.)
1. Speeches, addresses, etc., American—African American authors.
2. African Americans—History—Sources.   3. African American orators.
I. Ellis, Catherine, 1964–   II. Smith, Stephen, 1960–

PS663.N4S39   2005
815'.508896073—dc22   2004057646

The New Press was established in 1990 as a not-for-profit alternative to
the large, commercial publishing houses currently dominating the book
publishing industry. The New Press operates in the public interest rather
than for private gain, and is committed to publishing, in innovative
ways, works of educational, cultural, and community value that are often
deemed insufficiently profitable.

www.thenewpress.com

Composition by dix!

Printed in the United States of America

2   4   6   8   10   9   7   5   3   1

For Nina and Kobe,
Henry and Ben

CONTENTS

Preface   Catherine Ellis and Stephen Drury Smith   xi

Acknowledgments   xv

Introduction   James Oliver Horton   xvii

 1. Booker T. Washington
   Speech to the Atlanta Cotton States and International
   Exposition, 1895   1

 2. Marcus Garvey
   "Explanation of the Objects of the Universal Negro
   Improvement Association," 1921   7

 3. Mary McLeod Bethune
   "What Does American Democracy Mean to Me?" 1939   11

 4. Walter White
   Speech at NAACP Annual Convention, 1947   15

 5. Charles Hamilton Houston
   Personal Recording, 1949   21

6. Thurgood Marshall
Argument Before the U.S. Supreme Court in
Cooper v. Aaron, 1958   29

7. Howard Thurman
"Community and the Self," 1961   33

8. Dick Gregory
Speech at St. John's Baptist Church, 1963   41

9. Fannie Lou Hamer
Testimony Before the Credentials Committee, Democratic
National Convention, 1964   49

10. Stokely Carmichael
Speech at University of California, Berkeley, 1966   55

11. Martin Luther King Jr.
"I've Been to the Mountaintop," 1968   75

12. John Hope Franklin
Martin Luther King Jr. Lecture, The New School for
Social Research, 1969   87

13. Shirley Chisholm
"The Black Woman in Contemporary America," 1974   105

14. Barbara Jordan
Statement at the U.S. House Judiciary Committee
Impeachment Hearings, 1974   113

15. Benjamin L. Hooks
Speech at Gustavus Adolphus College, 1978   121

16. Joseph Lowery
"The Black Presence in America," 1980   137

17. Louis Farrakhan
Address to the National Press Club, 1984   149

18. Jesse Jackson
"Keep Hope Alive"
Democratic National Convention, 1988   163

19. Johnetta B. Cole
"Defending Our Name," 1994   179

20. Lani Guinier
"Different Voices, Common Talk: Why We Need a National
Conversation About Race," 1994   187

21. Clarence Thomas
    "Be Not Afraid," 2001   197
22. Randall Robinson
    "The Debt and the Reckoning," 2002   213
23. Julian Bond
    "The Broken Promise of *Brown*," 2004   227

Notes   243
Permissions   253

PREFACE

Say it Plain is the first published anthology of African American political oratory designed for the ear and the eye. All of the speeches, sermons,
and statements we selected feature an excerpt on the accompanying com-
pact discs. This fact shaped the collection in ways that might not be obvious to the listener and reader. *Say It Plain* does not claim to be the
definitive collection of rhetoric by African Americans. It is a sampling
from the great stream of words spoken by black Americans, exhorting the
nation to make good on its democratic principles. We cast down our buck-
ets into that broad, deep current. Reading the texts of these speeches
should be a satisfying, moving experience. But the words were meant to
be heard.

One influence on this project is the history of technology. Audio
recording of public figures dates back only to the late nineteenth century. Early recording equipment was too primitive to capture live events.
Most records were cut in a studio or a private room.[1] Phonograph and
wire recorders became better and less expensive over time, but until
the 1960s the practice of making audio recordings was generally left to

professionals in the music and radio industries.[2] Furthermore, African Americans were generally excluded from much of mainstream America's public discourse, whether written on paper or cut into the grooves of a phonograph record.

Another challenge was finding—and getting permission to use— historic recordings of black oratory. We got generous help from a number of archivists, librarians, and scholars in our search for sound. Family members and descendants of important African American orators also assisted. But many audio collections remain unpreserved or uncatalogued for lack of money or lack of institutional interest. In some cases, copyright holders demanded such high permission fees that important, historic speeches were placed outside the reach of this project. In other cases, the copyright holders declined our request outright, including the heirs of Malcolm X.

Finally, there are the limits of space, both in the book and on the CDs. We've tried to present a compelling and illuminating cross section of black political oratory from the past one hundred years. But there remain legendary speakers, significant events, and important political perspectives we wanted to include that had to be left out. We hope future projects—in books, over the airwaves, and on the Internet—will coax more of this great legacy of African American oratory back into our hearing.

About the Transcripts

The transcripts for this book were drawn from the accompanying recordings. In some cases, we were able to start with existing transcripts in the public domain and check them against the recordings. In other instances, we produced the transcripts ourselves, with the help of dedicated colleagues.

On some occasions the available text of a speech differed from the recording. Speakers commonly diverge from their written texts—which are sometimes speeches they give repeatedly—but no one takes the time to document the extemporaneous remarks. Each transcript here has been checked against the recordings by at least three sets of ears. But, occasionally, words in some of the recordings can be difficult to hear. We've used our best judgment to make the most faithful transcripts we can.

Catherine Ellis and Stephen Drury Smith

ACKNOWLEDGMENTS

We would like to thank Marc Favreau at The New Press for offering us the chance to assemble this anthology of African American oratory. We received tremendous help from our colleagues at American Radio Works and American Public Media, especially the redoubtable Ellen Guettler. We are also indebted to Neil Tassoni, Carey Biron, Bente Birkeland, Samantha Kennedy, Misha Quill, and Sasha Aslanian. We are grateful to Bill Buzenberg for his support of this project, and to Sara Meyer for her archival assistance.

We have enjoyed the goodwill and intellectual generosity of many researchers and archivists, including: Marilyn Costanzo at Boston University's School of Theology Archive, Kai Jackson at the Howard Thurman Center at Morehouse College, Chuck Howell at the University of Maryland's Library of American Broadcasting, Mark Torres and Brian De Shazor at Pacifica Radio Archives, and J. Fred MacDonald at his archive in Chicago. We are also grateful to the staff of the Miller Center of Public Affairs at the University of Virginia, the staff of the Vincent Voice Library at Michigan State University, and to Shola Lynch and Patricia Thompson. Several scholars helped guide our research. Thanks go especially to

James Cone, Randall Burkett, Barbara D. Savage, David Levering Lewis, and James Horton.

Finally, we are most grateful to the wonderful orators—or, in some cases, their heirs—who gave us permission to include the speeches in this collection.

INTRODUCTION

Rooted in the strong oral traditions of African culture, the act of public speech-making has historically been much more than just a means of communication for the African American people. Ancient Egyptians produced the earliest known written theoretical discussions of oratory, and formal instruction in rhetoric was an important part of their education system. "Speech is explicitly recognized as an important instrument of social life," observed anthropologist Ethel Albert, commenting on the culture of Burundi. "[E]loquence is one of the central values of the cultural worldview; and the way of life affords frequent opportunity for its exercise."[1] For early American blacks, bound in service to a land that claimed to be freedom-loving, public speaking was more than an important social instrument: it was a practical weapon against the power of slavery that sought to be all-controlling, a means to psychological and emotional survival, and a vehicle for maintaining personal dignity and self-respect. It was a means of resisting slavery's intent to reduce its victims to the level of subhuman property taking value solely from a master's appraisal.

Frederick Douglass, himself a former slave and a great advocate of antislavery, found his self-image in the language of freedom that allowed him to speak against the bondage into which he had been born. When he was a slave, thirteen years old and living in Baltimore, he happened upon a copy of *The Columbian Orator,* a collection of historically significant speeches compiled by New England educator Caleb Bingham. Having been taught to read by his master's wife, who broke both law and tradition in so doing, Douglass found the words in this little book inspiring and empowering. He purchased his own copy for fifty cents and read it over and over, practicing the rhetoric and taking courage from its message. He was especially attracted to a dialogue between a master and a slave in which the slave, after convincing his master to set him free, argued for the God-given right of human liberty and explained how much slaves hate those who withhold their freedom. As Douglass later recalled, "I got a bold and powerful denunciation of oppression and a most brilliant vindication of the rights of man." It was with this foundation that Douglass felt "equal to a contest with the religious advocate of slavery."[2]

Most slaves encountered the rhetoric of protest in words spoken by community leaders. By the mid nineteenth century, the oratory of the black preacher had become legendary among African Americans, slave and free alike. His message of hope and deliverance, of protest and resistance, served as both admonition and prescription. He spoke to men and women struggling to maintain relationships and to hold families together in the face of overwhelming odds and the unrelenting power of slaveholders' quest for ever-increasing profit. He spoke through biblical stories of the Israelites escaping slavery to the promised land, guided by wise men and protected by a mighty God. Christianity appealed to people of African ancestry bound in an unchristian-like slavery, in large part because it offered a message of redemption and salvation under the reign of a just God. Empassioned words confirming this belief provided the strength enslaved people needed to hope in the face of the hopelessness.

In northern freedom, African Americans regarded the art of public speaking as a critical tool for organization against slavery and for the establishment and maintenance of civil rights. In the free black communities, black schools and juvenile debating societies prepared young people to participate in the mutual aid and abolition societies. During the 1830s and 1840s, black Bostonians established the Boston Philomathean Society and the Young Men's Literary Debating Society to instruct African American youth in the ways of public oratory. Similar groups were organized in Philadelphia, New York, Cincinnati, and in many other urban black communities. The young people emerging from these groups became the community's leading voices of abolition.[3]

The power of the preacher's message was not only in his words but in his delivery and his ability to draw visual images with his inflection, his cadence, and the tonal and rhythmic quality of his articulation. African American secular speakers were deeply influenced by the preacher's style, and, like the men of the church, they often moved their listeners as much by the emotional impact of their presentation as by the power of their words. Douglass, who understood the importance of the logical argument, innovative conceptual structure, and the rhythm of rhetoric, was also moved and inspired by the power of good preaching. He understood, as did many who came before and after him, the importance of combining the message of faith and God's concern for the humans he created with the political messages of organization and alliance-building.

The importance of spoken words that moved listeners to action became the staple of American politics in the years before the Civil War. In some of the most important African American literature of the period, the spoken word often preceded written words. Much of Douglass's writings came directly from his abolitionist speeches and the stories he told on the antislavery speakers' circuit. *David Walker's Appeal*, the stinging indictment of American slavery and the hypocrisy of Christian slaveholders published in 1829 by a black Boston abolitionist, was first a speech that Walker delivered three years earlier before a gathering of the Massachusetts Colored Association, an early black antislavery organization.

These early speeches, as well as those throughout the antebellum and Civil War years, set a standard for those that followed during the late nineteenth century and into the twentieth century. They called to the conscience of the nation, to white America to live up to its creed that promised freedom and equality. They also called to black America to persist in demanding the rights of a free people. The speeches contained in this collection illustrate the range of rhetorical styles and strategic arguments adopted by black leaders over the last century and throughout history. They address the racial issues that have shaped American life and the African American struggle toward freedom. Differences in racial circumstances over time and in various regions of the country have evoked different approaches to protest and a variety of responses to the persistent racial injustice that has characterized American history.

These speeches were shaped by the changing nature of America's racial climate. Most are easily interpreted, calling out for racial justice and denouncing prejudice and discrimination. A few are more subtle, indicating the pressure under which the speaker was delivering the message. Booker T. Washington's "Atlanta Compromise Address," as his speech at the Atlanta Exposition of 1895 came to be known, was an appeal to the white South to continue its dependence on black labor and a call to African Americans not to abandon their Southern homes for the urban, industrializing North. Delivered at the height of the Jim Crow system of racial segregation and in the wake of the rising tide of Southern lynching and white terrorism directed at preventing African American political equality, Washington's words carried the weight of increasing racial oppression throughout the South. He urged black Southerners to settle for social and political inequality in exchange for limited economic opportunity. He assumed that the vast majority of African Americans would remain in the South and would need to reconcile themselves to slow progress within the context of the racial traditions of that region. His rhetoric encouraged blacks and whites of the South not to abandon one another, but to agree to immediate social stability, with the hope of eventual racial reconciliation.

Washington's message was challenged by other African Americans who refused to compromise their civil rights and the benefits of freedom. Throughout the 1890s the voices of black protest delivered a different, more militant demand for political and social equality. In the summer of 1905, twenty-nine black intellectuals, led by Dr. W.E.B. Du Bois, met in Niagara Falls, Canada, to draw up a manifesto calling for full civil liberties and the abolition of the Jim Crow system taking legal form throughout the American South. Subsequent annual meetings led to the formation in 1909 of the National Association for the Advancement of Colored People, the premier civil rights organization of the first half of the twentieth century.

Other twentieth-century speeches were more militant in tone, often reflecting the fact that they were given in the North, distant from the racial violence of the Jim Crow South. Some of the most stinging indictments of racial injustice in twentieth-century America came from Marcus Garvey, the Jamaican-born founder of the Universal Negro Improvement and Conservation Association and African Communities League. Garvey established the organization in 1914 to work for the worldwide improvement of the conditions of black people. Inspired by Washington's autobiography, *Up from Slavery,* and its message of racial self-help, Garvey wrote to Washington, who invited him to visit the United States. Washington died a few months before Garvey arrived, but the Jamaican found broad support for his program, which encouraged independent black economic organization and an aggressive appeal to racial pride. Although Garvey's tone and his personality differed greatly from that of the more conciliatory Washington, the men shared a belief in a determined use of American-style capitalism as the most effective route to racial opportunity. Chapters of Garvey's Universal Negro Improvement Association sprang up all across the country. By the 1920s it had become the largest mass organization of African Americans in U.S. history. Estimates of its membership range from two to four million. In the speech included in this volume, Garvey issues a call for African Americans to join with the UNIA as a point of racial solidarity and pride. He argued that black people around the world needed a nation of their own, where they could be self-governing and have wide opportunities to demonstrate their abilities and develop their talents.

In 1923, Garvey was convicted—falsely, many claim—of mail fraud and sentenced to five years in prison. Four years later, he was deported from the United States. By that time the tide of civil rights was running against his "back to Africa" program. The voices of black protest demanded equal rights and social justice in the United States. Leaders like Mary McLeod Bethune and Walter White guided major civil rights organizations, building the structure of the modern civil rights movement that burst on the national scene in the postwar years of the late 1940s. In the North a new group of black elected leaders gained prominence, lending their voices to the struggle. New York representative Adam Clayton Powell became a powerful spokesman for the Harlem community and for urban blacks across the nation. He demanded universal equality of opportunity and recognized the significant role blacks continued to play in broadening civil rights for all Americans.

During the 1950s and 1960s the voices of African America rose to a crescendo. The Supreme Court ruling in the 1954 *Brown v. Board of Education of Topeka, Kansas,* which came as the result of a half century of legal struggle against Jim Crow, struck down the legal basis for racial segregation in public education and paved the way for a broad assault on racial discrimination. In December of 1955, the arrest of Rosa Parks for refusing to give up her seat to a white passenger on a city bus in Montgomery, Alabama, led to an African American boycott of that city's bus system and signaled a quickening of the nonviolent direct-action civil rights movement. It also catapulted a young minister, Dr. Martin Luther King Jr., into the national spotlight as a major movement leader. During 1956, the fight to end racial discrimination in public transportation spread to other cities in the South, such as in Birmingham and Tallahassee, where blacks mounted effective campaigns. In all these efforts, the African American voice of protest was critical in rallying support in what, even as recently as the mid twentieth century, was a difficult and dangerous cause. Many blacks suffered the wrath of white resistance to the prospect of the end of white supremacy. In 1956 alone, black singer Nat King Cole was attacked on stage in a Birmingham theater by a white supremacist; the home of Martin Luther King Jr. in Montgomery, and that of Rev. F.L. Shuttlesworth, a civil rights leader in Birmingham, were bombed; and white mobs rioted at the University of Alabama, at Mansfield High School in Mansfield, Texas, and in Clay, Kentucky, in attempts to prevent school integration. As if to encourage such action, one hundred Southern members of the U.S. Senate and House of Representatives signed a manifesto condemning the Supreme Court's ruling against school segregation.

Clearly, there was determined opposition to the movement, yet the struggle for civil rights that had continued since the nineteenth century now moved more rapidly. It became ever more of a national issue as the new medium of television brought it live and often uncensored into the living rooms of middle-class America. Minute by minute coverage gave it even greater urgency and a more shocking impact. Now African American voices of protest were heard across the nation and around the world, making the rhetoric of equality and freedom an especially powerful weapon for civil rights advocates within the context of the Cold War. America's call for freedom from Communism abroad was weighed against America's response to the internal demands for racial justice. The ever-present media made it clear that when civil right protestors were attacked by white supremacist mobs, or when Southern law officials denounced efforts to enforce court decisions, it was not done in isolation. At the height of the Cold War, voices from the civil rights movement demanded that America live up to its professed beliefs in human rights, or acknowledge its hypocrisy before the eyes of the world. The bright lights of the visual media changed the equation, and as civil rights speakers painted verbal pictures of their efforts to overcome the forces of white supremacy and to make the basic rights of citizenship available to African Americans in the South, the message carried a credibility as never before, and "the whole world was watching."

The TV cameras were there in 1958 when baseball star Jackie Robinson, who had a decade earlier integrated the major leagues, joined with African American singer and actor Harry Belafonte and labor organizer A. Philip Randolph to lead ten thousand students in a Youth March for Integration of Schools in Washington, D.C. Two years later, when four North Carolina A&T college students sat down at a lunch counter in Greensboro to demand that they be served a cup of coffee, the violent response of local whites was also captured for the general TV audience. And as the movement spread rapidly, to Chattanooga, Nashville, Montgomery, Atlanta, Jacksonville, and elsewhere around the South, the student sit-in campaign became a regular major news event, drawing TV viewers and creating a national and international uproar.

African Americans felt that they had lost a powerful friend when President John F. Kennedy was assassinated in the fall of 1963, but President Johnson's works and actions in pressing for the passage of the 1964 Civil Rights Act served to reassure many. Obviously the presidential election of 1964 was a critical moment for the movement, and the outcome at the Democratic National Convention in Atlantic City, New Jersey, that year was an important test of the new Johnson administration's civil rights resolve. The integrated Mississippi Freedom Democratic Party (MFDP) appeared before the Democratic credentials committee and asked to be seated at the convention as Mississippi's official delegation. They argued that the all-white delegation presenting itself to the convention was not representative of the state's Democrats, since Mississippi blacks were barred from registering to vote by a series of racially restrictive state regulations. African Americans faced racial barriers to their voting throughout the South, but in Mississippi, where only 6.4 percent of blacks had managed to successfully negotiate the obstacles of literacy and citizenship tests, poll taxes, and violence at registration and polling sites, the situation was extraordinary.

The Mississippi Freedom Democratic Party delegation, made up mainly of sharecroppers, small businessmen, maids, and schoolteachers, had traveled to the convention by bus, to stay, four to a room, at the decaying Gem Hotel, a mile from Convention Hall, to represent the true Democratic constituency of their state. Most knew that their action would cost them their jobs or worse. That summer, civil rights workers in Mississippi had suffered thirty-five shootings, six murders, sixty-five home and church burnings, and at least eighty beatings. Still, they came to Atlantic City that August, dressed in their "Sunday-go-to-meeting best," to ask for an official place at the convention.

Among those testifying before the credentials committee on behalf of the Mississippi Freedom Democratic Party was Fannie Lou Hamer, a forty-six-year-old ex-sharecropper and one of the oldest field organizers of the Student Nonviolent Coordinating Committee of the period. She had been beaten and ejected from her sharecropping plantation when the landowner for whom she worked learned that she had tried to register to vote. In a powerful message to the committee, she argued that if the Freedom party was not seated after all it had risked to get to the convention, "I question America. Is this America, the land of the free and the home of the brave, where we have to sleep with our telephones off the hooks because our lives be threatened daily, because we want to live as decent human beings, in America?" she asked. Most African Americans shared Hamer's frustration, and many said so. From the determined message of SNCC leader Ella Baker to Stokely Carmichael's strident call for black power, the voice of black America refused to be hushed. By the mid 1960s, Malcolm X became a dominant spokesman, especially for young blacks. His appeal was in both his message of black pride and his style of defiance, confronting white authority. Malcolm's father had been a Garveyite, and Malcolm mixed Garvey's philosophy with the teachings of Nation of Islam founder Elijah Muhammad to indict white racism and those who used it as a weapon against black people. In the middle years of the sixties, black frustration boiled over into the violence of urban riots in Los Angeles; Newark, New Jersey; Detroit; and other American cities. The message was clear. Black America was "sick and tired of being sick and tired."

The preeminent civil rights spokesman of the period, Dr. Martin Luther King Jr., confronted white American complacency with nonviolent direct action against the most obvious signs of racial discrimination and stirred all America with his powerful rhetoric. King's last public address, "I've Been to the Mountaintop," delivered in Memphis, is one of his most moving, especially in the context of his assassination just hours later. The minister of nonviolence had met a violent death at the hands of a white sniper, but his words lived far beyond his death. For the next two generations and more, his words and those of other African Americans spoke to the conscience of America, appealing to national ideals and confronting the national self-image. In the inspiring words of Congresswoman Shirley Chisholm, calling black women to continue their traditional role as political organizers and leaders, or those of Jesse Jackson, urging America to "keep hope alive," or those of civil rights attorney Lani Guinier, issuing a reasoned call for a meaningful conversation on race, African Americans have continued to *say it plain,* to a nation that often seems bent on ignoring their voices.

The speeches in this collection span the twentieth century and beyond. They are the words of political activists, civil rights organizers, celebrities, and religious leaders, all critical symbols of the centuries-old struggle for American democracy. Here are some of the most important speeches by African Americans engaged in the most critical work that any citizen can perform, their voices a clarion call to the national conscience.

—James Oliver Horton
George Washington University

Say It Plain

1.

BOOKER T. WASHINGTON (1856–1915)

Speech to the Atlanta Cotton States and International Exposition

Atlanta, Georgia—October 18, 1895

One of the first African American speeches ever recorded in sound was one of great significance: Booker T. Washington's address at the Atlanta Cotton States and International Exposition. The fact that a black man was invited to speak to this all-white Southern audience was itself a historic event. Washington's words sparked a fundamental debate over race relations that burned for decades to follow: should black people concentrate on a gradual accumulation of skills and economic security or demand the full and immediate rights simply due them as American citizens?

Booker T. Washington was one of the last major black leaders born in slavery. He epitomized the American ideal of a self-made man, escaping poverty through relentless work and pursuit of education, and achieving international fame. Washington founded the Tuskegee Institute in Alabama in 1881. The black-run institution was designed to prove the worth of African Americans through self-improvement, education, moral uplift, and skilled labor. The students made the bricks for their new schools by hand.

Washington became a national figure with his Atlanta speech. He

urged African Americans to discard Reconstruction-era notions of social equality. Instead, he argued, most Southern blacks should pursue a
modest, methodical program of self-improvement through service and
labor. Washington beseeched whites to recognize how valuable this
loyal and unresentful workforce could be. He climaxed the speech with
a promise that many whites—uneasy about the threat that black ambi-
tions posed to their supremacy—found appealing: whites and blacks
could simultaneously live together and apart. "In all things that are
purely social, we can be as separate as the fingers, yet one as the hand
in all things essential to mutual progress."

The applause was described as thunderous, the scene extraordinary. Former slaveholders and Confederate officers gripped the hand
of the man born in slavery. White women tossed flowers to him.[1]

Historian David Levering Lewis counts Washington's Atlanta Exposition speech as "one of the most consequential pronouncements in
American History."[2] Washington's message was printed in newspapers across the country; white politicians North and South embraced
the speech and its author. So did most other black leaders—for a time.
The 1895 Atlanta speech came at a time when black hopes for an equi-
table place in American society were being decimated by the white
backlash against Reconstruction. Segregation laws multiplied across
the South as lynchings and other racial violence increased. To many,
Washington's message of modesty, rectitude, and service offered a
soothing promise of social order and gradual change. Before long,
though, other black leaders would assail Washington as an accommo-
dationist and, ultimately, a traitor to the race.

Eleven years after he made the Atlanta speech, Washington recorded portions of it in a Columbia Phonograph Company studio. The
recording date is known—December 5, 1906—but the location is not. It
is also unclear why Washington recorded the speech. Tim Brooks, a
historian of recorded sound, speculates the cylinder may have been
made for fund-raising or simply as a family heirloom. It is the only known
recording of Washington's voice.[3]

The recording is only three minutes and twenty-nine seconds long
and captures roughly a third of the speech. The maximum length of a
cylinder recording was about four minutes. Washington abridges his
speech by dropping the fifth paragraph. The recording ends after the

sixth paragraph. It is possible that Washington continued the address on additional cylinders that have not survived or been located.

By the time he made the recording, Washington's Atlanta speech—and his enormous power as a black leader—had come under growing attack from other African Americans, most famously by W.E.B. Du Bois. He was criticized for accommodating white supremacy and using his authority as the de facto spokesman for black America to suppress his rivals. Still, Washington was an enormously influential figure in African American history and a powerful speaker at a time when black social activism was under fierce attack in the South.

MR. PRESIDENT and Gentlemen of the Board of Directors and Citizens:

One-third of the population of the South is of the Negro race. No enterprise seeking the material, civil, or moral welfare of this section can disregard this element of our population and reach the highest success. I but convey to you, Mr. President and Directors, the sentiment of the masses of my race when I say that in no way have the value and manhood of the American Negro been more fittingly and generously recognized than by the managers of this magnificent Exposition at every stage of its progress. It is a recognition that will do more to cement the friendship of the two races than any occurrence since the dawn of our freedom.

Not only this, but the opportunity here afforded will awaken among us a new era of industrial progress. Ignorant and inexperienced, it is not strange that in the first years of our new life we began at the top instead of the bottom; that a seat in Congress or the state legislature was more sought than real estate or industrial skill; that the political convention or stump speaking had more attraction than starting a dairy farm or a stockyard.

A ship lost at sea for many days suddenly sighted a friendly vessel. From the mast of the unfortunate vessel was seen a signal, "Water, water; we die of thirst!" The answer from the friendly vessel at once came back, "Cast down your bucket where you are." A second time the signal, "Water, send us water!" went up from the distressed vessel, and was answered, "Cast down your bucket where you are." A third and fourth signal for water was answered, "Cast down your bucket where you are." The captain of the distressed vessel, at last heeding the injunction, cast down his bucket, and it came up full of fresh, sparkling water from the mouth of the Amazon River.

To those of my race who depend on bettering their condition in a foreign land or who underestimate the importance of cultivating friendly relations with the Southern white man who is their next-door neighbor, I would say: "Cast down your bucket where you are"—cast it down, making friends in every manly way of the people of all races by whom you are surrounded.

Cast it down in agriculture, mechanics, in commerce, in domestic service, and in the professions. And in this connection it is well to bear in mind that whatever other sins the South may be called to bear, when it comes to business, pure and simple, it is in the South that the Negro is given a man's chance in the commercial world, and in nothing is this Exposition more eloquent than in emphasizing this chance. Our greatest danger is that in the great leap from slavery to freedom we may overlook the fact that the masses of us are to live by the productions of our hands, and fail to keep in mind that we shall prosper in proportion as we learn to dignify and glorify common labor and put brains and skill into the common occupations of life, shall prosper in proportion as we learn to draw the line between the superficial and the substantial, the ornamental gewgaws of life and the useful. No race can prosper till it learns that there is as much dignity in tilling a field as in writing a poem. It is at the bottom of life we must begin, and not at the top. Nor should we permit our grievances to overshadow our opportunities.

"Cast down your bucket where you are!"

To those of the white race who look to the incoming of those of foreign birth and strange tongue and habits for the prosperity of the South, were I permitted I would repeat what I have said to my own race, "Cast down your bucket where you are." Cast it down among the eight millions of Negroes whose habits you know, whose fidelity and love you have tested in days when to have proved treacherous meant the ruin of your firesides. Cast down your bucket among these people who have, without strikes and labor wars, tilled your fields, cleared your forests, builded your railroads and cities, and brought forth treasures from the bowels of the earth, and helped to make possible this magnificent representation of the progress of the South. Casting down your bucket among my people, helping and encouraging them as you are doing on these grounds, and to education of head, hand, and heart, you will find that they will buy your surplus land, make blossom the waste places in your fields, and run your factories.

While doing this, you can be sure in the future, as in the past, that you and your families will be surrounded by the most patient, faithful, law-abiding, and unresentful people that the world has seen. As we have proved our loyalty to you in the past, in nursing your children, watching by the sick-bed of your mothers and fathers, and often following them with tear-dimmed eyes to their graves, so in the future, in our humble way, we shall stand by you with a devotion that no foreigner can approach, ready to lay down our lives, if need be, in defense of yours, interlacing our industrial, commercial, civil, and religious life with yours in a way that shall make the interests of both races one. In all things that are purely social, we can be as separate as the fingers, yet one as the hand in all things essential to mutual progress.

There is no defense or security for any of us except in the highest intelligence and development of all. If anywhere there are efforts tending to curtail the fullest growth of the Negro, let these efforts be turned into stimulating, encouraging, and making him the most useful and intelligent citizen. Effort or means so invested will pay a thousand percent interest. These efforts will be twice blessed—blessing him that gives and him that takes. There is no escape through law of man or God from the inevitable:

> *The laws of changeless justice*
> *Bind oppressor with oppressed;*
> *And close as sin and suffering joined*
> *We march to fate abreast.*

Nearly sixteen millions of hands will aid you in pulling the load upward, or they will pull against you the load downward. We shall constitute one-third and more of the ignorance and crime of the South, or one-third its intelligence and progress; we shall contribute one-third to the business and industrial prosperity of the South, or we shall prove a veritable body of death, stagnating, depressing, retarding every effort to advance the body politic.

Gentlemen of the Exposition, as we present to you our humble effort at an exhibition of our progress, you must not expect overmuch. Starting thirty years ago with ownership here and there in a few quilts and pumpkins and chickens (gathered from miscellaneous sources), remember the path that has led from these to the inventions and production of agricultural implements, buggies, steam-engines, newspapers, books, statuary, carvings, paintings, the management of drug stores and banks, has not been trodden without contact with thorns and thistles.

While we take pride in what we exhibit as a result of our independent efforts, we do not for a moment forget that our part in this exhibition would fall far short of your expectations but for the constant help that has come to our educational life, not only from the Southern states, but especially from Northern philanthropists, who have made their gifts a constant stream of blessing and encouragement.

The wisest among my race understand that the agitation of questions of social equality is the extremist folly, and that progress in the enjoyment of all the privileges that will come to us must be the result of severe and constant struggle rather than of artificial forcing. No race that has anything to contribute to the markets of the world is long in any degree ostracized. It is important and right that all privileges of the law be ours, but it is vastly more important that we be prepared for the exercise of these privileges. The opportunity to earn a dollar in a factory just now is worth infinitely more than the opportunity to spend a dollar in an opera-house.

In conclusion, may I repeat that nothing in thirty years has given us more hope and encouragement, and drawn us so near to you of the white race, as this opportunity offered by the Exposition; and here bending, as it were, over the altar that represents the results of the struggles of your race and mine, both starting practically empty-handed three decades ago, I pledge that in your effort to work out the great and intricate problem which God has laid at the doors of the South, you shall have at all times the patient, sympathetic help of my race; only let this be constantly in mind, that, while from representations in these buildings of the product of field, of forest, of mine, of factory, letters, and art much good will come, yet far above and beyond material benefits will be that higher good, that, let us pray God, will come, in a blotting out of sectional differences and racial animosities and suspicions, in a determination to administer absolute justice, in a willing obedience among all classes to the mandates of law.

This, coupled with our material prosperity, will bring into our beloved South a new heaven and a new earth.

2.

Marcus Garvey (1887–1940)

"Explanation of the Objects of the
Universal Negro Improvement Association"

New York City—July 1921

In the wake of World War I, a fiery Jamaican named Marcus Garvey created the largest black organization in America as well as a popular movement for African American self-reliance, racial pride, and economic power. Garvey inspired millions of African Americans with the dream of a separate, parallel society built on black-owned business and industry. He also preached about the need for international unity among peoples of African origin.

Garvey's Universal Negro Improvement Association (UNIA) was an ambitious, flamboyant, and doomed enterprise. From its Harlem office, the UNIA grew to hundreds of chapters in the U.S. and abroad. Garvey was a charismatic leader and an object of ridicule. He indulged a liking for parades and plumed military uniforms, which drew mockery from his opponents. He launched an array of business enterprises, including the Black Star Line, a shipping company. Bad management undermined Garvey's business schemes. The shipping line foundered. In 1923, Garvey was convicted of mail fraud for Black Star Line stock deals. He served two years in jail and was deported to Jamaica.

Garvey was deeply influenced by Booker T. Washington's example of self-reliance and moral uplift, but did not agree with Washington's accommodating stance on race relations. Rather than compromise with white Americans, Garvey urged blacks to abandon them. He railed against race mixing and openly distrusted light-skinned blacks (who often dominated leadership positions in rival organizations such as the NAACP). One of Garvey's most controversial acts was to meet with Ku Klux Klan leaders in Atlanta in 1922 to demonstrate his agreement with the KKK's view on miscegenation.

By all accounts, Marcus Garvey was a brilliant public speaker. He attracted much of his enormous political following with words. As a boy in Kingston, Jamaica, Garvey was captivated by raucous street debaters and the stirring cadences of black preachers. He practiced oratory at home, reading aloud from his school reader and watching himself in the mirror.[1] In America, Garvey scolded blacks for abetting their own oppression through moral lassitude. "Sloth, neglect, indifference caused us to be slaves. Confidence, conviction, action will cause us to be free men today," he proclaimed.[2]

The Liberty Halls Garvey and his followers bought in a number of major American cities became the center of UNIA activity. Garvey's home base was the Liberty Hall in Harlem, where nightly meetings drew up to six thousand people at a time.[3] In July of 1921, Garvey recorded two short speeches on a 78 rpm record at a studio in New York. One side was a version of the UNIA's mission statement, "Explanation of the Objects of the Universal Negro Improvement Association," the other, a complaint about federal efforts to deny Garvey a reentry visa after a foreign trip.[4]

These are the only known recordings of the famous public speaker. Garvey's performance on the disc hardly sounds like the work of a stem-twisting orator, but bellowing into a lifeless microphone or a recording horn was nothing like exhorting a throng of excited followers. Many performers froze up—or at least stiffened—in front of the recording machine. The time limits of three to seven minutes on early discs and cylinders also made true oration difficult.[5] Garvey's recorded speech is hard to hear at times. Early 78 rpm discs were prone to a high level of surface noise that competed with the music or voice being played back. Repeated playing made the problem worse as the surface of the disc wore away beneath the weight of a steel needle.[6]

The three-and-a-half-minute recording is less than a third the length of Garvey's complete membership appeal. Whether it was intended for mass production or simply to preserve Garvey's voice is unclear.

FELLOW CITIZENS of Africa, I greet you in the name of the Universal Negro Improvement Association and African Communities League of the World. You may ask, what organization is that? It is for me to inform you that the Universal Negro Improvement Association is an organization that seeks to unite into one solid body the 400 million Negroes of the world; to link up the 50 million Negroes of the United States of America, with the 20 million Negroes of the West Indies, the 40 million Negroes of South and Central America with the 280 million Negroes of Africa, for the purpose of bettering our industrial, commercial, educational, social and political conditions.

As you are aware, the world in which we live today is divided into separate race groups and different nationalities. Each race and each nationality is endeavoring to work out its own destiny to the exclusion of other races and other nationalities. We hear the cry of England for the Englishman, of France for the Frenchman, of Germany for the Germans, of Ireland for the Irish, of Palestine for the Jews, of Japan for the Japanese, of China for the Chinese.

We of the Universal Negro Improvement Association are raising the cry of Africa for the Africans, those at home and those abroad. There are 400 million Africans in the world who have Negro blood coursing through their veins. And we believe that the time has come to unite these 400 million people for the one common purpose of bettering their condition.

The great problem of the Negro for the last 500 years has been that of disunity. No one or no organization ever took the lead in uniting the Negro race, but within the last four years the Universal Negro Improvement Association has worked wonders in bringing together in one fold four million organized Negroes who are scattered in all parts of the world, being in the 48 states of the American union, all the West Indian Islands, and the countries of South and Central America and Africa. These 40 million people are working to convert the rest of the 400 million scattered all over the world and it is for this purpose that we are asking you to join our ranks and to do the best you can to help us to bring about an emancipated race.

If anything praiseworthy is to be done, it must be done through unity. And it is for that reason that the Universal Negro Improvement Association calls upon every Negro in the United States to rally to its standard. We want to unite the Negro race in this country. We want every Negro to work for one common object, that of building a nation of his own on the great continent of Africa. That all Negroes all over the world are working for the establishment of a government in Africa means that it will be realized in another few years.

We want the moral and financial support of every Negro to make the dream a possibility. Already this organization has established itself in Liberia, West Africa, and has endeavored to do all that's possible to develop that Negro country to become a great industrial and commercial commonwealth.

Pioneers have been sent by this organization to Liberia and they are now laying the foundation upon which the 400 million Negroes of the world will build. If you believe that the Negro has a soul, if you believe that the Negro is a man, if you believe the Negro was endowed with the senses commonly given to other men by the Creator, then you must acknowledge that what other men have done, Negroes can do. We want to build up cities, nations, governments, industries of our own in Africa, so that we will be able to have the chance to rise from the lowest to the highest positions in the African commonwealth.

3.

MARY MCLEOD BETHUNE
(1875–1955)

"What Does American Democracy Mean to Me?"

America's Town Meeting of the Air, New York City—November 23, 1939

In the New Deal era, educator and activist Mary McLeod Bethune was called the "First Lady of the Struggle" for her influence on the Roosevelt administration on civil rights issues. In 1904, Bethune founded a small school for black girls in Florida that she quickly built into a thriving college-prep and vocational training program. In 1923, she merged the school with Cookman College to create the first fully accredited black institution of higher learning in the state.

Bethune was born to former slaves in 1875. One of seventeen children, she grew up picking cotton in Sumter County, South Carolina. Her parents owned a five-acre parcel of land, and her mother continued to work for the family that once owned her. Though her parents and siblings were illiterate, Bethune knew as a child that she wanted to escape "the dense darkness and ignorance" in which she found herself.[1] Her ambition to read was only fueled by a white girl who once commanded her to put down a book, saying, "You can't read."[2]

Bethune was one of the first youngsters to sign up for a new mission school for black children built near her home. She recalled, "That first morning on my way to school I kept the thought uppermost, 'put that down—you can't read,' and I felt that I was on my way to read."[3] Bethune was not only on her way to read, she was on her way to a life-long career devoted to educating a people only a generation or two away from slavery.

As an adult, Bethune's influence soon extended far beyond the South. She was a gifted organizer and became a leader in the effort to build coalitions among black women fighting for equal rights, better ed-ucation, jobs, and political power. After leading numerous local, re-gional, and national women's clubs, Bethune founded a new umbrella organization in 1935, the National Council of Negro Women. Through this work Bethune became close friends with Eleanor Roosevelt, who encouraged Franklin D. Roosevelt to name Bethune director of the Of-fice of Minority Affairs in the National Youth Administration in 1935. Bethune lunched regularly with Mrs. Roosevelt in the White House.[4]

As a member of FDR's "black cabinet," Bethune was the only African American woman to hold an influential post in the administra-tion. She met every Friday night at home with her black colleagues and civil rights leaders such as Charles H. Houston, Walter White, and A. Philip Randolph. She called the men together to stay apprised of their work and to use her influence to improve the lives of African Americans and fight inequality.[5]

Bethune's position gave her access not only to the president but, on occasion, to a radio audience of millions. On the eve of America's en-trance into World War II, she joined a panel discussion on NBC radio's weekly public affairs broadcast of "America's Town Meeting of the Air." The panelists addressed the question, What does American democ-racy mean to me? With her Victorian elocution and a thunderous tone, Bethune reminded her listeners that African Americans had always been willing to die for American democracy but were still shut out from its promise of freedom.

DEMOCRACY IS FOR ME, and for 12 million black Americans, a goal towards which our nation is marching. It is a dream and an ideal in whose ultimate realization we have a deep and abiding faith. For me, it is based on Christianity, in which we confidently entrust our destiny as a people. Under God's guidance in this great democracy, we are rising out of the darkness of slavery into the light of freedom. Here my race has been afforded [the] opportunity to advance from a people 80 percent illiterate to a people 80 percent literate; from abject poverty to the ownership and operation of a million farms and 750,000 homes; from total disfranchisement to participation in government; from the status of chattels to recognized contributors to the American culture.

As we have been extended a *measure* of democracy, we have brought to the nation rich gifts. We have helped to build America with our labor, strengthened it with our faith and enriched it with our song. We have given you Paul Lawrence Dunbar, Booker T. Washington, Marian Anderson and George Washington Carver. But even these are only the first fruits of a rich harvest, which will be reaped when new and wider fields are opened to us.

The democratic doors of equal opportunity have not been opened wide to Negroes. In the Deep South, Negro youth is offered only one-fifteenth of the educational opportunity of the average American child. The great masses of Negro workers are depressed and unprotected in the lowest levels of agriculture and domestic service, while the black workers in industry are barred from certain unions and generally assigned to the more laborious and poorly paid work. Their housing and living conditions are sordid and unhealthy. They live too often in terror of the lynch mob; are deprived too often of the Constitutional right of suffrage; and are humiliated too often by the denial of civil liberties. We do not believe that justice and common decency will allow these conditions to continue.

Our faith in visions of fundamental change as mutual respect and understanding between our races come in the path of spiritual awakening. Certainly there have been times when we may have delayed this mutual understanding by being slow to assume a fuller share of our national responsibility because of the denial of full equality. And yet, we have always been loyal when the ideals of American democracy have been attacked. We have given our *blood* in its defense—from Crispus Attucks on Boston Commons to the battlefields of France. We have fought for the democratic principles of equality under the law, equality of opportunity, equality at the ballot box, for the guarantees of life, liberty and the pursuit of happiness. We have fought to preserve one nation, conceived in liberty and dedicated to the proposition that *all* men are created equal. Yes, we have fought for America with all her imperfections, not so much for what she is, but for what we *know* she can be.

Perhaps the greatest battle is before us, the fight for a new America: fearless, free, united, morally re-armed, in which 12 million Negroes, shoulder to shoulder with their fellow Americans, will strive that this nation under God will have a new birth of freedom, and that government of the people, for the people and by the people shall not perish from the earth. This dream, this idea, this aspiration, *this* is what American democracy means to me. [applause]

4.

WALTER WHITE
(1893–1955)

Speech at NAACP Annual Convention

Lincoln Memorial, Washington, D.C.—June 29, 1947

Walter White was known as "Mr. NAACP." He joined the staff of the National Association for the Advancement of Colored People (NAACP) in 1918, after serving as an NAACP volunteer in Atlanta. When asked to speak at a mass meeting he had organized in his hometown in 1917, White stood up and cried, "We have got to show these white people that we aren't going to stand being pushed around any longer. As Patrick Henry said, so must we say, 'Give me liberty, or give me death!' "[1] It was the start of a long career as the NAACP's primary spokesman.

Founded in 1909 by W.E.B. Du Bois and a group of liberal whites, the NAACP was the nation's most influential civil rights organization through the 1950s. Walter White ran it from 1931 to 1955.

White began to investigate lynchings in the South as soon as he joined the NAACP's national staff in New York. With light skin and blue eyes, he often passed as a white man, getting firsthand accounts of hideous crimes. The NAACP regularly protested lynchings, sending letters to government officials and newspapers and generating publicity for their anti-lynching campaign. With White on board, they had a new weapon for exposing such crimes. As White's biographer, Kenneth Janken, reports, "From 1918 to 1930 [White] investigated forty-one lynchings, and eight race riots . . . His easy manner, Atlanta roots, and white appearance gave him sources in mobs and Ku Klux Klan circles that were the journalists' envy. On one occasion he was deputized and given permission to shoot blacks . . ."[2] The work was dangerous, but White reveled in it. He "delighted in making fools of unsuspecting white supremacists and utilizing his ambiguous appearance to demonstrate the absurdity of racial categorization," Janken writes.[3]

White took over as executive secretary of the NAACP in 1931. He was by turns charming and imperious, affable and demanding. He alienated important co-workers, including Du Bois himself, but he was also adept at gaining friends in high places, among them Eleanor Roosevelt. White had her help securing FDR's support for various civil rights initiatives, though he could not get the president to endorse an antilynching bill.[4]

President Harry Truman was more responsive to White's entreaties. Following a race riot in Columbia, Tennessee, in which 106 black men were arrested and 2 shot dead in jail, White met with Truman to discuss mob violence against blacks. According to historian Adam Fairclough, Truman reacted quickly to the problem, appointing a fifteen-member commission to recommend effective ways to protect the civil rights of blacks. The commission's report, *To Secure These Rights*, would become a milestone in civil rights history. It called for the elimination of segregation in every area of American life.[5]

As the commission prepared its report, Truman agreed to another of White's requests: to speak at an NAACP mass meeting at the Lincoln Memorial in June 1947. Historian Barbara Savage notes that White was "a skilled publicist."[6] He arranged for the four major radio networks, a host of independent radio stations, and even the State Department to broadcast Truman's speech. The first president to address the NAACP's convention would be heard by millions of listeners around the world. So would Walter White.

White's introduction to Truman's speech, presented here, reflects the increasingly forceful demands for equality that African Americans made following World War II. This was one of many public speeches

White made against segregation. He often emphasized the hypocrisy of asking black soldiers to fight for American democracy abroad while denying them fundamental rights, and basic human dignities, at home.

LADIES AND GENTLEMEN, many thousands are here today at the feet of Abraham Lincoln in Washington. I am told that between 30 and 40 million other Americans may be listening to the radio at this hour. Countless other millions listen overseas by short-wave broadcast.

We are gathered together because of our deep concern for human rights. This is in great contrast to another meeting on Lincoln's birthday in 1909, 38 years ago. Then there were but a handful: men and women, white and Negro. They had been moved to meet by a Southern white man, who had just returned from Springfield, Illinois, Abe Lincoln's old home. There this man, the late William English Wally, had witnessed and written about a bloody race riot. He couldn't take it, just as you and I can't take it today. He felt something had to be done about race-hate and violence, just as you and I feel something must be done right now. That day the National Association for the Advancement of Colored People began.

Pessimists say the race question is insoluble. Insoluble? See what has been done in a single generation. 600,000 Americans, Negro and white, are banded together in 1,509 branches of the NAACP. They have helped to work a quiet, bloodless revolution in public opinion on this question. Although that change is sometimes obscured by the shocking acquittal of self-confessed lynchers in South Carolina or by obscenities of speech and action on the floor of the Congress. Let's look at the record. In a government of laws the chief bulwark of freedom for the oppressed is the courts.

Negroes know all too well that there's many a slip between law and living. But during its 38 years, the NAACP has taken to the United States Supreme Court 24 cases involving fundamental human and citizenship rights. It has won 22. [applause] As a result, every American, white as well as Negro, is assured a fair trial in a court not dominated by a mob. No man can legally be denied the right to vote in a primary election because of his color, although there still are some who would deny that right despite the Supreme Court and the Constitution. No man or woman because of color can legally be denied equal education in tax-supported schools. Every man, regardless of race, is legally entitled to first-class travel accommodations in return for payment of first-class fare. No labor union can legally deny a man the right to work by excluding him because of color.

Substantial progress has been made in gaining court decisions requiring equality, but it is the Association's conviction and contention that there will never be complete equality until the courts and America abandon the myth of separate but equal accommodation. [applause] None of us is naïve enough to believe that court decisions or legislation by themselves are enough, but legal action and laws set the pattern, both in restraining the lawless and in the education of decent public opinion.

The NAACP came into being 38 years ago because decent Americans just could not take the evils of mob violence and racial bigotry. We carry on today because we just can't take the gouging out of the eyes of a Negro war veteran by a South Carolina policeman, who was speedily set free. We just can't take the acquittal of men who have taken the law into their own hands and thereby lynched, not only American citizens, but the law as well. We just can't take the denial to any American citizen of the right to work, to vote, to live outside a ghetto, to share the privileges, as well as the responsibilities of citizenship, solely because of the color of his skin.

The NAACP operates on the proved principle that no nation can exist half free, half slave. We know that throughout history, bigots have grown powerful by first attacking the most vulnerable minority in a nation and then proceeding to attack others, until liberty was destroyed for everybody, including the bigots. Hitler did that in Germany. Mussolini did it in Italy. Racist bigots backed by selfish and frightened economic groups are attempting to set race against race, creed against creed, class against class in America today. They must not, they will not, be permitted to succeed. [applause]

Today there sit among the special guests upon the platform ambassadors from many of the nations of the earth. We ask you, Gentlemen, to tell your countrymen that although the stories of lynching and denial of justice to Americans because of race, creed, or national origin are all too often true, these outrages do not represent the majority of American citizens. [applause] We confess to our shame that ours is not yet a perfect democracy. We have grievous faults, but this great assemblage of American citizens and the presence of the President of the United States, of Mrs. Roosevelt, and of the distinguished Republican senator from Oregon attest that a determined and incessant attack is being made upon our national shortcomings. We are resolved to make our nation truly a government of the people, by the people and for the people. [applause] We know full well that what is done here in America has immediate and far-reaching effect upon the fortunes and aspirations of the two-thirds of the world's people whose skins are colored.

The NAACP has done its work, not through large endowments, but by the voluntary contributions of thousands of Americans, white as well as Negro, who want to make democracy real. We are proud that our national office is housed in the Wendell Willkie Memorial building in New York City, dedicated to the memory of a great American who fought for freedom for all men, everywhere. No political party has ever been permitted or ever will be permitted to influence the Association's policy. We firmly believe that our way of life can be destroyed only from within and not from without. If we, as Americans, assure that no man is denied any right of citizenship because he is dark of skin or worships his God in a different place or was born elsewhere, then democracy can never be destroyed. But we also know that human freedom must be in the hearts of men and not solely on paper. To this high objective, today we dedicate our every energy. We welcome to the struggle, whose outcome will help to determine the future of mankind, every citizen who believes that the Bill of Rights means what it says.

Ladies and Gentlemen, the President of the United States. [applause]

5.

CHARLES HAMILTON HOUSTON (1895–1950)

Personal Recording

Washington, D.C.—December 1949

Charles Hamilton Houston was endowed with a formidable intellect, relentless drive, and a heart that couldn't keep up. The only child of a lawyer and a hairdresser in Washington, D.C., he attended M Street High School, the city's elite African American college-preparatory school. In 1915, Houston graduated from Amherst College.

In World War I, Houston was sent to a segregated officers' training camp. He was commissioned as a second lieutenant and shipped to France in 1918. Houston never saw combat, but the racism against black soldiers he witnessed and experienced during the war made him determined to fight segregation when he got home.

Houston attended Harvard Law School, where he specialized in constitutional law. "I made up my mind," Houston said, "that I would never get caught . . . without knowing . . . my rights; that I would study law and use my time fighting for men who could not strike back."[1] He did just that. From the mid-1920s until the time of his death, Houston was the chief architect of the legal strategy to defeat Jim Crow segregation, especially in America's public schools.

While in private practice in the mid-1920s, Houston began teaching at all-black Howard University's night law school. In 1929, he became dean of that school and, in the span of a couple years, transformed it into a premier training ground for black lawyers. One of Houston's star pupils was future Supreme Court Justice Thurgood Marshall. Marshall recalled Houston as an unrelenting perfectionist: "If we did a slipshod job, boy, he would lay it on you. . . . We nicknamed him Iron Pants and Cement Shoes. We named him everything. But he insisted on perfection." Ultimately, Marshall said, there was little he did in the practice of law "that wasn't the result of what Charlie Houston banged into my head."[2]

In 1934, Houston left Howard University to become special counsel to the National Association for the Advancement of Colored People (NAACP). There he directed a range of legal assaults on Jim Crow laws. Thurgood Marshall soon joined him at the NAACP. Houston toured the South by automobile, documenting the world of segregation on film and in notebooks, delivering speeches, meeting with state officials, and campaigning for local NAACP branches. In his first year with the organization, he logged nearly twenty-five thousand miles.[3]

Though Houston left the NAACP in 1940 to return to private practice, he continued the fight against unfair treatment of blacks, including discrimination in work and housing. By the time of his death in 1950, Houston saw the campaign for civil rights in the United States as part of a larger struggle by oppressed people in every corner of the world.

In the fall of 1949, Houston began suffering chest pains. His good friend and doctor Edward Mazique diagnosed heart disease. After spending weeks confined to a hospital bed, Houston, along with his five-year-old son, Charles Hamilton Houston Jr. ("Bo"), moved in with Mazique and his wife over Christmas. (Houston's wife had been hospitalized for some temporary health problems.) While there, Houston gave the Maziques one of his prized possessions, a 1930s poster advertising a rally in Amsterdam for nine black teenage boys on trial in Scottsboro, Alabama. Charged with raping two white women, the boys faced the death penalty. When the Maziques asked Houston if he had any thoughts he wanted to share with them—or to preserve for five-year-old Bo—Houston asked them to pull out their tape recorder.[4] Here is the transcript of that tape, the only known recording of Houston's voice.

Four months after he made the recording, Charles Houston died of heart failure. Friends say Houston literally worked himself to death. He was fifty-four years old.[5]

The first few minutes of the tape are hard to hear; unintelligible portions have been indicated by ellipses.

I THINK I'LL START with you just about the time that I began to get acquainted with Bill Patterson, who was the Secretary of the ILD [International Labor Defense]. I'd known Bill Patterson as a young lawyer in New York at 200 West 135th Street. At the time he had . . . I used to come by the office all the time on my way from law school. Pat was . . . feeling his way along, he was discontented; finally he joined the Communist Party, and then the next thing I knew about him, he went to Russia. I didn't hear anything more from him for about four or five years, and the next thing I knew he turned up as a member of the International Labor Defense. . . .

About this time, the freight trains were . . . hobos looking like blackbirds and all at once Scottsboro burst on the scene. At the time, the NAACP [and] the ILD [were] trying to get a hold of the Scottsboro case.

The ILD won—and it was very important that the ILD did win—because it marked a historic departure in the struggle for Negro life in the South; certainly a departure since the days when the Negroes in the South had lost their franchise and the masses of the Negroes in the South had ceased to be vocal, articulate, and powerful, in the sense of being masters of their own destiny.

I'm not dealing so much with the matter of the trial of the Scottsboro cases, although even there, there was a new approach in the handling and fighting of Negro cases in the South. I've always said that in the preliminary struggle for the admission of Negroes on the jury, which took place in the second trial that was handled by Sam Leibovitz, who is now a judge in Brooklyn. When Sam Leibovitz stood up before Tom Knight, who was then Attorney General of Alabama, and shouted at him, "Take your finger out of those witnesses' face. Stand back and call him Mister." In addressing a Negro witness—there was a new day in the manner of the insistence, the absolute insistence, without any apology whatsoever, that Negro witnesses *and* Negroes be given the same rights in the Southern court as anybody else. I witnessed the argument of the first Scottsboro case by Walter

Pollak in the Supreme Court of the United States, which established the historic principle that every defendant accused of crime is entitled to counsel. I witnessed Leibovitz argue the second case. But even more fundamental than that, the significance of the Scottsboro case is in the new approach and the identification of the masses of the people in the struggle for liberation.

Prior to the Scottsboro case, certainly within my history, when Negroes in the South had been lynched, or where they had been persecuted in the courts, struggle and effective struggle was made for them. But the masses of Negroes themselves were not identified with the struggle. Rather, the tendency in the South up to that time had been for the masses of Negroes to try to stay away from those Negroes who found themselves in trouble, with the idea of not letting trouble spread, and also with the idea of avoiding consequences to themselves. This probably stemmed from the terror of the Ku Klux Klan days, and also the general disfranchisement and the oppression under which the South finally culminated its domination of the Negro in the revision of the Virginia Constitution of 1901.

But in the Scottsboro case, for the first time, the masses of Negroes were identified with the struggle itself, were made to feel it was *their* struggle, were made to feel that even without the ordinary weapons of democracy, they still had the force of what you might call primeval pressures with which they themselves could bring to bear pressure and affect the results of the trial and of the cases which were pending. On top of that, the whole struggle was interpreted to them in a different way, and the people who, up to that time, had been considered to be almost unorganizable suddenly were transformed into an articulate protesting mass bent upon their own freedom.

They were taught for almost the first time in the Scottsboro cases that the whole setup of the Southern government was an instrumentality which was not designed to give them justice but to keep them in their places and to keep them subject to domination. They were taught, as a matter of fact, that the courts were instrumentalities of the status quo and that they must ultimately depend for their liberation upon their *own* power and the solidarity of the white and the black masses of the South.

There were lots of crude things done. There were lots of things done which had no immediate effect. For example, I am quite certain that there was no immediate effect in the hundreds of telegrams which were poured in. But you've got to consider even this situation from two aspects: the aspect of the effect on the judge, which was perhaps in the immediate instance nothing, and the effect of the sending of the telegram upon the man who sent it—and there, of course, there was the identification with the struggle, the recognition of the struggle, and the commitment to the struggle. Because nobody who ever sent a telegram of protest to any of the Scottsboro judges, whether on the trial court, Supreme Court of Alabama, or the United States Supreme Court, ever inside himself accepted the fact that he was willingly from then on going to tolerate the system and the oppression to which he hitherto had been unresistingly subject to.

But even more important than the domestic aspects of the Scottsboro case—and the reason why I say that it was historically necessary that this Scottsboro case be fought out by the ILD instead of the NAACP—was its international aspect. To my mind the most significant part of Scottsboro was not the judicial process in the United States of America, where after three appeals to the United States Supreme Court, the sentences were finally affirmed in substance—under the theory that if you try a case long enough, if the government tries a case long enough, the defense will finally run out of errors on which to seek a conviction. And inevitably, if the government, with all of its power, keeps the case or defendant in court long enough, the defendant ultimately will be convicted—especially if he belongs to a minority oppressed group. The whole purpose of this trial is to establish the dominance of the ruling class over this oppressed minority. So that from the standpoint of judicial maneuvering and judicial process, the significance of the case is not that it finally resulted in the convictions of the Scottsboro boys drawing out for years of their lives, some 20 years of their lives or 10 years of their lives, until they were finally paroled. But the historical significance of the Scottsboro case and its new departure is the identification of the masses of the *world* with the struggle of the masses of the Negroes in the United States. And that was done by the protest meetings in foreign countries, by the demonstrations before the United States consulates, and by the speaking and the crusade that was carried on in these other countries.

And there we come down now to the picture of this poster of the great open-air protest meeting in Amsterdam, Holland. I think it's significant in this picture, and also prophetic, that one of the speakers is from Indonesia. And that in 17 years after the Scottsboro meeting, the Indonesians have now achieved a status of equality and independence inside of the Dutch federation of nations, if you want to speak of it that way. I think it is also significant that here, inside of 17 years, you have seen, not necessarily out of Scottsboro, but as a part of a struggle which Scottsboro itself symbolized, the movement of the great masses of the people.

The other thing is that it is necessary to establish the principle of the indivisibility of liberty, so that the masses recognize that no matter where liberty is challenged, no matter where oppression lifts its head, it becomes the business of *all* the masses. So, the protest meetings in Amsterdam, the protest meetings in Argentina, the protest meetings in Cuba, in France, in England and other places against Scottsboro, tended to educate the masses of the people locally as to their own situation and as to the relationship between their situation and the situation here in America.

There's nothing new in this approach of appealing to foreign countries for aid in local situations—we did it in the revolution when we sent Benjamin Franklin to France; we did it in the Civil War at the time when we sent Frederick Douglass to England. The only thing revolutionary is in the people who did it! The fact that here the masses begin to turn, the masses begin to arise. When I say *begin,* I don't mean *begin* in the strict grammatical sense that they had never done anything until then. But any new struggle is a beginning, it is a new commitment; and in that sense, the international aspect of the Scottsboro case is the most significant thing which has happened in my generation, so far as the struggle of the Negro in America is concerned.

W.E.B. Du Bois had organized the pan-African conferences immediately after World War I. And Du Bois was right, in the sense that it was the obligation of the Negro in America, as the most advanced politically positioned group, to take the lead in speaking out and holding conferences for the liberation of Africans. But you see, the Scottsboro case cuts deeper because it is the liberation of all of oppressed humanity; it was a message carried to all of oppressed humanity. So far as I am concerned, looking at that picture from day to day, it has taught me the indivisibility of the struggle for liberty.

When I was about to take sick, I had on my desk the bills pending in Congress for the relief of the Indians. I had made contacts in the West so that we could identify through me the struggle of the Indians with the struggle of the Negro. I made contacts in Latin America, I made contacts in Mexico, I made contacts with the migrant foreign workers in California so that the point could be that all groups who feel the same type of oppression may realize their mutual inter-responsibility of struggling each for the other's freedom in order that they may accomplish freedom for themselves. Same goes for the Japanese Americans; the same goes for the struggle for the Jewish; the same goes for the struggle of the displaced persons. As a matter of fact, in the articles that I have written for the newspapers, the important thing that I have stressed is the fact that it is the international aspect of the struggle for freedom which now should most concern us in the United States.

There come times when it is possible to forecast the results of a contest, of a battle, of a lawsuit, or of a struggle long before the final event has taken place. And, so far as our struggle for civil rights is concerned, I'm not worried about that now. The struggle for civil rights in America is won. What I am more concerned about is the fact that the Negro shall not be content simply with demanding an equal share in the existing system. It seems to me that his fundamental responsibility and his historical challenge is to use his weight, since he has less to lose in the present system than anybody else or any other group, to make sure that the system which shall survive in the United States of America—I don't care what system you call it—shall be a system which guarantees justice and freedom for everyone. The way I usually put it is, "Sure, we're being invited now in to take a front seat, but there's no particular honor in being invited to take a front seat at one's own funeral."

So in the office, when I get discouraged, when things go wrong, I look up at this picture and then realize, one, that we are fighting a system, that we are trying to remove the lid off of the oppressed peoples everywhere. Also I regard what I am doing and my work as a lawyer not as an end in itself, but simply as the means of a technician probing in the courts, which are products of the existing system, *how far* the existing system will *permit* the exercise of freedom before it clamps down. I have seen several instances as to the limitations on which the existing system, as represented by its courts, will go. Beyond that, the appeal must be through the education of the masses themselves, to educate them in an *intelligent* use of their own power. There again we go to the process of teaching, the process of the open meeting, the process of carrying the message to the masses, of interpreting it to them so that they may recognize the relationship between the particular issue and the whole broad aspect.

Someday, if things get worse—and I don't see how they can avoid getting worse, because we are in a situation where we have got to have an expanding economy and our markets are contracting and we are losing our markets, we are losing the power to exploit colonial and other peoples—the struggle for freedom having accomplished itself politically in Asia will soon shift to Africa. So that I say I can't see how we can avoid a crisis. And we've seen enough in the present day to know that the first reaction of the powers that be is going to be silence and oppression, censorship, and other things. They are going to try to cut off the intellectuals from the masses. So that in this day, while there is still a little time, the primary task is to probe, to struggle, but even more than probing and struggle, to teach—to teach the masses to think for themselves, to teach the masses to know their place and to recognize their power and to apply it intelligently.

So this is the significance of the great open-air protest meeting. I hope that you will get the same pleasure out of this picture that I have gotten. I hope you will get the same inspiration, because I know that you are interested, basically, in the same things that I have always been interested in. And I hope that you'll turn this picture over to Bo when he gets to be a man and *tell* him that it was one of the great influences in his daddy's life.

6.

THURGOOD MARSHALL (1908–1993)

Argument Before the U.S. Supreme Court in
Cooper v. Aaron

Washington, D.C.—September 11, 1958

Thurgood Marshall was the first African American appointed to the United States Supreme Court. Before that, he led a long, distinguished career as the nation's most famous civil rights lawyer. Marshall was the lead attorney in the fight against segregation that led to the Supreme Court's 1954 *Brown v. Board of Education* ruling.

Marshall liked to tell people he was born way up South in Baltimore, Maryland. On the southern rim of the Mason-Dixon line, the Baltimore of Marshall's boyhood was rigidly segregated. But there was also a thriving black business district and a well-organized black middle class.

Marshall's parents were ambitious and determined. His mother, Norma, was a schoolteacher. His brash, outgoing father, Willie, was a railroad porter and a steward at a fashionable Maryland country club.

Marshall attended the prestigious, all-black Lincoln University in Pennsylvania where he decided to be a lawyer instead of a dentist. But the state university's law school in Baltimore was segregated, so Marshall commuted by train to all-black Howard University Law School in Washington, D.C. At sunrise, Marshall caught the train to Washington; he often took the last train home at night.[1]

Howard Law School had been overhauled by a demanding and ambitious Harvard Law School graduate named Charles Hamilton Houston. Thurgood Marshall started helping Houston, his mentor, fight legal cases while still a student.

Marshall graduated from Howard in 1933, at the top of his class. Houston left the university a year later to become chief lawyer for the National Association for the Advancement of Colored People (NAACP)—the nation's leading civil rights organization. Soon after, he recruited Marshall.

With Houston's guidance, Marshall won his first big civil rights case in 1935, when he sued the University of Maryland Law School for barring a black applicant, Donald Murray, from the school. This was Marshall's first attack on school segregation. He argued that excluding blacks from the public university violated the Supreme Court's doctrine of separate-but-equal because the school provided no separate—let alone equal—law school for blacks.

Legal scholar David Wilkins says that Marshall and Houston took a step-by-step approach to school desegregation for nearly two more decades: "[They] challenged both the factual equality between the black and the white schools," Wilkins explains, "as well as the general principle that separate could be equal in some meaningful constitutional sense. Each victory then built up to the next victory and the next victory, and by the late 1940s they had won a series of cases. *Brown* was the culmination of that twenty-year campaign."[2]

From 1938 through 1961, Thurgood Marshall headed the NAACP's Legal Defense and Educational Fund (LDF).[3] With a team of brilliant and dedicated lawyers, Marshall conducted a courtroom crusade against Jim Crow. He and his colleagues used the U.S. Constitution to defeat discrimination in voting laws, interstate transportation, and housing codes, as well as other inequities. They achieved their greatest victory in the 1954 *Brown* decision, in which the Supreme Court struck down the principle of separate-but-equal—the heart of Jim Crow law. *Brown* is widely regarded as one of the most significant American legal decisions of the twentieth century.

When the Supreme Court issued the *Brown* ruling, it was the sole branch of the federal government in support of integration. Southern white leaders immediately launched a campaign known as "massive resistance" to evade or defy the Court's order. The LDF had to fight harder than ever in court to get school districts to comply with *Brown*. Massive resistance reached its peak in Little Rock, Arkansas, in 1957, when Governor Orval Faubus called out the National Guard to prevent nine black children from attending Central High School. Escorted by federal troops, the "Little Rock Nine" finally made it into Central High School, but endured a year of harassment.

The Little Rock school board, citing fears of more racial upheaval, tried to suspend desegregation. Marshall fought the move all the way to the Supreme Court. In August 1958, the Court agreed to hold a special session to hear arguments in the case.

On September 11, 1958, Marshall, representing the "Little Rock Nine," appeared before the High Court. His argument was recorded on tape, a practice the court began in 1955. Rather than worry for the black children he was representing, Marshall expressed concern for the education of white students: what would *they* learn about their country if a white mob could trump the law of the land? With unusual speed the Supreme Court issued a strongly worded and unanimous ruling: Little Rock schools must obey the law and desegregate immediately.

Despite the Court's unambiguous ruling, Governor Faubus figured out another way to avoid the Court's order: he shut down the Little Rock public school system. It took a year of court battles and political turbulence before the schools reopened in 1959.

In 1961, Marshall left his career as the nation's leading civil rights lawyer to become a judge on the United States Second Circuit Court of Appeals. In 1965, Lyndon Johnson appointed Marshall as the first African American solicitor general of the United States. In 1967, Thurgood Marshall became the first African American to sit on the United States Supreme Court, where he served for twenty-five years. Marshall retired from the Court in 1991 and died two years later at the age of eighty-four.

THE TRUTH of the matter is, these entire proceedings, starting with the filing of the petition of the school board way back in February asking for time, the whole purpose of these proceedings is to get time. The objective of the proceedings is that the Little Rock schools be returned from desegregated to segregated status as of September school term.

I think we have to think about these children and their parents, these Negro children that went through this every day and their parents that stayed at home wondering what was happening to their children, listening to the radio about the bomb threats and all of that business. I don't see how anybody under the sun could say that after those children and those families went through that for a year to tell them: All you have done is gone. You fought for what you considered to be democracy and you lost. And you go back to the segregated school from which you came. I just don't believe it. And I don't believe you can balance those rights.

Education is not the teaching of the three R's. Education is the teaching of the overall citizenship, to learn to live together with fellow citizens, and above all to learn to obey the law.

And the damage to the education in Arkansas and in Little Rock and in Central High comes about through the order of Judge Lemley, which says that not only the school board and the state can and should submit to mob violence and threats of mob violence, but that the federal judiciary likewise should do so.

I don't know of any more horrible destruction of principle of citizenship than to tell young children that those of you who withdrew rather than to go to school with Negroes, those of you who were punished last year—the few that the school board did punish: Come back, all is forgiven, you win.

And therefore, I am not worried about the Negro children at this stage. I don't believe they're in this case as such. I worry about the white children in Little Rock who are told, as young people, that the way to get your rights is to violate the law and defy the lawful authorities. I'm worried about their future. I don't worry about those Negro kids' future. They've been struggling with democracy long enough. They know about it.

The way this case stands, there must be a definitive decision—I hate to use the two together, it's bad English but it's the best way I can do it—that there be no doubt in Arkansas that the orders of that district court down there must be respected and cannot be suspended and cannot be interfered with by the legislature or anybody else. And less than that I don't think will give these young children the protection that they need and they most certainly deserve.

7.

HOWARD THURMAN (1899–1981)

"Community and the Self"

Marsh Chapel, Boston University, Boston, MA—April 16, 1961

Theologian Howard Thurman offered spiritual guidance and rejuvenation to some of the most prominent Christian activists of the American civil rights movement. They included Mary McLeod Bethune, James Farmer, Martin Luther King Jr., Jesse Jackson, and Barbara Jordan. Thurman believed deeply in the interconnection of all human beings. He was one of the earliest exponents of nonviolent direct action in the African American struggle for equal rights.[1]

Thurman's religious training began at the knee of his grandmother Nancy Ambrose, a former slave. She reassured the boy that he was not a "nigger"—an epithet he often heard from whites—but a child of God. It was a lesson she repeated with young Thurman, one she had heard from a black preacher who sometimes visited the slave plantation where she had lived.[2]

Born into a poor family in Daytona, Florida, in 1899, Thurman was profoundly influenced by the spiritual liberation "Grandma Nancy" experienced through her Christian faith. He said he became "deeply convinced that the legacy of slave religion was of lasting importance: 'By some amazing but vastly creative spiritual insight, the slave undertook the redemption of a religion that the master had profaned in his midst.' "[3]

Thurman attended high school in Jacksonville and entered Morehouse College, an all-black school in Atlanta, in 1919. There he studied government and economics and was valedictorian of his class. In 1923, Thurman was selected for one of two spots allotted to black students at Rochester Theological Seminary in New York. In that virtually all-white setting, Thurman began to contemplate the virtues of racial integration. Thurman and two white friends defied rules against interracial living by rooming together on campus. He graduated from Rochester in 1926 at the top of his class.[4]

In 1929, Thurman studied under the Quaker mystic Rufus Jones, leader of the interracial Fellowship of Reconciliation. Thurman's interest in a multiracial fellowship of peace deepened, and in 1935 he led the first black "Delegation of Friendship" to South Asia. On the trip, Thurman was invited to meet Mohandas K. Gandhi, leader of the nonviolent revolution against British colonialism in India. Gandhi encouraged Thurman to use the teachings of Jesus as a tool for challenging white supremacy in America. It is thought to be the first formal exchange between the Indian pacifist and an African American leader. Their conversation inspired Thurman as he developed his own ideas about Christianity and the black liberation struggle.[5]

After serving as dean of the Rankin Chapel at Howard University, Thurman moved to San Francisco in 1943 to help open the maiden church of the Fellowship of Reconciliation, the first known interfaith, multiracial church in the country. During these years, he shared his ideas with budding civil rights activists like James Farmer, founder of the nonviolent Congress of Racial Equality, and Martin Luther King Jr. In 1953, Thurman moved to Boston to become dean of Marsh Chapel at Boston University. He was the first African American dean at a predominantly white university.

Life magazine once named Thurman one of the twelve greatest preachers of the twentieth century.[6] His sermons were marked by their slow, suspenseful unfolding, by deep ruminations on the nature of humanity, and by long, meditative pauses. In this sermon, Thurman tells how his grandmother recounted visits from the slave preacher. It is a powerful example of the oral tradition from the time of slavery finding its way into twentieth-century African American oratory.

As we wait together in the presence of God, our thoughts are full of forebodings and distresses and uneasiness because there is so much that is broken and bleeding in our world. We find ourselves unable to manage the degree of our involvement in much that is at work in our world. The stark sense of guilt, which is every man's portion, when we remember the terrible days of the gas chambers and the ovens, the mute, numb misery of the condemned and the long empty silence of all the world, while the agonies ascended to God. How may we become clean again?

When we remember, the catalogue is long and limitless. The sense of personal guilt that revolves around the deliberate act, the responsible private act, which is ours and in some sense ours alone. And the need for forgiveness, for reconciliation, for a mounting experience of harmony with those who walk the way with us in order that we may find some measure of peace and tranquility in our own hearts. We turn to thee, our Father, with the great hunger for wholeness and cleanliness that before our own eyes, even as before thee, we shall not be ashamed. Teach us thy forgiveness that we may learn, our Father, how to forgive ourselves. Oh God, God, God. Teach us while there is still time. [organ music]

As a background for our thinking on community and the self, continuing our series, will you listen to these words?

> Look round our world; behold the chain of love
> Combining all below and all above.
> See plastic Nature working to this end,
> The single atoms each to other tend,
> Attract, attracted to, the next in place
> Form'd and impell'd its neighbor to embrace.
> See matter next, with various life endur'd
> Press to one centre still, the gen'ral good.
> See dying vegetables life sustain,
> See life dissolving vegetate again:
> All forms that perish other forms supply,

(By turns we catch the vital breath, and die)
Like bubbles on the sea of matter born,
They rise, they break, and to that sea return.
Nothing is foreign: parts relate to whole;
One all-extending, all Preserving Soul
Connects each being, greatest with the least;
Made beast in aid of man, and man of beast;
All serv'd, all serving: nothing stands alone;
The chain holds on, and where it ends, unknown.

[excerpt from *An Essay on Man: Epistle III* by Alexander Pope]

And then this,

No man is an Island, entire of its self;
Every man is a piece of the Continent,
A part of the main;
If a clod be washed away by the sea,
Europe is the less,
As well as if a promontory were,
As well as if a manor of thy friends
or of thine own were;
Any man's death diminishes me,
Because I am involved in Mankind
And therefore never send to know
For whom the bell tolls;
It tolls for thee.

[excerpt from "Meditation XVII" by John Donne]

The working definition of community is the experience of wholeness, of completeness, of inner togetherness, of integration, and wherever this is experienced, at whatever level of life, at that particular level there is community. We pointed out last week that the individual human being experiences in his organism this definition of community. As if the organism, all the parts, had committed to memory a sense of the whole, a social sense which is the overtone of the biological inner-continuity.

Now this is the heritage. It is this that is the essential and necessitous equipment of the little child, of the baby when the baby is born, if all is well.

We do not know what the self is precisely, but there seems to be a considerable body of thought, and if I may put it this way, a considerable body of thoughtful thought that insists that we are not born human, that the self is a discovery of the organism, that the self emerges as the organism begins to discriminate between this-ness and that-ness, between the self and the not-self. The sense, first I suppose, of self is rooted in the sense of one's own body.

You may remember the incident to which I referred last—well that's awful—last year. I was babysitting with a friend of mine. That is, he was babysitting and I was sitting with him. His little son was in the next room asleep while we were visiting. And then suddenly the baby began whimpering and then the whimper became a little more dramatic, and then it almost became full blown, but not quite. And we were disturbed and we went in and we found a very interesting thing. This little boy, baby, was gumming his big toe. And his gums were rather firm and he was gumming his big toe and it was hurting him. And he was crying but he couldn't quite cry full-blown because he had to keep on gumming his toe. He didn't *know* that it was his toe; he had no sense of toe-ness. [laughter] It was not a part of his organism. He was yet to *discover* his body as distinguished from that which was *not* his body.

It is in this development, this kind of tension, that the sense of self emerges, and as the self begins to develop it is in a sense a gift, which is embraced by the individual, but a gift from other selves. And this, wherever this happens, the self becomes articulate. Always, you see, the sense, then, of belonging to some primary social unit is but an extension of the sense of biological community that the baby has when the baby is born. As if all through the corridors of his little organism there were a social sense. And now when, in relation to human beings, the same sense of harmony, the same sense of belonging, the same sense of continuity, can be experienced, then the child grows up with what may be called a kind of emotional stability.

But you see there is always implicit in this process the elements that make for crisis, you see. Because the needs which the child has are immediate needs. And the environment in its early stages, in the child's early stages, is conditioned to meeting those needs, those immediate needs, immediately. This means then, that for the little child, the time interval between what the child wishes in terms of its needs, its felt needs, and the fulfillment of these needs is zero. Now as long as it remains zero, there is the experience of harmony, the experience of community, the experience of the little integrated self. But when, for various reasons, the time interval between wish and fulfillment is tampered with, then the child senses the enemy and he finds himself placed over against that which threatens him. And the threat takes the form of the unwillingness or the unavailability of the things which the child needs, and needs now. So that growth then becomes a part of the experience through which the child goes, as the child begins to negotiate the expanding time interval between what the child desires and the meeting of those desires.

Now once the sense of self becomes articulate, then the individual is always on the *search* for the kind of relationships that will *restore* the original sense of community. It is for this reason, for instance, that if you are contemplating an act, the first question that you're apt to raise is about that deed you're about to do is not whether it is right or wrong. Theoretically, if you are of good conscience, this is the first question you raise. But actually the first question you're apt to raise is, what is the relationship between this act that I contemplate and that little world of human beings to whom I relate in terms of community? If I do this deed, will it rupture my relationship, will it break the thing that guarantees my persona, that gives to me my sense of community? And if I decide that I will run the risk of cutting myself off so that I will no longer be a person but an individual, then immediately I must see this deed in terms of a new sense of community that I may develop. And it is for this reason then that all persons who are concerned about social change understand very clearly that it is never ever enough merely to try to change the insides of people's hearts. This is important, it is crucial, it is necessitous, but it is not enough because the thing that guarantees the sense of private and personal stability for the individual is a sense of being supported, sustained, maintained in community.

Now, with that background let me hasten to do two things. First, how then may we develop the self in community? And by that I do not mean merely the self in relation to other human beings, but the sense of inner wholeness, so that the deep, piercing dichotomies that rift my tranquility can somehow be resolved.

Now we do this in various ways. One, we seek to relate ourselves to something that is to us more significant, more important, than whether we as human beings live or die. Some transcendent purpose or cause, which in the impact that it makes upon us in terms of demand will be so crucial that on its behalf we are brought into focus. Some need that galvanizes the personality into focus, something that transcends all of the fragmentation of our lives and is so important to us that for its sake we give up *anything*.

A second thing: this possibility may be out of our reach. We may say that I don't, I can't relate myself to any cause that will give to me a sense of inner togetherness, that I'm too insignificant and I have no particular talent, or no particular gift. I'm just myself, I don't have any things that any cause can use. Or the causes to which I'm exposed are so overwhelming that I'm immobilized, I'm rendered completely ineffective because I have a profound sense of being stymied.

Now this is one of the tragedies of our time. We have been so surfeited by all kinds of violences, all kinds of suffering and agonies. I found myself looking at my insides yesterday afternoon while the movie that was a part of our Near East exhibition yesterday, while this movie was being played and the pictures revealed of the plight of some 750,000 refugees. I found that the *mass attack* of that upon my emotions, just rendered me with a sense of complete impotence and finally a kind of devastated *deadness*. And this is our plight! What would it take to *arouse* you, at the *deep* place in you, so that when you *touched* this depth, everything in you would be sucked into it?

I wish I knew the answer to this, but I have one simple suggestion. I think that one of the things that we must do is to cultivate—how to say this—to cultivate our inner, to cultivate our inner life. To take time in withdrawal and plumb our own depths, and here I'm not talking about the things that make for morbidity and inward turning of that sort, but to plumb our own depths until we hit the place in us that is the common ground not only of human life, but of life! For there is such a thing, and it may be that if day after day after day, we learn how to do this, it is entirely possible that the insight that comes will so renew all of our activities that these activities will be become more and more expressive of something that is central in us. And the self will no longer be splintered and fragmented but it will be a channel of one piece through which the living energy of the living God pours itself out. And this perhaps is what is meant by being a child of God. It is this discovery of the depth that is available to each of us that makes the difference in the center of focus and integration and community: wholeness, tranquility of the self.

I shall always remember this very personal reference. But when I was a boy and having to spend most of my time with my grandmother who was a young woman at the time of the Civil War. She was a slave in Tallahassee, Florida. And sometimes when life seemed very, so fragmented for me that I didn't know where to take hold, and I could not find any authentic way to belong, she used to talk to me about what it really meant to be a child of God.

I shall always remember one of the things she said to me one Sunday morning. She told me about how she made that discovery as a little girl on this plantation. The minister, who was one of the slaves, was permitted now and then to have a religious service for all the slaves on that plantation and the neighboring plantation. And he always had the same sermon to preach, the essence of which was this. "Look at you, look at you. You, you are not slaves. You, you are God's children." And after the long silence that passed after she'd tell me this then she would add, "Nothing else really matters."

Now that may *seem* like a very naïve defense mechanism that has no significance beyond the temporary reinforcement of the ego at a moment of attack. But no! It gave to her and to those like her and to their offspring, a sense of roots that was watered by the underground river of existence. And this is the discovery that the prodigal son made in the lesson, when he came to himself, when he cut down through all the levels until he hit this hard core, it was, at once to him, going back to his father. When he came to himself, he came to his father. When you come to yourself, you come to your father. And the tranquility that pervades all the levels of your life announces in everything you do, community, wholeness, integration!

This after all, our Father, is the deep desire of our hearts. May we never give up the quest until at last we come to ourselves, in thee.

8.

DICK GREGORY
(1932–)

Speech at St. John's Baptist Church

Birmingham, Alabama—May 20, 1963

He might have chosen to stay home and protect his lucrative career as a nationally acclaimed comedian, but Dick Gregory was ready to go to jail in Birmingham, Alabama. May 6, 1963, marked the largest single day of nonviolent arrests in American history as civil rights groups took on a city with a reputation as "the Bastille of segregation."

Gregory flew in from Chicago to help. He led the first group of what became a wave of children and teenagers marching out of church doors to get arrested for protesting peacefully for equal rights. More than 3,300 people were already in Birmingham's jails when thousands more took part in what became known as "The Children's March." Birmingham's notorious police chief, Bull Connor, turned high-pressure fire hoses and snarling police dogs loose on the orderly protestors. The news coverage sparked international outrage.[1]

After spending four days in jail, Gregory flew home to Chicago, then returned to Birmingham about a week later to address a Monday night mass meeting with the story of his arrest. Gregory was a veteran of civil rights protests. In 1961, he was asked by voting rights activist Medgar

Evers to speak at a rally in Jackson, Mississippi. He lent his hand and his humor to other groups as well.[2]

Gregory was born in 1932 in St. Louis, where he grew up poor, especially after his father deserted his mother and five siblings. Gregory attended public schools and won a track scholarship to Southern Illinois University, which he attended until he was drafted in 1954. Gregory made a name for himself in army talent shows, and after his discharge in 1956, he quit college to pursue a career in comedy. His first big break came at the Chicago Playboy Club when he filled in for an ailing white actor and, defying the odds, entertained a group of Southern businessmen with his racially barbed routine.

At the height of the Birmingham protests, Gregory gave confidential advice to Attorney General Robert F. Kennedy on how the Kennedy administration could work with civil rights leaders. It led to a secret New York meeting between RFK and a group of African American leaders, artists, and others organized by author James Baldwin.[3]

Gregory remained active in politics and civil rights. In 1967, he fasted for forty days to protest the Vietnam War. He also ran for mayor of Chicago and the U.S. presidency. In the 1970s and 1980s, Gregory became a widely quoted advocate of dieting and nutrition.

I'LL TELL YOU ONE THING, it sure is nice being out of that prison over there. Lot of people asked me when I went back to Chicago last night, they said, "Well how are the Negroes in Birmingham taking it? What did they act like? What did they look like?" I said, "Man, I got off a plane at 10:30, arrived at the motel at 11 and by one o'clock I was in jail." [laughter] So I know what you all mean when you refer to the good old days. I asked one guy, "What is the 'good old days'?" and he said, "10 B.C. and 15 B.C." And I said, "Baby, you're not that old" and he said, "Nah, I mean 10, 15 years before Bull Connor got here." [laughter]

Man they had so many Negroes in jail over there, the day I was there, when you looked out the window and see one of them walking around free, you knew he was a tourist. I got back to Chicago last night and a guy said, "Well how would you describe the prison scene?" and I said, "Baby, just wall to wall *us*." [laughter]

So I don't know, really, when you stop to think about it. That was some mighty horrible food they were giving us over there. First couple of days, it taste bad and look bad and after that it tasted like home cooking. [laughter] Matter of fact, it got so good the third day it got so good that I asked one of the guards for the recipe. [laughter]

Of course you know, really, I don't mind going to jail myself, I just hate to see Martin Luther King in jail. For various reasons: one, when the final day get here, he is going to have a hard time trying to explain to the boss upstairs how he spent more time in jail than he did in the pulpit. [laughter] When I read in the paper in Chicago that they had him in jail on Good Friday, I said that's good. And I was praying and hoping when they put him in Good Friday they had checked back there Easter Sunday morning and he would have been *gone*. That would have shook up a lot of people, wouldn't it? [laughter]

I don't know how much faith you have in newspapers, but I read an article in the paper a couple days ago, where the Russians—did you see this, they gave it a lot of space—the Russians claim they found Hitler's head. Well I want to tell you that's not true. You want to find Hitler's head, just look right up above Bull Connor's shoulders. [laughter] To be honest with you, I don't know why you call him 'Bull Connor.' Just say bull, that's half of it. Couple of them hep sisters over there in the corner.

I don't know, when you stop and think about it, I guess little by little when you look around, it kind of looks like we're doing alright. I read in the paper not too long ago, they picked the first Negro astronaut. That shows you so much pressure is being put on Washington, these cats just reach back and they trying to pacify us real quickly. A lot of people was happy that they had the first Negro astronaut, well I'll be honest with you, not myself. I was kind of hoping we'd get a Negro airline pilot first. They didn't give us a Negro airline pilot; they gave us a Negro astronaut. You realize that we can jump from back of the bus to the moon? [laughter] That's about the size of it. I don't know why this cat let 'em trick him into volunteering for that space job, they not even ready for a Negro astronaut. You have never heard of no dehydrated pig's feet.

I never would have let them give me that job, myself. No, I wouldn't, that's one job I don't think I could take. Just my luck, they'd put me in one of them rockets and blast it off, we'd land on Mars somewhere. A cat'd walk up to me with 27 heads, 59 jaws, 19 lips, 47 legs and look at me and say, "I don't want you marrying my daughter neither." Oh I'd have to cut him.

So I don't know, when you stop and think about it, we're all confused. I'm very confused—I'm married, my wife can't cook. No, it's not funny. How do you burn Kool-Aid? [laughter] You know, raising kids today is such a difficult task. These kids are so clever. They're so hip. My son walked up to me not too long ago, he said, "Daddy, I'm going to run away from home. Call me a cab." [laughter] I remember when I was a kid, I told my father the same thing, I said, "Pa if you don't give me a nickel, I'm leaving home." He said, "Son I'm not gonna give you one penny and take your brothers with you." [laughter] I remember when I was a kid, if my parents wanted to punish me, it was simple, they told me, "Get upstairs to your room," which was a heck of a punishment because there was no upstairs. [laughter]

And I just found out something not too long ago I didn't know. You don't walk into a kid's room anymore. You have to knock first. My daughter told me, "I'm three years old, I've got rights." What do you mean you have rights? You haven't even got a job. I said, "Honey, you don't know how fortunate you are: you have a room by yourself, a bed by yourself." I said, "Honey, do you realize when I was three years old, so many of us slept in the same bed together, if I went to the washroom in the middle of the night, I had to leave a bookmark so I wouldn't lose my spot." [laughter] She said, "Daddy aren't you happy you're living with us now?" [laughter]

Let me tell you about this daughter of mine. Last Christmas Eve night, I walked into my daughter's room, I said, "Michelle, tonight's Christmas Eve, it's 11:30, you're three years old, go to bed and get ready for Santa Claus." She said, "I don't believe in Santa Claus." I said, "What in the world you mean you don't believe in Santa Claus and I'm picking up the tab?" She said, "Daddy, I don't care what you picking up, I don't believe in Santa Claus." I said, "Why?" She said "Because you know darn good and well there ain't no white man coming into our neighborhood after midnight." [laughter] So you see, we have problems.

I'd like to say, it's been a pleasure being here. A lot of people wonder, why would I make a decision to go to Greenwood, Mississippi? Why would I make a decision to come to Birmingham? When I lay in my bed at night and I think if America had to go to war tonight, I would be willing to go to any of the four corners of the world; and if I am willing to go and lay on some cold dirt, away from my love ones and my friends and take a chance on losing my life to guarantee some foreigner that I've never met equal rights and dignity, I must be able to come down here.

You know it is such a funny thing how the American mind works—and this is white and Negro alike—how many on both sides of the fence say, "Well did he go down for publicity?" One, I don't *need* publicity. But the amazing thing is if I had decided to quit show business and join the Peace Corps and go to South Vietnam, nobody would have said anything about publicity. Only when you decide to help us, you get a complaint.

You people here in the South are the most beautiful people alive in the world today. The only person in this number one country in the world, that knows where he's going and have a purpose, is the Southern Negro—bar none. When you break through and get your freedom and your dignity, then we up North will also break through and get our freedom and our dignity. Because up North we have always been able to use the South as our garbage can. But when you make these white folks put that lid on this garbage can down here, we are going to have to throw our garbage in our own backyard, and it's going to stink worse than it stinks down here. [applause]

One of greatest problems the Negro has in America today is that we have never been able to control our image. The man downtown has always controlled our image. He has always told us how we're supposed to act. He has always told us a nigger know his place—and he don't mean this, because if we knew our place he wouldn't have to put all those signs up. [applause] And if you think we know our place, let one of us get $2 uptight on our rent and 50 cents in our pocket and we'll kick the hinges off them doors downtown to open up.

But we have never been able to control our image. He's always told us about a Negro crime rate, to the extent that you have finally decided to believe it. This is the bad part about not being able to control your image. I've always said, "What Negro crime rate?" Look at it, we not raping three-year-old kids. We haven't put forty sticks of dynamite in mother's luggage and blew one of them airplanes out the sky. And I don't care what they say about us, we've never lynched anybody [applause]. So what Negro crime rate? If you want to see a true Negro crime rate, watch television. Look at all them gangster movies, you never see us. Of course now, you can look at TV, week in and week out and look at all those doctor series they have on television and you'd be led to believe a Negro never gets sick. [laughter]

For some reason, not being able to control our image has made us almost ashamed of us. Because anything he decides to tell us, about us, we believe it, and become ashamed of it. Negro crime rate? Sure, a lot of us get arrested. Why? The answer is right out there in the street, everyday. You got a Southerner out there in the police department that is probably the lowest form of man walking the earth today. Now here's a man out there, didn't like you in the first place, now he's got a gun. What is your crime rate supposed to look like?

They have gotten to the point where they've made you ashamed of relief. "Don't talk to so and so, she's on ADC." I was on relief twenty years, back home. It wasn't funny, but I wasn't ashamed of it, because had they gave my daddy the type of job he deserved to have, we wouldn't have needed no relief. And the day this white man—not only in the South, but in America—gives us fair housing, fair jobs, equal schools and the other things the Constitution say we supposed to have, we will relieve him of relief. [applause] Until that day rolls around, let him pay his dues. The check ain't much, but it's steady.

And then you read a lot and hear a lot about Negro women with illegitimate kids. Oh this really makes you ashamed. Each time you pick up one of them newspapers, one of them magazines, reading about Negro women with illegitimate kids, check the article out and see who wrote it. Some chick living in a neighborhood where they've got abortion credit cards.

Never been able to control our image, all at once we're ashamed. Talked about us for so long, we started believing it. Talked about our hair for so long, for a hundred years now we've been trying to straighten our wig out. Wouldn't it be wild if you find out one day that we had natural hair and there was something wrong with theirs?

Every time you look around, they're talking about a Negro with a switchblade to the extent we don't want to carry switchblades no more. Well I keep me a switchblade. I got a deal going with the white folks, I don't say nothing about their missiles and they don't say nothing about my switchblade. [laughter] Here's a man who owns half the missiles in the world and want to talk about my switchblade. I don't know one Negro in

America that manufactures switchblades—now he going to sell me some and then talk about it after I get it.

He made a lot of mistakes and had all you older people been able to figure out the mistakes he made like the younger people figured them out, we would have had this a long time ago. [applause] Yep, he made a lot of mistakes. Here's a man that got over here and didn't even know how to work segregation. Didn't even know how prejudice worked. He just wanted to try it. He said, "We got a bunch of them niggers, let's try it" and he messed up. 'Cause any clown knows that if you want to segregate somebody and keep them down forever, you put them up front. They made the great mistake of putting us in the back; we've been watching them for 300 years. [applause] Yeah, that was a big mistake they made. We know how dirty they get their underwear, because we wash them for them. They don't even know if we wear them or not.

They made a couple of mistakes. It is beginning to catch up with them now. One of the biggest mistakes they made, is that white lady. All at once they think all we want is a white lady. And they don't understand why we want one. It's their fault. Bufferins can't advertise Bufferins without one of them white ladies and so we feel we need a white lady to get rid of our headache. [laughter] Every year General Motors advertise them Cadillacs with them blonds and know we gonna get one of them cars. Every time I go to the movie, I can't see none of them pretty little chocolate drops in them dynamite love scenes—show me one of them white ladies. Every time I look at Miss America, I can't see no Mau Mau queens—show me one of them white ladies. So what am I supposed to watch? But I'll make a deal with the good white brother, yes, if he let me turn on television and see some of my women advertising some of them products we use so much of, if he let me go to the movie and see some of my folks in some of them good scenes, and if he let me turn on television this year and see seven of us on Miss America to make up, then anytime he see me with a white woman I'll be holding her for the police. [laughter]

Again, I'd like to say it is completely and totally my pleasure being here. I don't know how many of you in the house have kids that was in jail. Four days I was in jail. Had you been there, as I was, walking through, listening, it was really something to be proud of, really something to be proud of. And if something ever happens and you have to do it again, don't hesitate.

[applause] Because the only thing we have left now that's gonna save this whole country and eventually the world is us. He taught us honesty and he forgot how it worked himself. Nothing wrong with that white man downtown—we just have to teach him how to act. He don't know how to be fair. He don't know—we'd never complain if he was fair. "Keep me a second-class citizen, but just don't make me pay first-class taxes. Send me to the worst schools in America, if you must, but when I go downtown to apply for that job, don't give me the same test you give that white boy." Now we are going to have to teach him how to be fair and the only thing we have to do it with is ourselves.

This is it, this is all we have. He has *all* the police, *all* the dogs; never thought I'd see the day the fireman would turn water on us in summertime and make us hotter, but they did. What these white folks don't realize is a terrific amount of police brutality that I have witnessed down here, what they fail to realize is when you let a man bend the law and aim it at us, he'll aim that same law at you. [applause]

These are the problems that we have. Again, I am as far away from you as Delta Airline is; anytime there is any problem, I will be back. Thank you very much and God bless you. [applause]

9.

FANNIE LOU HAMER (1917–1977)

Testimony Before the Credentials Committee, Democratic National Convention

Atlantic City, New Jersey—August 22, 1964

Fannie Lou Hamer's life took a dramatic turn the day she showed up for a mass meeting to learn about voting. It was August 1962 and Hamer, who was forty-four years old, wasn't even sure what a "mass meeting" was. "I was just curious to go, so I did," she said.[1] The meeting was organized by the Student Nonviolent Coordinating Committee (SNCC) and Hamer was told something she'd never heard before: black people had the right to vote.

One of twenty children born to a family of sharecroppers in the Mississippi Delta, Hamer grew up picking cotton and cutting corn and attended school through the sixth grade. She married a fellow sharecropper and the two scratched out a living doing hard, menial work on a plantation near Ruleville, Mississippi.

According to biographer Sina Dubovoy, when Hamer heard SNCC's presentation, she asked herself, "What did she really have? Not even security." A lynching in a nearby town in 1904 had terrorized blacks then, and the ever-present KKK still kept them quiet. As Dubovoy notes, "The Mississippi Delta was the world's most oppressive place to live if you were black."[2] Hamer decided on the spot to register to vote.

On August 31, 1962, she boarded a bus to Indianola with seventeen others to try to register to vote. The next day she was kicked off the plantation where she had lived and worked for eighteen years. Her husband lost his job, too.

Hamer immediately went to work as a field organizer for SNCC. Returning home from a training workshop in June 1963, Hamer's bus was intercepted by policemen. She and two others were taken to jail in Winona, Mississippi, and mercilessly beaten. Hamer suffered permanent damage to her kidneys. After recovering from her injuries, she traveled across the U.S. telling her story. With her genuine, plainspoken style, Hamer raised more money for SNCC than any other member.

In 1964, with the support of the Mississippi Freedom Democratic Party (MFDP), Hamer ran for Congress. The incumbent was a white man who had been elected to office twelve times. In an interview with the *Nation,* Hamer said, "I'm showing the people that a Negro can run for office." The reporter observed: "Her deep, powerful voice shakes the air as she sits on the porch or inside, talking to friends, relatives and neighbors who drop by on the one day each week when she is not campaigning. Whatever she is talking about soon becomes an impassioned plea for a change in the system that exploits the Delta Negroes. 'All my life I've been sick and tired,' she shakes her head. 'Now I'm sick and tired of being sick and tired.' "[3]

SNCC had formed the MFDP to expand black voter registration and challenge the legitimacy of the state's all-white Democratic Party. MFDP members arrived at the 1964 Democratic National Convention intent on unseating the official Mississippi delegation or, failing that, getting seated with them. On August 22, 1964, Hamer appeared before the convention's credentials committee and told her story about trying to register to vote in Mississippi. Threatened by the MFDP's presence at the convention, President Lyndon Johnson quickly preempted Hamer's televised testimony with an impromptu press conference. But later that night, Hamer's story was broadcast on all the major networks.

Support came pouring in for the MFDP from across the nation.[4] But the MFDP's bid to win a seat at the Atlantic City convention still failed. At the Democratic National Convention in Chicago four years later the

MFDP succeeded. On that occasion, Dubovoy recounts, "Hamer received a thunderous standing ovation when she became the first African American to take her rightful seat as an official delegate at a national-party convention since the Reconstruction period after the Civil War, and the first woman ever from Mississippi."[5]

MR. CHAIRMAN, and to the Credentials Committee, my name is Mrs. Fannie Lou Hamer, and I live at 626 East Lafayette Street, Ruleville, Mississippi, Sunflower County, the home of Senator James O. Eastland, and Senator Stennis.

It was the 31st of August in 1962 that eighteen of us traveled twenty-six miles to the county courthouse in Indianola to try to register to become first-class citizens.

We was met in Indianola by policemen, Highway Patrolmen, and they only allowed two of us in to take the literacy test at the time. After we had taken this test and started back to Ruleville, we was held up by the City Police and the State Highway Patrolmen and carried back to Indianola where the bus driver was charged that day with driving a bus the wrong color.

After we paid the fine among us, we continued on to Ruleville, and Reverend Jeff Sunny carried me four miles in the rural area where I had worked as a timekeeper and sharecropper for eighteen years. I was met there by my children, who told me that the plantation owner was angry because I had gone down to try to register.

After they told me, my husband came, and said the plantation owner was raising Cain because I had tried to register. Before he quit talking the plantation owner came and said, "Fannie Lou, do you know—did Pap tell you what I said?"

And I said, "Yes, sir."

He said, "Well I mean that." He said, "If you don't go down and withdraw your registration, you will have to leave." Said, "Then if you go down and withdraw," said, "you still might have to go because we are not ready for that in Mississippi."

And I addressed him and told him and said, "I didn't try to register for you. I tried to register for myself."

I had to leave that same night.

On the 10th of September 1962, sixteen bullets was fired into the home of Mr. and Mrs. Robert Tucker for me. That same night two girls were shot in Ruleville, Mississippi. Also Mr. Joe McDonald's house was shot in.

And June the 9th, 1963, I had attended a voter registration workshop; was returning back to Mississippi. Ten of us was traveling by the Continental Trailway bus. When we got to Winona, Mississippi, which is Montgomery County, four of the people got off to use the washroom, and two of the people—to use the restaurant—two of the people wanted to use the washroom.

The four people that had gone in to use the restaurant was ordered out. During this time I was on the bus. But when I looked through the window and saw they had rushed out I got off of the bus to see what had happened. And one of the ladies said, "It was a State Highway Patrolman and a Chief of Police ordered us out."

I got back on the bus and one of the persons had used the washroom got back on the bus, too.

As soon as I was seated on the bus, I saw when they began to get the five people in a highway patrolman's car. I stepped off of the bus to see what was happening and somebody screamed from the car that the five workers was in and said, "Get that one there." When I went to get in the car, when the man told me I was under arrest, he kicked me.

I was carried to the county jail and put in the booking room. They left some of the people in the booking room and began to place us in cells. I was placed in a cell with a young woman called Miss Ivesta Simpson. After I was placed in the cell I began to hear sounds of licks and screams, I could hear the sounds of licks and horrible screams. And I could hear somebody say, "Can you say, 'yes, sir,' nigger? Can you say 'yes, sir'?"

And they would say other horrible names.

She would say, "Yes, I can say 'yes, sir.' "

"So, well, say it."

She said, "I don't know you well enough."

They beat her, I don't know how long. And after a while she began to pray, and asked God to have mercy on those people.

And it wasn't too long before three white men came to my cell. One of these men was a State Highway Patrolman and he asked me where I was from. I told him Ruleville and he said, "We are going to check this."

They left my cell and it wasn't too long before they came back. He said, "You are from Ruleville all right," and he used a curse word. And he said, "We are going to make you wish you was dead."

I was carried out of that cell into another cell where they had two Negro prisoners. The State Highway Patrolmen ordered the first Negro to take the blackjack.

The first Negro prisoner ordered me, by orders from the State Highway Patrolman, for me to lay down on a bunk bed on my face.

I laid on my face and the first Negro began to beat. I was beat by the first Negro until he was exhausted. I was holding my hands behind me at that time on my left side, because I suffered from polio when I was six years old.

After the first Negro had beat until he was exhausted, the State Highway Patrolman ordered the second Negro to take the blackjack.

The second Negro began to beat and I began to work my feet, and the State Highway Patrolman ordered the first Negro who had beat me to sit on my feet—to keep me from working my feet. I began to scream and one white man got up and began to beat me in my head and tell me to hush.

One white man—my dress had worked up high—he walked over and pulled my dress—I pulled my dress down and he pulled my dress back up.

I was in jail when Medgar Evers was murdered.

All of this is on account of we want to register, to become first-class citizens. And if the Freedom Democratic Party is not seated now, I question America. Is this America, the land of the free and the home of the brave, where we have to sleep with our telephones off the hooks because our lives be threatened daily, because we want to live as decent human beings, in America?

Thank you.

10.

STOKELY CARMICHAEL (1941–1998)

Speech at University of California, Berkeley

October 29, 1966

Stokely Carmichael was the brilliant and impatient young civil rights leader who, in the 1960s, popularized the phrase "black power." Carmichael was initially an acolyte of the Reverend Martin Luther King Jr. and his philosophy of nonviolent protest. Carmichael became a leader in the Student Nonviolent Coordinating Committee (SNCC), but was radicalized when he saw peaceful protestors brutalized in the South.

In the mid 1960s, Carmichael challenged the civil rights leadership by rejecting integration and calling on blacks to oust whites from the freedom movement. Following his arrest during a 1966 protest march in Mississippi, Carmichael angrily demanded a change in the rhetoric and strategy of the civil rights movement. "We've been saying 'Freedom' for six years," Carmichael said. "What we are going to start saying now is 'Black Power.' "[1]

Historian Adam Fairclough writes that King was "aghast" at Carmichael's use of a slogan that sounded so aggressive. "Black power" was condemned by whites as a motto for a new form of racism. Some whites feared that black power was a call for race war. King urged

Carmichael to drop the phrase but he refused.[2] NAACP leader Roy Wilkins condemned the slogan as "the father of hate and the mother of violence," predicting that black power would mean "black death."[3]

Fellow civil rights organizer John Lewis, later a Democratic congressman from Georgia, remembered Carmichael as tall, lanky, and up-front. "He didn't wait to be asked his opinion on anything—he told you and expected you to listen," Lewis wrote. The two became estranged when Carmichael toppled Lewis from the SNCC chairmanship.[4]

In 1966 and 1967, Carmichael toured college campuses giving increasingly belligerent speeches. He coauthored a radical manifesto titled *Black Power,* in which he argued that civil rights groups had lost their appeal to increasingly militant young blacks. The movement's voice, he wrote, had been hopelessly softened for "an audience of middle class whites."[5]

Carmichael didn't shrink from these views when he addressed mostly white audiences in places like Berkeley. He spoke with a dry sense of humor, a jagged edge of anger, and a confidence described as strutting while standing still. "He became the personification of raw militancy," Lewis said.[6]

In 1967, SNCC severed ties with Carmichael. He became honorary prime minister of the Black Panthers but soon left that group over disagreements on seeking support from whites. Carmichael moved to the West African nation of Guinea in 1969. He changed his name to Kwame Ture in honor of Sekou Ture, the Marxist leader of Guinea, and Kwame Nkrumah, the deposed independence leader of Ghana. Kwame Ture lived in self-imposed exile for thirty years but returned to the U.S. for speeches and political activity. In 1996, he sought treatment in New York for prostate cancer, still answering the phone, "Ready for the Revolution!" He died two years later at his home in Africa.[7]

THANK YOU VERY MUCH. It's a privilege and an honor to be in the white intellectual ghetto of the West. [laughter] We wanted to do a couple of things before we started. The first is that based on the fact that SNCC, through the articulation of its program by its chairman, has been able to win elections in Georgia, Alabama, Maryland, and by our appearance here will win an election in California, in 1968 I'm gonna run for president of the United States. [applause] I just can't make it cause I wasn't born in the United States. That's the only thing holding me back.

We wanted to say that this is a student conference, as it should be, held on a campus, and that we're not ever to be caught up in the intellectual masturbation of the question of Black Power. That's a function of the people who are advertisers that call themselves reporters. [applause] Oh, for my members and friends of the press, my self-appointed white critics: I was reading Mr. Bernard Shaw two days ago, and I came across a very important quote, which I think is most apropos for you. He says, "All criticism is autobiography." Dig yourself. [applause]

OK. The philosophers Camus and Sartre raise the question whether or not a man can condemn himself. The black existentialist philosopher who is pragmatic, Frantz Fanon, answered the question. He said that man could not. Camus and Sartre does not. We in SNCC tend to agree with Camus and Sarte that a man cannot condemn himself. Were he to condemn himself he would then have to inflict punishment upon himself. An example would be the Nazis. Any of the Nazi prisoners who admitted, after he was caught and incarcerated, that he committed crimes, that he killed all the many people that he killed, he committed suicide. The only ones who were able to stay alive were the ones who never admitted that they committed a crime against people—that is, the ones who rationalized that Jews were not human beings and deserved to be killed, or that they were only following orders.

On a more immediate scene, the officials and the population—the white population—in Neshoba County, Mississippi (that's where Philadelphia is) could not condemn [Sheriff] Rainey, his deputies, and the other fourteen men who killed three human beings. They could not because they elected Mr. Rainey to do precisely what he did; and that for them to condemn him would be for them to condemn themselves.

In a much larger view, SNCC says that white America cannot condemn herself. And since we are liberal we have done it. You stand condemned. Now a number of things that arises from that answer, how do you condemn yourselves? It seems to me the institutions that function in this country are clearly racist and that they're built upon racism. And the question then is, how can black people inside of this country move? And then how can white people who say they're not a part of those institutions begin to move? And how then do we begin to clear away the obstacles that we have in this society, that make us live like human beings? How can we begin to build institutions that will allow people to relate with each other as human beings? This country has never done that, especially around the country of white and black.

Now, several people have been upset because we've said that integration was irrelevant when initiated by blacks, and that in fact it was a subterfuge, an insidious subterfuge for the maintenance of white supremacy. Now we maintain that in the past six years or so, this country has been feeding us a "thalidomide drug of integration," and that some Negroes have been walking down a dream street talking about sitting next to white people. And that that does not begin to solve the problem.

That when we went to Mississippi we did not go to sit next to Ross Barnett, we did not go to sit next to Jim Clark, we went to get them out of our way. And that people ought to understand that. That we were never fighting for the right to integrate, we were fighting against white supremacy. [applause]

Now then, in order to understand white supremacy, we must dismiss the fallacious notion that white people can give anybody their freedom. No man can give anybody his freedom. A man is born free. You may enslave a man after he is born free. And that is in fact what this country does. It enslaves black people after they're born. So that the only act that white people can do is to stop denying black people their freedom. That is, they must stop denying freedom. They never give it to anyone.

Now we want to take that to its logical extension so that we can understand then what its relevancy would be in terms of new civil rights bills. I maintain that every civil rights bill in this country was passed for white people, not for black people. [applause] For example, I am black. I know that. I also know that while I am black I am a human being. Therefore I have the right to go into any public place. White people didn't know that. Every time I tried to go into a place they stopped me. So some boys had to write a bill to tell that white man, "He's a human being; don't stop him." That bill was for that white man, not for me. I knew it all the time. I knew it all the time. [applause]

I knew that I could vote and that that wasn't a privilege, it was my right. Every time I tried I was shot, killed or jailed, beaten or economically deprived. So somebody had to write a bill for white people to tell them,

"When a black man comes to vote, don't bother him." That bill, again, was for white people, not for black people. So that when you talk about open occupancy I know I can live anyplace I want to live. It is white people across this country who are incapable of allowing me to live where I want to live. You need a civil rights bill, not me! I *know* I can live where I want to live. [applause]

So that the failure to pass a civil rights bill isn't because of Black Power, isn't because of the Student Nonviolent Coordinating Committee, is not because of the rebellions that are occurring in the major cities. It is the incapability of whites to deal with their own problems inside their own communities. That is the problem of the failure of the civil rights bill. [applause]

And so in a larger sense we must then ask, how is it that black people move? And what do we do? But the question in the greater sense is, how can white people who are the majority, and who are responsible for making democracy work, make it work? They have miserably failed to this point. They have never made democracy work. Be it inside the United States, Vietnam, South Africa, the Philippines, South America, Puerto Rico, wherever America has been, she has not been able to make democracy work. [applause] So that in a larger sense, we not only condemn the country for what is done internally, but we must condemn it for what it does externally. We see this country trying to rule the world, and someone must stand up and start articulating that this country is not God and cannot rule the world. [applause]

Now then, before we move on we ought to develop the [concept of] white supremacy attitudes, that we're either conscious or subconscious of, and how they run rampant through the society today. For example, the missionaries were sent to Africa. They went with the attitude that blacks were automatically inferior. As a matter of fact, the first act the missionaries did, you know, when they get to Africa was to make us cover up our bodies, because they said it got them excited. We couldn't go barebreasted any more because they got excited! [laughter] Now when the missionaries came to civilize us because we were uncivilized, educate us because we were uneducated, and give us some literate studies because we were illiterate, they charged a price. The missionaries came with the Bible, and we had the land. When they left, they had the land, and we still have the Bible. [applause]

And that has been the rationalization for Western civilization as it moves across the world, and stealing and plundering, and raping everybody in its path. Their one rationalization is that the rest of the world is uncivilized and they are in fact civilized. And they are uncivilized. [applause]

And that runs on today, you see, because what we have today is that we have what we call modern-day Peace Corps . . . uh . . . missionaries. And they come into our ghettos and they Head Start, Upward Lift, Bootstrap, and Upward Bound us into white society. 'Cause they don't want to face the real problem. Which is a man is poor for one reason and one reason only: because he does not have money. Period. If you want to get rid of poverty you give people money. Period. And you ought not tell me about people who don't work, and you can't give people money without working, because if that were true, you'd have to start stopping Rockefeller, Bobby Kennedy, Lyndon Baines Johnson, Lady Bird Johnson, the whole of Standard Oil, the Gulf Club [Gulf Corporation]—all of them. [applause] Including probably a large number of the board of trustees of this university. [applause]

So the question, then, clearly is not whether or not one can work. It's who has power? Who has power to make his or her acts legitimate? That is all. And that [in] this country that power is invested in the hands of white people, and they make their acts legitimate. It is now, therefore, for black people to make our acts legitimate. [applause]

Now we are engaged in a psychological struggle in this country. And that is whether or not black people have the right to use the words they want to use without white people giving their sanction to it. [applause] And that we maintain whether they like it or not we gonna use the word "Black Power" and let them address themselves to that. [applause] But that we are not going to wait for white people to sanction Black Power. We're tired of waiting; every time black people move in this country, they're forced to defend their position before they move. It's time that the people who are supposed to be defending their position do that, that's white people. They ought to start defending themselves as to why they have oppressed and exploited us.

Now it is clear that when this country started to move in terms of slavery, the reason for a man being picked as a slave was one reason—because of the color of his skin. If one was black one was automatically inferior, inhuman, and therefore fit for slavery. So that the question of whether or not we are individually suppressed is nonsensical, and it's a downright lie. We are oppressed as a group because we are black. Not because we are lazy. Not because we're apathetic. Not because we're stupid. Not because we smell. Not because we eat watermelon and have good rhythm. [applause] We are oppressed because we are black.

And in order to get out of that oppression one must wield the group power that one has, not the individual power which this country then sets the criteria under which a man may come into it. That is what is called in this country as integration. "You do what I tell you to do and then we'll let you sit at the table with us." And that we are saying that we have to be opposed to that. We must now set a criteria and that if there's going to be any integration it's going to be a two-way thing. If you believe in integration, you can come live in Watts, you can send your children to the ghetto schools. Let's talk about that. If you believe in integration then we're going to start adopting us some white people to live in our neighborhood. [applause]

So it is clear that the question is not one of integration or segregation. Integration is a man's ability to want to move in there by himself. If someone wants to live in a white neighborhood, and he is black, that is his choice. It should be his right. It is not because white people will not allow him. So vice versa if a black man wants to live in the slums that should be his right. Black people will let him. That is the difference. And it's the difference on which this country makes a number of logical mistakes when they begin to try to criticize a program articulated by SNCC.

Now we maintain that we cannot afford to be concerned about six percent of the children in this country—black children—who you allow to come into white schools. We have ninety-four percent who still live in shacks. We are going to be concerned about those ninety-four percent. You ought to be concerned about them too. The question is, are we willing to be concerned about those ninety-four percent? Are we willing to be concerned about the black people who will never get to Berkeley, who will never get to Harvard, and cannot get an education so you'll never get a chance to rub shoulders with them and say, "Well, he's almost as good as we are. He's not like the others." [applause]

The question is, how can white society begin to move to see black people as human beings? I am black, therefore I am. Not that I am black and I must go to college to prove myself. I am black, therefore I am. And don't deprive me of anything and say to me that you must go to college before you gain access to X, Y, and Z. It is only a rationalization for one's oppression.

The political parties of this country do not meet the needs of the people on a day-to-day basis. The question is, how can we build new political institutions that will become the political expressions of people on a day-to-day basis? The question is, how can you build political institutions that will begin to meet the needs of Oakland, California? And the needs of Oakland, California, is not one thousand policemen with submachine guns. They don't need that. They need that least of all. [applause] The question is how can we build institutions where those people can begin to function on a day-to-day basis, where they can get decent jobs, where they can get decent houses, and where they can begin to participate in a policy and major decisions that affect their lives? That's what they need, not Gestapo troops, because this is not 1942, and if you play like Nazis, we playing back wit' you this time around—get hip to that. [applause]

The question then is, how can white people move to start making the major institutions that they have in this country function the way it is supposed to function? That is the real question. And can white people move inside their own community and start tearing down racism where in fact it does exist? Where it exists. It is you who live in Cicero and stopped us from living there.[8] It is white people who stopped us from moving into Grenada.[9] It is white people who make sure that we live in the ghettos of this country. It is white institutions that do that. They must change. In order . . . in order for America to really live on a basic principle of human relationships a new society must be born. Racism must die. And the economic exploitation of this country of non-white peoples around the world must also die. Must also die. [applause]

Now there are several programs we have in the South, mostly in poor white communities where we're trying to organize poor whites on a base where they can begin to move around the question of economic exploitation and political disfranchisement. We know, we've heard the theory several times. But few people are willing to go into there. The question is, can the white activist not try to be a Pepsi generation who comes alive in the black community, but can he be a man who's willing to move into the white community and start organizing where the organization is needed? [applause] Can he do that? The question is, can the white society, or the white activist disassociate himself with two clowns who waste time parrying with each other rather than talking about the problems that are facing people in this state? Can you disassociate yourself with those clowns and start to build new institutions that will eliminate all idiots like them? [applause] And the question is, if we are going to do that, when and where do we start and how do we start? We maintain that we must start doing that inside the white community.

Our own personal position politically is that we don't think the Democratic Party represents the needs of black people. We know it don't. [applause] And that if, in fact, white people really believe that the question's if they going to move inside that structure, how are they going to organize around a concept of whiteness based on true brotherhood and based on stopping economic exploitation, so that there will be a coalition base for black people to hook up with? You cannot form a coalition based on national sentiment. That is not a coalition. If you need a coalition to redress itself to real changes in this country, white people must start building those institutions inside the white community. And that is the real question I think facing the white activists today. Can they, in fact, begin to move into and tear down the institutions that have put us all in the trick bag that we've been into for the last hundred years?

I don't think that we should follow what many people say. That we should fight to be leaders of tomorrow. Frederick Douglass said the youth should fight to be leaders today. And God knows we need to be leaders today, because the men who run this country are sick. Are sick. [applause] So that we on a larger sense can begin today to start building those institutions and to fight to articulate our position, to fight to be able to control our universities—we need to be able to do that—to fight to control the basic institutions which perpetuate racism by destroying them and building new ones. That's the real question that faces us today, and it is a dilemma because most of us do not know how to work. And that the excuse that most white activists find is to run into the black community.

Now we maintain that we cannot have white people working in the black community—and we've made it on a psychological ground. The fact is that all black people often question whether or not they are equal to whites, because every time they start to do something, white people are around showing them how to do it. If we are going to eliminate that for the generation that comes after us, then black people must be seen in positions of power, doing and articulating for themselves. [applause] For themselves. That is not to say that one is a reverse racist. It is to say that one is moving on a healthy ground. It is to say what the philosopher Sartre says, one is becoming an "anti-racist racist." [laughter] And this country can't understand that. Maybe it's because it's all caught up in racism. But I think what you have in SNCC is an anti-racist racism. We are against racists. Now if everybody who's white see themselves as racist and then see us against him, they're speaking from they're own guilt position, not ours. Not ours. [applause]

Now then the question is, how can we move to begin to change what's going on in this country? I maintain, as we have in SNCC, that the war in Vietnam is an illegal and immoral war. [applause] And the question is, what can we do to stop that war? What can we do to stop the people who, in the name of our country, are killing babies, women, and children? What can we do to stop that? And I maintain that we do not have the power in our hands to change that institution. To begin to re-create it so that they learn to leave the Vietnamese people alone. And that the only power we have is the power to say, "Hell no to the draft." We have to say, [applause] we have to say to ourselves that there's a higher law than the law of a racist named McNamara. There is a higher law than the law of a fool named Rusk. There's a higher law than the law of a buffoon named Johnson. [applause] It's the law of each of us. The law of each of us. [applause]

It is the law of each of us saying that we will not allow them to make us hired killers. We will stand pat. We will not kill anybody that they say kill. And if we decide to kill, we're gonna to decide who we gonna kill. [applause] And this country will only be able to stop the war in Vietnam when the young men who are made to fight it begin to say, "Hell, no, we ain't going." [applause]

Now there's a failure because the peace movement has been unable to get off the college campuses where everybody has a 2S and [is] not gonna get drafted anyway. The question is how can you move out of that into the white ghettos of this country and begin to articulate a position for those white students who do not want to go? We cannot do that. It is sometimes ironic that many of the peace groups have begun to call us [SNCC] violent and say they can no longer support us, and we are in fact the most militant organization for peace or civil rights or human rights, against the war in Vietnam in this country today. There isn't one organization that has begun to meet our stance on the war in Vietnam. Because we not only say we are against the war in Vietnam, we are against the draft. We are against the draft. No man has the right to take a man for two years and train him to be a killer. A man should decide what he wants to do with his life. [applause]

So the question then is, it becomes crystal clear for black people because we can easily say that anyone fighting in the war in Vietnam is nothing but a black mercenary. And that's all he is. Any time a black man leaves the country where he can't vote to supposedly deliver the vote for somebody else, he's a black mercenary. [applause] Any time a black man leaves this country, gets shot in Vietnam on foreign ground, and returns home and you won't give him a burial in his own homeland, he's a black mercenary. [applause] A black mercenary.

And that even if we're to believe the lies of Johnson—if I were to believe his lies that we're fighting to give democracy to the people in Vietnam, as a black man living in this country I wouldn't fight to give this to anybody. [applause] I wouldn't give it to anybody. So that we have to use our bodies and our minds in the only way that we see fit. We must begin, like the philosopher Camus, to come alive by saying no. That is the only act in which we begin to come alive. And we have to say no to many, many things in this country. This country is a nation of thieves. It has stole everything it has, beginning with black people. [applause] Begining with black people. And the question is then how do we move this country to begin changing this country from what it is—a nation of thieves. This country cannot justify any longer its existence. We have become the policeman of the world. The marines are at our disposal to always bring democracy, and if the Vietnamese don't want democracy, well damn it we'll just wipe them the hell out, because they don't deserve to live if they won't have our way of life. [applause]

There is then in a larger sense what do you do on your university campus? Do you raise questions about the hundred black students who were kicked off campus a couple of weeks ago? Eight hundred? Eight hundred? And how does that question begin to move? Do you begin to relate to people outside of the ivory tower and university wall? Do you think you're capable of building those human relationships as the country now stands? You're fooling yourself. It is impossible for white and black people to talk about building a relationship based on humanity when the country is the way it is, when the institutions are clearly against us.

We have taken all the myths of the country and we found them to be nothing but downright lies. This country told us that if we worked hard we would succeed, and if that were true we would own this country lock, stock, and barrel. [applause] Lock, stock, and barrel. Lock, stock, and barrel. It is we who have picked the cotton for nothing. It is we who are the maids in the kitchens of liberal white people. It is we who are the janitors, the porters, the elevator men. We who sweep up your college floors. Yes it is we who are the hardest workers and the lowest paid. And the lowest paid. And that it is nonsensical for people to start talking about human relationships until they are willing to build new institutions. Black people are economically insecure. White liberals are economically secure. Can you begin to build an economic coalition? Are the liberals willing to share their salaries with the economically insecure black people they so much love? Then if you're not, are you willing to start building new institutions that will provide economic security for black people? That's the question we want to deal with. [applause] That's the question we want to deal with.

We have to seriously examine the histories that we have been told. But we have something more to do than that. American students are perhaps the most politically unsophisticated students in the world. [applause] In the world. In the world.

Across every country in this world, while we were growing up, students were leading the major revolutions of their countries. We have not been able to do that. They have been politically aware of their existence. In South America, our neighbors down below the border, have one every 24 hours just to remind us that they are politically aware. And that we have been unable to grasp it because we've always moved in the field of morality and love while people have been politically jiving with our lives. And the question is, how do we now move politically and stop trying to move morally. You can't move morally against a man like Brown and Reagan. You've got to move politically to cut them out of business. [applause] You've got to move politically.

You can't move morally against Lyndon Baines Johnson because he is an immoral man. He doesn't know what it's all about. So you've got to move politically. [applause] You've got to move politically. And that we have to begin to develop a political sophistication, which is not to be a parrot: [mimicking] The two-party system is the best system in the world. [laughter] There's a difference between being a parrot and being politically sophisticated. We have to raise questions about whether we do need new types of political institutions in this country, and we in SNCC maintain that we need them now. [applause] We need new political institutions in this country.

Any time Lyndon Baines Johnson can head a party which has in it Bobby Kennedy, Wayne Morse, Eastland, Wallace, and all those other supposed-to-be-liberal cats, there's something wrong with that party. They're moving politically, not morally. And that if that party refuses to seat black people from Mississippi and goes ahead and seats racists like Eastland and his clique, it's clear to me that they're moving politically, and that one cannot begin to talk morality to people like that. We must begin to think politically and see if we can have the power to impose and keep the moral values that we hold high. We must question the values of this society, and I maintain that black people are the best people to do that because we have been excluded from that society. And the question is we ought to think whether or not we want to become a part of that society. [applause]

And that that is precisely what it seems to me that the Student Nonviolent Coordinating Committee is doing. We are raising questions about this country. I do not want to be a part of the American pie. The American pie means raping South Africa, beating Vietnam, beating South America, raping the Philippines, raping every country you've been in. I don't want any of your blood money. I don't want it. Don't want to be part of that system. And the question is, how do we raise those questions? [applause] How do we raise them as activists? How do we begin to raise them?

We have grown up and we are the generation that has found this country to be a world power. That has found this country to be the wealthiest country in the world. We must question how she got her wealth. That's what we're questioning. And whether or not we want this country to continue being the wealthiest country in the world at the price of raping everybody else across the world. That's what we must begin to question. And that because black people are saying we do not now want to become a part of you, we are called reverse racists. Ain't that a gas? [laughter]

Now then we want to touch on nonviolence because we see that again as the failure of white society to make nonviolence work. I was always surprised at Quakers who came to Alabama and counseled me to be nonviolent, but didn't have the guts to start talking to James Clark to be nonviolent. That is where nonviolence needs to be preached—to Jim Clark, not to black people. They have already been nonviolent too many years. [applause] The question is, can white people conduct their nonviolent schools in Cicero where they belong to be conducted, not among black people in Mississippi? Can they conduct it among the white people in Grenada? Six-foot-two men who kicked little black children—can you conduct nonviolent schools there? That is the question that we must raise. Not that you conduct nonviolence among black people. Can you name me one black man today who has killed anybody white and is still alive? Even after a rebellion, when some black brothers throw some bricks and bottles, ten thousands of them has to pay the crime. 'Cause when the white policeman comes in, anybody who's black is arrested because we all look alike. [applause]

So that we have to raise those questions. We, the youth of this country, must begin to raise those questions. And we must begin to move to build new institutions that gonna speak to the needs of people who need it. We are going to have to speak to change the foreign policy of this country. One of the problems with the peace movement is that it's just too caught up in Vietnam, and if we pull out the troops from Vietnam this week, next week you'd have to get another peace movement for Santo Domingo. And the question is how do you begin to articulate needs to change the foreign policy of this country. A policy that is decided upon rape. A policy in which decisions are made upon getting economic wealth at any price. At any price.

Now we articulate that we therefore have to hook up with black people around the world. And that that hookup is not only psychological but becomes very real. If South America today were to rebel, and black people were to shoot the hell out of all the white people there—as they should, as they should—then Standard Oil would crumble tomorrow. [applause] If South Africa were to go today, Chase Manhattan Bank would crumble tomorrow. [applause] If Zimbabwe, which is called Rhodesia by white people, were to go tomorrow, General Electric would cave in on the East Coast.

The question is, how do we stop those institutions that are so willing to fight against "Communist aggression" but closes their eye to racist oppression? That is the question that you raise. Can this country do that? Now many people talk about pulling out of Vietnam. What will happen if we pull out of Vietnam [is] there will be one less aggressor there. We won't be there. We won't be there. And so the question is how do we articulate those positions? And we cannot begin to articulate them from the same assumptions that the people in the country speak 'cause they speak from different assumptions than I assume the youth in this country are talking about.

That we're not talking about a policy of aid or sending Peace Corps people in to teach people how to read and write and build houses while we steal their raw materials from them. Is that what we're talking about? 'Cause that's all we do. What underdeveloped countries need is information about how to become industrialized, so they can keep their raw materials where they have it, produce them and sell them to this country for the price it's supposed to pay. Not that we produce it and send it back to them for a profit, and keep sending our modern day missionaries there, calling them the sons of Kennedy. And that if the youth are going to participate in that program, how do you raise those questions where you begin to control that Peace Corps program? How do you begin to raise them?

How do you raise the questions of poverty? The assumption for this country is that if someone is poor, they are poor because of their own individual blight, or they weren't born on the right side of town, they had too many children, they went in the army too early, their father was a drunk, they didn't care about school, they made a mistake. That's a lot of nonsense. Poverty is well calculated in this country. It is well calculated. And the reason why the poverty program won't work is because the calculators of poverty are administering it. That's why it won't work. [applause]

So how can we, as the youth in this country, move to start tearing those things down? We must move into the white community. We are in the black community. We have developed a movement in the black community. The challenge is that the white activist has failed miserably to develop the movement inside of his community. And the question is, can we find white people who are gonna have the courage to go into white communities and start organizing them? Can we find them? Are they here and are they willing to do that? Those are the questions that we must raise for the white activist. And we're never gonna get caught up in questions about power. This country knows what power is. Knows it very well. And it knows what Black Power is 'cause it's deprived black people of it for four hundred years. So it knows what Black Power is. But the question of why do white people in this country associate Black Power with violence, and the [answer] is because of their own inability to deal with blackness. If we had said "Negro Power" nobody would get scared. [laughter] Everybody would support it. If we said power for colored people, everybody'd be for that. But it is the word "black." It is the word "black" that bothers people in this country, and that's their problem, not mine. [applause] Their problem.

Now there's one modern-day lie that we want to attack and then move on very quickly—and that is the lie that says anything all black is bad. Now, you're all a college university crowd. You've taken your basic logic course. You know about a major premise, minor premise. So people have been telling me anything all black is bad. Let's make that our major premise.

Major premise: Anything all black is bad.

Minor premise or particular premise: I am all black.

Therefore. [laughter] I'm never going to be put in that trick bag; I'm all black and I'm all good. [applause] Anything all black is not necessarily bad. Anything all black is only bad when you use force to keep whites out. Now that's what white people have done in this country, and they're projecting their same fears and guilt on us, and we won't have it, we won't have it. [applause] Let them handle their own affairs and their own guilt. Let them find their own psychologists. We refuse to be the therapy for white society any longer. We have gone mad trying to do it. We have gone stark, raving mad trying to do it.

I look at Dr. King on television every single day, and I say to myself, "Now there is a man who's desperately needed in this country. There is a man full of love. There is a man full of mercy. There is a man full of compassion." But every time I see Lyndon on television, I say, "Martin, baby, you got a long way to go." [laughter]

So that the question stands as to what we are willing to do, how we are willing to say no, to withdraw from that system and begin, within our community, to start the function and to build new institutions that will speak to our needs. In Lowndes County, we developed something called the Lowndes County Freedom Organization—it is a political party. The Alabama law says that if you have a party, you must have an emblem. We chose for the emblem a black panther—a *beautiful* black animal—which symbolizes the strength and dignity of black people. An animal that never strikes back until he's backed so far into the wall that he's got nothing to do but spring out. And when he springs, he does not stop.

Now there is a party in Alabama that is called the Alabama Democratic Party. It is all white. It has as its emblem a white rooster and the words "white supremacy for the right." Now the gentlemen of the press, because they are advertisers and because most of them are white and because they are produced by that white institution, never calls the Lowndes County Freedom Organization by its name—but rather they call it the Black Panther Party. Our question is, why don't they call the Alabama Democratic Party the White Cock Party? [laughter] It is clear to me that just points out America's problem with sex and color—not our problem, [laughter] not our problem. It is now white America that is going to deal with those problems of sex and color.

If we were to be real and honest, we would have to admit, we would have to admit, that most people in this country see things black and white. We have to do that, all of us do: we live in a country that's geared that way. White people would have to admit that they are afraid to go into a black ghetto at night. They're afraid, that's a fact. They're afraid because they'd be "beat up," "lynched," "looted," "cut up," et cetera, et cetera. That happens to black people inside the ghetto every day, incidentally. And white people are afraid of that. So you get a man to do it for you—a policeman. And now you figure his mentality, where he's afraid of black people. The first time a black man jumps, that white man's gonna shoot him. He's gonna shoot him. So police brutality is going to exist on that level, because of the incapability of that white man to see black people come together and to live in the conditions.

This country is too hypocritical; and we cannot adjust ourselves to its hypocrisy. The only time I hear people talk about nonviolence is when black people move to defend themselves against white people. Black people cut themselves every night in the ghetto—don't anybody talk about nonviolence. Lyndon Baines Johnson is busy bombing the hell out of Vietnam—don't nobody talk about nonviolence. White people beat up black people every day—don't nobody talk about nonviolence. But as soon as black people start to move, the double standard comes into being. You can't defend yourself—that's what you're saying. 'Cause you show me a man who advocates aggressive violence that would be able to live in this country. Show him to me.

The double standards again come into itself. Isn't it ludicrous and hypocritical for the political shamelian who calls himself a vice president of this country [laughter] to stand up before this country and say, "Looting never got anybody anywhere?" [laughter] Isn't it hypocritical for Lyndon to talk about looting, that you can't accomplish anything by looting, and you must accomplish it by the legal ways? What does he know about legality? Ask Ho Chi Minh, he'll tell you. [laughter]

So that in conclusion, we want to say that, number one: it is clear to me that we have to wage a psychological battle on the right for black people to define their own terms; define themselves as they see fit; and organize themselves as they see it. Now, the question is, how is the white community going to begin to allow for that organizing, because once they start to do that, they will also allow for the organizing that they want to do inside their community. It doesn't make a difference, 'cause we're gonna organize our way, anyway. We gonna do it.

The question is how we're going to facilitate those matters, whether it's going to be done with a thousand policemen with submachine guns, or whether or not it's going to be done in a context where it's allowed to be done by white people warding off those policemen. That is the question. And the question is, how are white people, who call themselves activists, ready to start move into the white communities on two counts? On building new political institutions to destroy the old ones that we have, and to move around the concept of white youth refusing to go into the army. So that we can start, then, to build a new world. It is ironic to talk about civilization in this country. This country is uncivilized; it needs to be civilized, it needs to be civilized. [applause] We must begin to raise those questions of civilization—what it is and who do it. And so we must urge you to fight now to be the leaders of today, not tomorrow. We've got to be the leaders of today. This country, this country is a nation of thieves! It stands on the brink of becoming a nation of murderers! We must stop it! We must stop it! We must stop it! [applause]

And then therefore, in a larger sense, there is the question of black people. We are on the move for our liberation. We have been tired of trying to prove things to white people. We are tired of trying to explain to white people that we're not gonna to hurt them. We are concerned with getting the things we want, the things that we have to have to be able to function. The question is, can white people allow for that in this country? The question is, will white people overcome their racism and allow for that to happen in this country? If that does not happen, brothers and sisters, we have no choice but to say very clearly, "Move over, or we're gonna move on over you." Thank you. [applause]

11.

MARTIN LUTHER KING JR. (1929–1968)

"I've Been to the Mountaintop"

Memphis, Tennessee—April 3, 1968

Martin Luther King Jr. felt poorly the night he delivered this speech, the last one of his life. The venue was a mass meeting held in the Bishop Charles Mason Temple Church of God. Andrew Young, who was with him at the time, said King initially decided not to speak at all that night. King and his small entourage—including Ralph Abernathy, Jesse Jackson, and Benjamin Hooks—had led a march that day protesting low pay for black garbage collectors in Memphis. A rainstorm was gathering. King decided he was too sick to preach. He asked his best friend, Abernathy, to speak instead.[1]

Once in the church, Abernathy felt King would have to speak to the crowd, so he phoned King and asked him to come down. Abernathy promised that he would still do the preaching; King would just have to say a few words. Abernathy spoke for more than half an hour, his words energizing the crowd. That called up the spirit in Reverend King, and he spoke that night without a single note in hand.[2]

In a speech Benjamin Hooks delivered a decade after King's death (also featured in this anthology), he recalled King's final sermon: "I remember that night when he finished, he stopped by quoting the words of that song that he loved so well, 'Mine eyes have seen the glory of the coming of the Lord.' He never finished. He wheeled around and took his seat and to my surprise, when I got a little closer, I saw tears streaming down his face. Grown men were sitting there weeping openly because of the power of this man who spoke on that night."

King had warned in previous sermons that he might die before the struggle ended. It was not the first time he told listeners he'd "seen the promised land." King had been living with death threats for years. No one in King's circle thought this was his final address. Later, Young wrote: "Did [King] know? He always knew some speech would be his last. Was he afraid? Not on your life!"

Young said the next day was one of King's happiest. "Surrounded by his brother, his staff and close friends of the movement," Young wrote, "he laughed and joked all day until it was time to go to dinner at 6 PM."[3] King stepped onto the balcony of his room at the Lorraine Motel, checking the weather to decide whether to bring a coat. As he leaned over the railing, talking with Jesse Jackson and others below, King was fatally shot.[4]

Martin Luther King Jr. was born on January 15, 1929, in Atlanta, Georgia. His father, "Daddy King," was a pastor at Ebenezer Baptist Church, a self-made businessman, and an early civil rights activist. He founded the Atlanta branch of the NAACP and fought for equal pay for Atlanta's black teachers. King's mother had a college degree. King grew up in a comfortable, middle-class home. He delivered his first sermon at the age of eighteen; his father had ordained him as a minister just days earlier. King graduated from Morehouse College when he was nineteen years old and went on to study at Crozer Theological Seminary just outside Philadelphia. In 1951, he began his doctoral work at Boston University's theology school, and in 1954 King and his new wife, Coretta Scott, moved to Montgomery, Alabama, where he was appointed pastor of Dexter Avenue Baptist Church. On December 2, 1955, a day after Rosa Parks was arrested for refusing to give up her seat on a bus to a white man, King led a mass meeting in his church. Almost overnight, he became the spiritual leader of the modern civil rights movement.[5]

———

THANK YOU VERY KINDLY, my friends. As I listened to Ralph Abernathy in his eloquent and generous introduction and then thought about myself, I wondered who he was talking about. [laughter] It's always good to have your closest friend and associate say something good about you. And Ralph is the best friend that I have in the world. I'm delighted to see each of you here tonight in spite of a storm warning. You reveal that you are determined to go on anyhow.

Something is happening in Memphis; something is happening in our world. And you know, if I were standing at the beginning of time, with the possibility of taking a kind of general and panoramic view of the whole human history up to now, and the Almighty said to me, "Martin Luther King, which age would you like to live in?"—I would take my mental flight by Egypt and I would watch God's children in their magnificent trek from the dark dungeons of Egypt through, or rather across the Red Sea, through the wilderness on toward the promised land. And in spite of its magnificence, I wouldn't stop there. I would move on by Greece, and take my mind to Mount Olympus. And I would see Plato, Aristotle, Socrates, Euripides and Aristophanes assembled around the Parthenon. And I would watch them around the Parthenon as they discussed the great and eternal issues of reality. But I wouldn't stop there.

I would go on, even to the great heyday of the Roman Empire. And I would see developments around there, through various emperors and leaders. But I wouldn't stop there. I would even come up to the day of the Renaissance, and get a quick picture of all that the Renaissance did for the cultural and aesthetic life of man. But I wouldn't stop there. I would even go by the way that the man for whom I'm named had his habitat. And I would watch Martin Luther as he tacked his ninety-five theses on the door at the church of Wittenberg.

But I wouldn't stop there. I would come on up even to 1863, and watch a vacillating president by the name of Abraham Lincoln finally come to the conclusion that he had to sign the Emancipation Proclamation. But I wouldn't stop there. [applause]

I would even come up to the early thirties, and see a man grappling with the problems of the bankruptcy of his nation. And come with an eloquent cry that we have nothing to fear but fear itself.

But I wouldn't stop there. Strangely enough, I would turn to the

Almighty, and say, "If you allow me to live just a few years in the second half of the 20th century, I will be happy." [applause] Now that's a strange statement to make, because the world is all messed up. The nation is sick. Trouble is in the land; confusion all around. That's a strange statement. But I know, somehow, that only when it is dark enough can you see the stars. And I see God working in this period of the twentieth century in a way that men, in some strange way, are responding—something is happening in our world. The masses of people are rising up. And wherever they are assembled today, whether they are in Johannesburg, South Africa; Nairobi, Kenya; Accra, Ghana; New York City; Atlanta, Georgia; Jackson, Mississippi; or Memphis, Tennessee—the cry is always the same—"We want to be free."

And another reason that I'm happy to live in this period is that we have been forced to a point where we're going to have to grapple with the problems that men have been trying to grapple with through history, but the demand didn't force them to do it. Survival demands that we grapple with them. Men, for years now, have been talking about war and peace. But now, no longer can they just talk about it. It is no longer a choice between violence and nonviolence in this world; it's nonviolence or nonexistence! [applause] That is where we are today.

And also in the human rights revolution, if something isn't done, and done in a hurry, to bring the colored peoples of the world out of their long years of poverty, their long years of hurt and neglect, the whole world is doomed. Now, I'm just happy that God has allowed me to live in this period, to see what is unfolding. And I'm happy that He's allowed me to be in Memphis.

I can remember, I can remember when Negroes were just going around as Ralph has said, so often, scratching where they didn't itch, and laughing when they were not tickled. But that day is all over. We mean business now, and we are determined to gain our rightful place in God's world.

And that's all this whole thing is about. We aren't engaged in any negative protest and in any negative arguments with anybody. We are saying that we are determined to be *men*. We are determined to be *people*. We are saying that we are *God's* children. And that we don't have to live like we are forced to live.

Now, what does all of this mean in this great period of history? It means that we've got to stay together. We've got to stay together and maintain unity. You know, whenever Pharaoh wanted to prolong the period of slavery in Egypt, he had a favorite, favorite formula for doing it. What was that? He kept the slaves fighting among themselves. But whenever the *slaves* get together, something happens in Pharaoh's court, and he cannot hold the slaves in slavery. When the slaves get together, that's the beginning of getting out of slavery. Now let us maintain unity.

Secondly, let us keep the issues where they are. The issue is injustice. The issue is the refusal of Memphis to be fair and honest in its dealings with its public servants who happen to be sanitation workers. Now, we've got to keep attention on that. That's always the problem with a little violence. You know what happened the other day, and the press dealt only with the window-breaking. I read the articles. They very seldom got around to mentioning the fact that one thousand, three hundred sanitation workers were on strike, and that Memphis is not being fair to them, and that Mayor Loeb is in dire need of a doctor. They didn't get around to that. [applause]

Now we're going to march again, and we've got to march again, in order to put the issue where it is supposed to be—and force everybody to see that there are thirteen hundred of God's children here suffering, sometimes going hungry, going through dark and dreary nights wondering how this thing is going to come out. *That's* the issue. And we've got to say to the nation: we know how it's coming out. For when people get caught up with that which is right and they are willing to sacrifice for it, there is no stopping point short of victory! [applause]

We aren't going to let any mace stop us. We are masters in our nonviolent movement in disarming police forces; they don't know what to do, I've seen them so often. I remember in Birmingham, Alabama, when we were in that majestic struggle there, we would move out of the 16th Street Baptist Church day after day; by the hundreds we would move out. And Bull Connor would tell them to send the dogs forth, and they did come; but we just went before the dogs singing, "Ain't gonna let nobody turn me around." Bull Connor next would say, "Turn the fire hoses on." And as I said to you the other night, Bull Connor didn't know history. He knew a kind of physics that somehow didn't relate to the transphysics that we knew about. And that was the fact that there was a certain kind of fire that *no water* could put out. And we went before the fire hoses; we had known water. If we were Baptist or some other denomination, we had been immersed. If we were Methodist, and some others, we had been sprinkled, but we knew water. That couldn't stop us.

And we just went on before the dogs and we would look at them; and we'd go on before the water hoses and we would look at it, and we'd just go on singing, "Over my head I see freedom in the air." And then we would be thrown in the paddy wagons, and sometimes we were stacked in there like sardines in a can. And they would throw us in, and old Bull would say, "Take them off," and they did; and we would just go on in the paddy wagon singing, "We Shall Overcome." And every now and then we'd get in the jail, and we'd see the jailers looking through the windows being moved by our prayers, and being moved by our words and our songs. And there was a power there which Bull Connor couldn't adjust to; and so we ended up transforming Bull into a steer, and we won our struggle in Birmingham. [applause]

Now we've got to go on in Memphis just like that. I call upon you to be with us when we go out Monday. Now about injunctions: We have an injunction and we're going into court tomorrow morning to fight this illegal, unconstitutional injunction. All we say to America is, "Be true to what you said on paper." [applause] If I lived in China or even Russia, or any totalitarian country, maybe I could understand some of these illegal injunctions. Maybe I could understand the denial of certain basic First Amendment privileges, because they hadn't committed themselves to that over there. But somewhere I read of the freedom of assembly. Somewhere I read of the freedom of speech. Somewhere I read of the freedom of the press. Somewhere I read that the greatness of America is the right to protest for right. And so just as I say we aren't going to let any dogs or water hoses turn us around, we aren't going to let any *injunction* turn us around. We are going on.

We need all of you. And you know what's beautiful to me, is to see all of these ministers of the Gospel. It's a marvelous picture. Who is it that is supposed to articulate the longings and aspirations of the people more than the preacher? Somehow the preacher must have a kind of fire shut up in his bones and whenever injustice is around, he must tell it. Somehow the preacher must be an Amos, and say, "When God speaks, who can but prophesy?" Again, with Amos, "Let justice roll down like waters and righteousness like a mighty stream." Somehow, the preacher must say with

Jesus, "The spirit of the Lord is upon me, because he hath anointed me to deal with the problems of the poor."

And I want to commend the preachers, under the leadership of these noble men: James Lawson, one who has been in this struggle for many years; he's been to jail for struggling; he's been kicked out of Vanderbilt University for this struggle, but he's still going on, fighting for the rights of his people. [applause] Rev. Ralph Jackson, Billy Kiles; I could just go right on down the list, but time will not permit. But I want to thank all of them. And I want you to thank them, because so often, preachers aren't concerned about anything but themselves. And I'm always happy to see a relevant ministry.

It's all right to talk about "long white robes over yonder," in all of its symbolism. But ultimately people want some suits and dresses and shoes to wear down here! It's all right to talk about "streets flowing with milk and honey," but God has commanded us to be concerned about the *slums* down here, and his children who can't eat three square meals a day. It's all right to talk about the new Jerusalem, but one day, God's preachers must talk about the new New York, the new Atlanta, the new Philadelphia, the new Los Angeles, the new Memphis, Tennessee. [applause] This is what we have to do.

Now the other thing we'll have to do is this: Always anchor our external direct action with the power of economic withdrawal. Now, we are poor people. Individually, we are poor when you compare us with white society in America. We are poor. Never stop and forget that collectively—that means all of us together—collectively we are richer than all the nations in the world, with the exception of nine. Did you ever think about that? After you leave the United States, Soviet Russia, Great Britain, West Germany, France, and I could name the others, the American Negro collectively is richer than most nations of the world. We have an annual income of more than thirty billion dollars a year, which is more than all of the exports of the United States, and *more* than the national budget of Canada. Did you know that? That's power right there, if we know how to pool it. [applause]

We don't have to argue with anybody. We don't have to curse and go around acting bad with our words. We don't need any bricks and bottles. We don't need any Molotov cocktails. We just need to go around to these stores, and to these massive industries in our country, and say, "God sent us by here, to say to you that you're not treating his children right. And we've come by here to ask you to make the first item on your agenda fair treatment, where God's children are concerned. Now, if you are not prepared to do that, we do have an agenda that we must follow. And our agenda calls for *withdrawing* economic *support* from you."

And so, as a result of this, we are asking you tonight, to go out and tell your neighbors not to buy Coca-Cola in Memphis. Go by and tell them not to buy Sealtest milk. Tell them not to buy—what is the other bread?— Wonder Bread. And what is the other bread company, Jesse? Tell them not to buy Hart's bread. As Jesse Jackson has said, up to now, only the garbage men have been feeling pain; now we must kind of redistribute the pain. [applause] We are choosing these companies because they haven't been fair in their hiring policies; and we are choosing them because they can begin the process of saying they are going to support the needs and the rights of these men who are on strike. And then they can move on downtown and tell Mayor Loeb to do what is right.

But not only that, we've got to strengthen black institutions. I call upon you to take your money out of the banks downtown and deposit your money in Tri-State Bank—we want a "bank-in" movement in Memphis. So go by the savings and loan association. I'm not asking you something we don't do ourselves at SCLC. Judge Hooks and others will tell you that we have an account here in the savings and loan association from the Southern Christian Leadership Conference. We're telling you to follow what we're doing. Put your money there. You have six or seven black insurance companies in the city of Memphis. Take out your insurance there. We want to have an "insurance-in."

Now these are some practical things we can do. We begin the process of building a greater economic base. And at the same time, we are putting *pressure* where it really hurts. I ask you to follow through here.

Now, let me say as I move to my conclusion that we've got to give ourselves to this struggle until the end. Nothing would be more tragic than to stop at this point, in Memphis. We've got to see it through. [applause] And when we have our march, you need to be there. If it means leaving work, if it means leaving school, be there. [applause] Be concerned about your brother. You may not be on strike. But either we go up together, or we go down together. [applause]

Let us develop a kind of dangerous unselfishness. One day a man came to Jesus; and he wanted to raise some questions about some vital matters in life. At points, he wanted to trick Jesus, and show him that he knew a little more than Jesus knew, and throw him off base. Now that question could have easily ended up in a philosophical and theological debate. But Jesus immediately pulled that question from mid-air, and placed it on a dangerous curve between Jerusalem and Jericho. And he talked about a certain man, who fell among thieves. You remember that a Levite and a priest passed by on the other side. They didn't stop to help him. And finally a man of another race came by. He got down from his beast, decided not to be compassionate by proxy. But he got down with him, administering first aid, and helped the man in need. Jesus ended up saying, this was the good man, this was the great man, because he had the capacity to project the "I" into the "thou," and to be concerned about his brother. Now you know, we use our imagination a great deal to try to determine why the priest and the Levite didn't stop. At times we say they were busy going to a church meeting—an ecclesiastical gathering—and they had to get on down to Jerusalem so they wouldn't be late for their meeting. At other times we would speculate that there was a religious law that "One who was engaged in religious ceremonials was not to touch a human body twenty-four hours before the ceremony." And every now and then we begin to wonder whether maybe they were not going down to Jerusalem, or down to Jericho, rather to organize a "Jericho Road Improvement Association." That's a possibility. Maybe they felt that it was better to deal with the problem from the causal root, rather than to get bogged down with an individual effort.

But I'm going to tell you what my imagination tells me. It's possible that those men were afraid. You see, the Jericho road is a dangerous road. I remember when Mrs. King and I were first in Jerusalem. We rented a car and drove from Jerusalem down to Jericho. And as soon as we got on that road, I said to my wife, "I can see why Jesus used this as the setting for his parable." It's a winding, meandering road. It's really conducive for ambushing. You start out in Jerusalem, which is about 1,200 miles, or rather 1,200 feet, above sea level. And by the time you get down to Jericho, fifteen or twenty minutes later, you're about 2,200 feet below sea level. That's a dangerous road. In the days of Jesus it came to be known as the "Bloody Pass." And you know, it's possible that the priest and the Levite looked over that man on the ground and wondered if the robbers were still around. Or it's possible that they felt that the man on the ground was merely faking. And he was acting like he had been robbed and hurt, in order to seize them over there, lure them there for quick and easy seizure. And so the first question that the Levite asked was, "If I stop to help this man, what will happen to me?" But then the Good Samaritan came by. And he reversed the question: "If I do not stop to help this man, what will happen to him?"

That's the question before you tonight. Not, "If I stop to help the sanitation workers, what will happen to my job?" Not, "If I stop to help the sanitation workers what will happen to all of the hours that I usually spend in my office every day and every week as a pastor?" The question is not, "If I stop to help this man in need, what will happen to me?" The question is, "If I do *not* stop to help the sanitation workers, what will happen to them?" That's the question. [applause]

Let us rise up tonight with a greater readiness. Let us stand with a greater determination. And let us move on in these powerful days, these days of challenge to make America what it ought to be. We have an opportunity to make America a better nation. And I want to thank God, once more, for allowing me to be here with you.

You know, several years ago, I was in New York City autographing the first book that I had written. And while sitting there autographing books, a demented black woman came up. The only question I heard from her was, "Are you Martin Luther King?" And I was looking down writing, and I said yes. And the next minute I felt something beating on my chest. Before I knew it I had been stabbed by this demented woman. I was rushed to Harlem Hospital. It was a dark Saturday afternoon. And that blade had gone through, and the X-rays revealed that the tip of the blade was on the edge of my aorta, the main artery. And once that's punctured, you drown in your own blood—that's the end of you.

It came out in the *New York Times* the next morning, that if I had merely sneezed, I would have died. Well, about four days later, they allowed me, after the operation, after my chest had been opened, and the blade had been taken out, to move around in the wheelchair in the hospital. They allowed me to read some of the mail that came in, and from all over the states, and the world, kind letters came in. I read a few, but one of them I will never forget. I had received one from the President and the Vice

President. I've forgotten what those telegrams said. I'd received a visit and a letter from the Governor of New York, but I've forgotten what the letter said. But there was another letter that came from a little girl, a young girl who was a student at the White Plains High School. And I looked at that letter, and I'll never forget it. It said simply, "Dear Dr. King: I am a ninth-grade student at the White Plains High School." She said, "While it should not matter, I would like to mention that I am a white girl. I read in the paper of your misfortune, and of your suffering. And I read that if you had sneezed, you would have died. And I'm simply writing you to say that I'm so happy that you didn't sneeze." [applause]

And I want to say tonight, I want to say that I too am happy that I didn't sneeze. Because if I had sneezed, I wouldn't have been around here in 1960, when students all over the South started sitting-in at lunch counters. And I knew that as they were sitting in, they were really standing up for the best in the American dream. And taking the whole nation back to those great wells of democracy which were dug deep by the Founding Fathers in the Declaration of Independence and the Constitution. If I had sneezed, I wouldn't have been around here in 1961 when we decided to take a ride for freedom and ended segregation in interstate travel. If I had sneezed, I wouldn't have been around here in 1962, when Negroes in Albany, Georgia, decided to straighten their backs up. And whenever men and women straighten their backs up, they are going somewhere, because a man can't ride your back unless it is bent! [applause] If I had sneezed, I wouldn't have been here in 1963, when the black people of Birmingham, Alabama, aroused the conscience of this nation, and brought into being the Civil Rights Bill. If I had sneezed, I wouldn't have had a chance later that year, in August, to try to tell *America* about a *dream* that I had had. If I had sneezed, I wouldn't have been down in Selma, Alabama, to see the great movement there. If I had sneezed, I wouldn't have been in Memphis to see the community rally around those brothers and sisters who are suffering. I'm so happy that I didn't sneeze. [applause]

And they were telling me, now it doesn't matter now. It really doesn't matter what happens now. I left Atlanta this morning, and as we got started on the plane, there were six of us, the pilot said over the public address system, "We are sorry for the delay, but we have Dr. Martin Luther King on the plane. And to be sure that all of the bags were checked, and to be sure that nothing would be wrong on the plane, we had to check out everything carefully. And we've had the plane protected and guarded all night."

And then I got to Memphis. And some began to say the threats, or talk about the threats that were out. What would happen to me from some of our sick white brothers?

Well, I don't know what will happen now. We've got some difficult days ahead. But it really doesn't matter with me now. Because I've been to the mountaintop. [applause] And I don't mind. Like anybody, I would like to live a long life. Longevity has its place. But I'm not concerned about that now. I just want to do God's will. And He's allowed me to go up to the mountain. And I've looked over. And I've seen the promised land. I may not get there with you. But I want you to know tonight, that we, as a people, will get to the promised land! So I'm happy, tonight. I'm not worried about *anything*. I'm not fearing any man. Mine *eyes* have seen the glory of the coming of the Lord! [applause]

12.

JOHN HOPE FRANKLIN
(1915–)

Martin Luther King Jr. Lecture,
The New School for Social Research

New York City   April 3, 1969

Historian John Hope Franklin is one of the most acclaimed American scholars of his time. He has been recognized with more than one hundred honorary degrees and the nation's highest civilian tribute, the Presidential Medal of Freedom, bestowed on him by President Bill Clinton in 1995. Franklin began his pioneering work on the American South when state-mandated segregation still had a firm grip on the region. He was obliged in a North Carolina archive to use a separate room from whites and in a Louisiana archive to do his research when the building was closed.[1]

Franklin's extraordinary output has changed the way Southern history is understood. His book *From Slavery to Freedom: A History of Negro Americans* (1947), now in its eighth edition, is a classic. Franklin also taught generations of new scholars and lent his skills to the struggle for civil rights. He contributed historical research to Thurgood Marshall's victory over legalized segregation in the U.S. Supreme Court's landmark *Brown v. Board of Education* decision, handed down in 1954.

Franklin was born in Rentiesville, Oklahoma, an all-black town. His father was a lawyer, his mother a teacher. Franklin said they moved to

Rentiesville to be free from the pressures of Jim Crow discrimination. But finding enough work there was difficult and the family eventually moved to Tulsa. A precocious child, Franklin learned to read and write by the age of four. He said his love for learning came from his parents, especially his father, who would read and write every night after work. "I grew up believing that in the evenings one either read or wrote," Franklin remembered. "It was easy to read something worthwhile, and if one worked hard enough he might even write something worthwhile."[2]

Franklin attended Tulsa's segregated schools and won a scholarship to Fisk University, a historically black college in Nashville, Tennessee. In his second year, his life was changed when his white history professor, Theodore Currier, encouraged him to pursue history. Franklin graduated in 1935 and went on to Harvard, with $500 in help from Currier. He earned his Ph.D. in 1941.[3]

Franklin taught at a number of schools, including Howard University, England's Cambridge University, and the University of Chicago. He retired from Duke University in 1985. Franklin has written more than a dozen books and scores of articles and essays, many challenging conventional ideas about black capacity, achievement, and historical agency. With his "easy amiability" and "icon-like status in his profession," Franklin is a revered and beloved scholar.[4]

IT IS INDEED A GREAT HONOR to be here this evening and to participate in the inauguration of the Martin Luther King lectures. In the presence of all of you, on the eve of the first anniversary of the martyrdom of Martin Luther King, I would like not only to dedicate these remarks to him this evening, but at the outset, to make a comment or two as we seek some meaning for us of his life and his death. It is, of course, no easy task to do this. We lack perspective; our emotions betray us. But a few things seem clear. What national anguish his death brought was short-lived, if indeed it ever existed at all. We do not seem to have moved significantly toward the goals he sought, or even in the direction of those goals. There has been no large enlistment of Americans in the causes for which he gave his life; no great national resolve to finish the task of creating a decent order. But his death can be viewed as a meaning and as a warning that the time is running out when we can solve any of our major problems peacefully.

The violent death of a man of peace triggered a period of convulsive and tragic violence. It provided yet another example of America's living and dying by the sword. The strain on our legal and our political institutions, of the murder of a president, and then a great national leader and then a United States senator, the strain on these institutions is incalculable. It pushes us clearer to the brink of anarchy; and the alarming deterioration of the rule under law is surely related to those violent and untimely deaths. Our young nation, the hope of the old world and the new, grows old and weary before its time. It seems unable to cope with the forces that propel it toward its own demise. It is the nature of our own life that has done this to it. A nation cannot be profligate and incontinent in its regard for its own people without draining itself of its own vitality, as well as of its own humanity. Perhaps it can recover, but not without some strong resolve, stronger than anything that we have yet witnessed—a resolve to become the vessel in which the lives and the hopes of all its people can flourish and thereby bring about the restoration of its own vitality.

Is this requiring too much? When a young poet of another nation learned of the death of Martin Luther King he wrote, "That bullet killed him, but by that bullet, I was reborn—and I was reborn a Negro." No one requires that a nation—surely not this nation—should do that much. But those lines may contain the key to our own salvation. If the death of Martin Luther King can somehow mean that the nation will experience a rebirth—a rebirth of simple humanity—then it can save itself and then all of his dreams can come true.

One of the most common words in the vocabulary of the professional historian is *revisionism*. Historians who make some claim of having new data, or a new way of looking at old data, or a new perspective afforded by time and detachment, then examine an event or a period in the light of their new vantage point. The result is a revised interpretation—sometimes successful, sometimes a complete failure, but an interpretation of some well established and widely accepted view of history. Thus, a half-century ago, Charles A. Beard challenged the long-held view that the members of the Constitutional Convention of 1787 were unselfish patriots who wanted merely to ensure the blessings of liberty to themselves and to their posterity. Beard claimed that the stake of the founding fathers in creating a more stable government was prompted largely, if not exclusively, by the government bonds that they possessed, by the land they owned and the offices they held or sought. More recently, some historians of the Reconstruction era have argued that the decade following the Civil War was not a long, dark night of dishonest Negro, carpetbag, scallywag rule, as has been claimed for generations. It was one, the revisionists said, that was not so long and was a mixture of good and bad, of white and black, of Northern and Southern management, that W.E.B. Du Bois, a pioneer revisionist, has called "a splendid failure," but for quite different reasons than his predecessors had dubbed a failure.

Revisionism had thus become a passion, if not a fad, among American historians, after they became scientific at the beginning of the 20th century. If, in the course of his career, the historian did *not* revise some longheld view of history, he had not altogether fulfilled his mission as an historian. But one of the curious developments in American historiography is that the truly pioneer developments in the revision of American historiography came from those historians who, more than a century ago and long before the principles of scientific inquiry characterized the modern historian, that these historians more than a century ago began to correct the errors, the omissions, and the distortions regarding the history of Negro Americans.

In the 1830s and '40s, George Bancroft, that great 19th-century historian, his views redolent with the ideas of Jacksonian democracy, was perhaps the most widely read historian of his time. And he was so concerned with advancing Jacksonian democracy, that he neglected to give much attention to those pioneers from Africa, who had done so much to tame the wilderness in the new world. Of course, his neglect was not strange, for none of his predecessors had given any attention to them either. Almost immediately, however, James W.C. Pennington, a runaway slave from Maryland, revised the exalted Bancroft, by publishing in 1841 his *Text Book of the Origin and History of the Colored People*. In this modest undertaking, Pennington, who was later to be honored by Heidelberg University with a degree of Doctor of Divinity, undertook to set the record straight, by indicating that Africans had enjoyed advanced civilizations in the Middle Ages and before and that they had contributed significantly to the founding and development of the New World experiment.

When Bancroft pursued the history of the United States and wrote several later volumes that brought it up through the Revolution, and when he neglected to mention the role of Negro Americans in the struggle for political independence of their own country and in the fight for their own freedom, it was W.C. Nell, a Negro American of Boston, who again had to set the record straight. In 1852 he published *Services of Colored Americans in the Wars of 1776 and 1812*. Three years later, he issued a substantially revised edition, under the elaborate and descriptive title of *The Colored Patriots of the American Revolution: With Sketches of Several Distinguished Colored Persons: To Which Is Added a Brief Survey of the Condition and Prospect of Colored Americans*. From that point on, no American who was really interested could not know of the exploits of Crispus Attucks, Peter Salem, Salem Poor and Prince Hall and Titus Coburn and hundreds of other brave black men who struggled successfully for the independence of the United States, but who fought in vain for the freedom of the slaves.

Now this revisionism on the part of Negro American historians became the pattern. At the close of the Civil War, there was a flood of books by white authors recounting the stories of the gallantry of the men who saved the Union. Virtually every Union regiment had its historian and the federal government itself smiled on those who extolled the virtues of the white Union fighting men. Even white Northerners avidly read of the exploits of the white Confederates in such magazines as *Field and Fireside* and *The Land We Love* and other publications of those who had stood steadfastly for four years against the Union. But scarcely a word was said of the incredible sacrifices of the black men who served in the segregated outfits known as the United States Colored Troops. Not only were they segregated, but they were also suffering discrimination, and were unable to draw compensation equal to that which the white soldier of the same rank and experience drew. No one reading the standard histories of the period had any idea of how many black men won the Medal of Honor or were slaughtered as rebels by the Confederates who denied them the ordinary protections under the laws of war. The white historians of the Civil War neglected to mention them.

It was the Negro revisionists who challenged the standard histories of the Civil War and introduced the black soldier as the forgotten but remarkable hero in the cause of union and freedom. See, for example, William Welles Brown's *The Negro and the American Revolution,* published in 1876 and having the very enticing subtitle *His Heroism and His Fidelity.* Or examine Joseph Wilson's *The Black Phalanx,* published a few years later. Or George Washington Williams's *History of the Negro Troops in the Rebellion,* published in 1887. It was George Washington Williams who published the first full-length history of the Negro people in the United States. A brilliant honor graduate of Andover Theological Seminary in Cambridge, a lawyer also, and the first Negro to serve in the Ohio State Legislature, Williams brought out in 1883 his monumental, two-volume *History of the Negro Race in America.* His work was so exhaustive, his style was so clear, and his contribution so indisputable that some reviewers referred to him as the Black Bancroft. But this was scarcely a compliment, for Williams was doing what Bancroft had failed to do: he was revising the written history of the United States and he was including in that history those whom Bancroft had ignored. And he was challenging the long-held and time-honored view that only white people had contributed to the making of America.

Surely one of the most important revisionists of American history was the Negro teacher. The Negro teacher of American history who, outraged by the kind of distorted history that he was required to teach the children of his own race, decided to do something about it. The leader in this group was a Negro high school teacher of Raleigh, North Carolina. His name was E.A. Johnson, who later was a distinguished member of the New York Bar and a respected member of the New York state legislature. In 1891, Johnson could no long bear to teach the kind of history that he had been required to teach. And in that year, he brought out his *School History of the Negro Race in America.* In the preface of his book, Johnson said, "During my experience of eleven years as a teacher, I have often felt that the children of the race ought to study some work that would give them a little information on the many brave deeds and noble characters of their own race. I have often observed," he said, "the sin of omission and commission on the part of the white authors, most of whom seem to have written exclusively for white children. And they have studiously left out the many credible deeds of the Negro. The general tone," he continued, "of most of the histories taught in our schools has been that of the inferiority of the Negro. Whether actually said in so many words, or implied from the highest laudation of the deeds of one race to the complete exclusion of the deeds of the other. How must the little colored child feel," Johnson continued, "when he has completed the assigned course in the United States history, and in it found not one word of credit, not one word of favorable comment for even one among the millions of his foreparents who have lived through nearly three centuries of his country's history." By writing his book, Johnson hoped that it would never again be possible for the Negro child to feel such slight as he had witnessed through the years.

But this was only the beginning of the revision. Soon W.E.B. Du Bois would be writing *The Suppression of the African Slave Trade*, the first volume published in the Harvard Historical Studies. Then he would go on to publish the *Philadelphia Negro*, *The Souls of Black Folk*, and many other sociological and historical studies of his people. Within a few years, Booker T. Washington would write a two-volume history of Negro Americans that is not terribly well known. And countless others would fill in the gaps by unearthing large quantities of hitherto unknown facts about the experiences of black people in the old world and the new. There were W.H. Crogman's *Progress of a Race*, T. Thomas Fortune's *Black and White*, W.J. Simmons's *Men of Mark*, to mention only a few.

Then finally in 1915, Dr. Carter G. Woodson and his associates organized the Association for the Study of Negro Life and History and in the following year they launched the *Journal of Negro History*. Then, for more than fifty years, this association and this journal would literally flood the country with a vast assortment of articles and monographs on Negro life and history. There would be studies of Africa, of free Negroes, of Negro soldiers, Negro schools, Negro churches, Negroes during the Reconstruction, countless other significant areas of Negro life were covered. And for more than a half-century, this association and this journal would lead, stimulate and inspire the Negro community about its own past and would lead in the fight to make the study of Negro life and history a respectable field of intellectual endeavor. In due time, the field would indeed become respectable. And before the middle of the 20th century, it would entice not only a large number of talented Negro scholars, who would join in the quest for a revised and more valid American history, but would also bring into its fold a considerable number of the ablest white historians, who could no longer tolerate biased, one-sided American history. Thus, Vernon Wharton's *The Negro in Mississippi*, Kenneth Stamp's *The Peculiar Institu-*

tion, and Louis Harlan's *Separate But Unequal,* to mention only three, rank among the best of the efforts that any historians, black or white, have made to revise the history of their own country. And in that role, they too became revisionists of the history of Negro Americans.

Even more exciting in some ways than the steady building of a vast literature on the subject of Negro American history is the extraordinary demand in recent years for the recognition of this history. It is indeed a part of the black revolution—the drive to secure for the black man his recognition as a man, as a citizen, and as an equal. It is strengthened by the realization that an understanding of the past will assist a people in discovering their own importance, and thus embolden them to formulate more clearly a program for securing their complete freedom.

It manifests itself in the demand that books on Negro American history be placed in the libraries; that materials on the subject be included in the general study of the history of the United States; and that courses on the subject be introduced at several levels of the educational experience. The response to these demands on the part of the white community have ranged from naïve to sinister and at various points in between. Some whites have decried the emphasis on Negro history, arguing that in a land where everyone is an American it would be unfortunate and misleading and distorting to single out persons of a particular color. In a word, they would advocate the kind of history which E.A. Johnson had to cope with back in 1891. Thus leaving the clear inference for everyone to draw that all participants worthy of mention were indeed white. Obviously such advocates of colorless and raceless history are mesmerized by the American myth of the melting pot, where all persons regardless of national origin, religion, or otherwise have blended into a new human being: the American, who knows no color, no race, no creed, or national origin. The myth persists, doubtless subscribed to by millions of adherents.

Others have suggested that any separate treatment of Negro Americans is distorting since it does for the black man what lily-white history has been doing for the white man for several generations. There is something to this argument. But it lacks appreciation not only for the principle of revisionism, but also for the damage that has been done to an entire race of people for some three centuries. If the balance is to be redressed at all, then it has to address itself to what Johnson called the errors of commission and omission. And it must employ the methods of criticism and of analysis to any so-called history that overlooks with impunity the words and the deeds of a people whose involvement in the history of this ante-dates the presence of most of those who now claim to deny that they had any place in the history at all.

Perhaps most distressing, is that group of whites who say that it is all very well to insist that the history of Negro Americans should be taught— in separate courses or even integrated in with the rest of American history—but who at the same time claim that it is impossible because of the lack of knowledge of the black man's history. To make such a claim is merely to admit ignorance. And one sees this ignorance in the willingness of the chairman of an English department who says that he would permit a course in Negro literature, but alas where are the poems, and the novels, and the short stories, and the dramas, and the essays that would make up such a course. It can be seen in the historian who admits that it would be good to have more about Negro Americans in the history courses, if only someone would *write* something on the Negro American or if only some-one would suggest where one could get the facts. It can also be seen in the secondary school curriculum chairman who, fearing some uprising in the ghetto, dispatches a few social studies teachers to a summer institute or even a weekend workshop where they can get some material on Negroes with which to enrich their courses in American history, [laughter] and in-cidentally to put out the fires of indignation that rage in the ghetto. Whether the response is naïve or sinister or somewhere in between, it is based on a set of fallacies regarding the nature of history in general, and especially the nature of American history.

Many persons confused about whether Negro Americans have a his-tory, or even more confused about what to do about it if they do have a his-tory, [laughter] believe that history is primarily an account of the great moments in the experience of mankind. For such persons, it is inconceiv-able that Negroes could be involved in history. Whether that history be past politics or the record of nations possessing a spiritual quality, or the account of a man solving the problems he encounters. They're great mo-ments and Negroes don't have great moments. They further believe that the history of the United States is a series of glorious triumphs—of tri-umphs over the wilderness, over Great Britain, over Mexico, over the mys-teries of science and industry. Many of these triumphs were forged by the labor and the sweat of Negro slaves. But the justification for anything so

barbarous as human bondage has to be that Negroes were inferior physio-
logically, intellectually, and spiritually. Thus it is inconceivable—white
Americans have convinced themselves—that people occupying such a low
point in the human family could have a history. Indeed, their inferior position in American life could be maintained only if the fiction of them as a
people with no history worth telling could be maintained.

With such a point of view it has been possible for historians of the glorious American Revolution to tell of the Declaration of Independence
without once mentioning that the first draft contained a condemnation of
the King of England for maintaining slavery and the slave trade. Now, this
portion of the Declaration of Independence was deleted from the final
draft for the simple reason that American patriots would not condemn an
institution that they had no intention of giving up. Such historians can tell
of the fight for independence without once mentioning the fact that it was
Negroes, slaves and free Negroes, who pointed out the inconsistency of
fighting for political independence while keeping black people in the de-
graded state of slavery. And the historians of the revolution can tell of the
glorious victories of Bunker Hill, of Utah Springs, and Yorktown, without
once mentioning that more than five thousand black patriots fought for
the freedom of the white men, who in turn then denied it to them. And of
course, such historians would obviously deny or would not mention the
fact that thousands of Negroes went over to fight on the side of the British
because the British came cleaner on the whole matter of their freedom
than did the American patriots.

With such a point of view it has been possible for historians to tell of
the building of the great nation without telling of the back man's part in
taming the wilderness, and planting the fields, and harvesting the crops.
They can tell of the institution of slavery without telling of the black man's
constant and bitter fight against slavery—of his revolts, of his running
away, of his sabotage and his malingering. They can tell of the fight to save
the union without once mentioning the fact that a hundred and eighty-six
thousand black men fought in a segregated army, refused to accept discriminatory pay, and did more than their share in saving the Union and
ridding the country of the barbarism of slavery. Now this is the kind of history that has been written and this is the kind of history that has been
taught in our schools and colleges. It is un-informed, arrogant, un-charita-
ble, un-democratic, and racist history.

It has thus spawned and perpetuated an ignorant, self-seeking, super-patriotic, ethnocentric group of white Americans, who can say in this day and time that they did not know that Negroes had a history. This is not the kind of history and this is not the kind of society of which a great nation should boast. And we must rid ourselves of the spurious and specious teachings of the past. And in its place we must teach a history that recognizes the worth of all the people who have worked and died to make this country whatever it is today. [applause]

As far as the history of Negro Americans is concerned, this does not involve nearly as much of an effort as some would believe. To be sure, we do need to do more research and write many more works on the history of Negro Americans, as indeed we do in many other fields in American history. Any graduate professor is happy that it hasn't all been done yet. But there are already hundreds and hundreds of first-rate historical works dealing with the history of Negro Americans that would occupy the attention of teachers and others for years to come and that would greatly illuminate their understanding of the history, not only of Negro Americans, but of the United States as a whole.

The book called *The Tragic Era,* written by Claude Bowers in 1929, castigates, misrepresents and blasphemes the role that Negro Americans played during Reconstruction. But that book has sold several hundred thousand copies since it was published in 1929. More than any other work in this century, it is responsible for the twisted, distorted and uninformed view of the Reconstruction era that prevails in 1969. On the other hand, *Black Reconstruction,* written by W.E.B. Du Bois, and that successfully refuted much that Bowers wrote and revised our understanding of Reconstruction—Du Bois's book went out of print shortly after its first modest printing in 1935 and did not appear again because of the lack of demand for it until 1964.

When Horace Mann Bonds's seminal book on Negro education in Alabama was published in 1938 and which gave us the best view we have of Alabama Reconstruction, it was ignored by historians and laymen alike and it remained out of print for nearly 30 years. Many other historical works of Negro Americans that have not gone out of print have remained on the shelves—dusty, unread, ignored. And this country is all the poorer for narrow view of what constitutes its own history.

We are now in the midst of a great renaissance regarding the history of

Negro Americans. Workshops, seminars, in-service courses, institutes and a dozen other arrangements herald a new day in the study of the history of Negro Americans. Colleges and universities are establishing divisions, and departments, and majors in what is now called Black Studies. Publishers are literally pouring handbooks, anthologies, workbooks, almanacs, documentaries and textbooks on the history of Negro Americans. Seldom has there been so much activity in a field so recently ignored and bypassed. Soon we shall have many more books than we can read; indeed, we shall have many more than we should read. Soon we shall have many more authorities on Negro history than we can listen to; and indeed many more than we should listen to. [laughter]

There's something both amusing and tragic about the way in which the great and not-so-great colleges and universities are reacting to the black revolution. It is reminiscent of the scramble to catch up with the Russians, after they sent up their first Sputnik in 1957. [laughter] Perhaps the older ones of you can recall the panic and desperation that characterized the approaches and the actions of officials, both in Washington and in higher education, to that momentous event. Enormous sums of money were spent to accelerate our space program, to set up language and area study programs, and to identify and encourage those who could benefit from such efforts. Soon resources were distributed too, in any and all directions; and it became possible for one to enjoy a national defense fellowship, not only to study astrophysics and the Russian language, but also to study the American frontier, as well as juvenile delinquency and family disorganization.

We have gone full circle now. Next year, at the University of Chicago, we expect to have a student specializing in the history of Negro Americans who will be on a national defense grant. [laughter] There must be some hidden significance in this development.

Left to its own devices, American higher education moves slowly, if at all, to adjust to the changes that take place all around it. And we see that after Sputnik, American higher education will never be the same. Today our colleges and our universities are engaged in a far-reaching revision of their curriculum to assimilate and accommodate black studies.

They also engage in a widespread talent search, not only for black students, but also for black professors. Some are even defying the Civil Rights Act of 1964 and setting up separate living and separate eating facilities for black students. Some of them have gone so far as to provide soul food for black students; [laughter] apparently not realizing in their effort to achieve peace in our time that fried chicken and turnip greens and cornbread are as important a part of the cuisine of Southern whites as it is of Southern blacks. [laughter]

It is clear that the most vigorous effort to revise the curriculum is in the field of history. Literally hundreds of colleges and universities have in the past two years introduced courses on the history of black Americans. Within the next year or two, several hundred more will add such courses. In this, as in other responses to the black revolution, many institutions are acting with a speed that can hardly be described as deliberate. Overnight they have established courses and placed them in the hands of persons whose greatest talent seems to be in wringing their hands and desperately trying to find out something about the history of Negro Americans before the beginning of the next meeting of the class. [laughter]

Ignorance abounds, not only among would-be white teachers of black history, but also among would-be black teachers of black history. My files are replete with calls for assistance. White teachers write with an air of desperation and helplessness and plead for assistance in the plans that their colleges have made to begin a course in black history immediately. Black teachers write with an air of triumph, saying they have forced the college to teach a course in black history and that they would appreciate it if I would send them, by return mail, [laughter] a course syllabus, a bibliography, and a suggestion for a textbook. [laughter]

The tragic fact is there are not sufficient competent teachers to meet the demands. Some institutions are without guilt, for they have not been engaged in the training of historians of any description. [laughter] Our distinguished universities, however, that have been the centers for the training of historians, including Negro historians, such institutions must share the responsibility for the present state of affairs. Until quite recently, they have not encouraged whites to study and write about the history of Negro Americans. And although they have trained almost all of the Negro historians, they have never encouraged any of them to join their own enterprise of teaching and research. Instead they seem to have no qualms about seeing their most gifted black historians become members of a segregated educational enterprise, where conditions not only discourage scholarly research and teaching, but stultify the human spirit as well. But the supreme irony is that now these same institutions are scouring the countryside in the effort to locate and offer professorships to those very black historians whom they trained and then sent into exile.

There's a story making the rounds these days that I'm insisting is apocryphal. I don't believe it. But it illustrates the point. It is reported that an Ivy League university has reestablished contact with a Negro teacher in Texas who received his Ph.D. from that university in 1936. A letter to him written by a former fellow student at that university—that fellow student is now chairman of the department—goes something like this: "Dear Joe. It has been ages since I have seen anything of you. [laughter] I heard that you were at the last several meetings of the MLA and I am terribly sorry that I did not see you, but you know how those awful meetings are. I've tried to keep up with you just the same and I remember that impressive thesis you wrote on the tragedy and sorrow in the poems of Phyllis Wheatley and I am delighted that you were able to get an article published from it in the 1938 issue of the *Journal of Higher Education Among Negroes*. By the way, Joe, we have decided to introduce a course in black literature. We were talking about it a few days ago with the students and they thought it was a good idea, too. They wondered where we could possibly get someone to teach it. That gave us a real laugh—we had you in mind all the time. [laughter] This opportunity comes at the right time, Joe, for old Professor Johnson—you remember him—is about to retire and we want to offer you his chair. It would be great to have you back here, at long last, and the black students would be delighted! Let me hear from you by return mail, Joe, and *tell* me that you will accept. Salary and fringe benefits are no problem at all. More detail later. All the best. Cordially yours, Tommy." [laughter]

One can almost hear the nervous laugh of the chairman as he tries to convince his former schoolmate that *he* should come and get him off the hook. One can also see the cold indifference of the chairman of this department to standards. That would not be the case in considering, say, the introduction on Anglo-Saxons or Chaucer or even Melville. His erstwhile buddy may well be the greatest living authority on black literature, but the chairman not only does not know that, but does not care. Somehow black literature is different—and if the students want it, and good old Joe will come and teach it, it won't do much harm and it will help to maintain peace. I hope this story is truly apocryphal; it was told to me by a friend.

But I'm afraid that if it is apocryphal, some stories like it are not. I'm afraid that there are a dozen similar, true stories today in economics, sociology, literature, perhaps even history.

It will take more than new books, new authorities, and new programs of study to achieve a new and urgently needed approach to the study and teaching of the history of Negro Americans. What is needed by all who would teach and who would write in this field is a new way of looking at the history of the United States and a new way of teaching that history in the future. The history of the United States is not merely the history of a few generals, a few presidents, a few planners and a few industrialists. It is the history of all the people, rich and poor, exalted and humbled, black and white and yellow. And all these people have been human beings, not sub-humans or pariahs, but people worthy of the blessings of liberty and the rights of equality. And all of them have been involved deeply in the history of this country, in every way at every step, even if the role that they played was by assignment if not by choice.

And if there was slavery, injustice, and unspeakable barbarities, the selling of babies from their mothers, the breeding of slaves, and the lynchings, and the burnings at the stake, and discrimination, and segregation—these things too are part of the history of the United States. If the patriots were more in love with slavery than freedom; if the founding fathers were more anxious to write slavery into the Constitution than they were to protect the rights of men; and if freedom was begrudgingly given and ineffectively denied for another century, these things too are a part of the nation's history. It takes a person with a stout heart and great courage and uncompromising honesty to look the history of this country squarely in the face and tell it like it is. But nothing short of this will make it possible to have a reassessment of American history and a revision of American history that will in turn permit the teaching of the history of Negro Americans.

And when that approach prevails, the history of the United States, and the history of the black man, can be written and can be taught by any person—white or black or otherwise. For there is nothing so irrelevant in telling the truth as the color of a man's skin. [applause]

But telling the history of the black man in America is to insist for ourselves what we have insisted from others. The history of Negro Americans is so rich, so full of drama, indeed so full of great moments that it needs neither embellishment nor exaggeration. Alexander Crummel of the 19th century and William Monroe Trotter of the 20th century do not need any assistance from any of us to transform them into great fighters for human dignity. Paul Cuthie, Martin Delaney, Marcus Garvey can stand on their own record and happily they were articulate enough to leave that record for all to see. But surely there were others—nameless, anonymous, despised, neglected, who were studiously ignored by earlier historians, but must not be neglected by those who would revise the history of the United States. The black strikebreaker had a cause that transcended the so-called principle of lily-white trade unionism and he must not be neglected. The black sharecropper had a part of transforming the economic life of the South and he must not be neglected. The new techniques that the new social history has developed will be especially important in enlarging our vision and knowledge of the inarticulate and even the oppressed. These techniques will be a boon to the future study of the history of Negro Americans.

And in the future, history must not become the exclusive tool for those who want to use it for narrow political purposes. Those who seek to use it in such a manner cannot be prevented from doing so; and perhaps it is just as well. For from the beginning of time, history has been used in this way. It must become and it must remain something else, something much more important, something much more intellectually defensible, and something much more significant than the mere handmaiden of the political advocate or even the social reformer.

For history must become and remain the searching and sobering force in American life, the balanced wheel in the American experience, the ground on which American historical scholarship can be tested. From the vantage point and perspective that it provides, it can be a most powerful factor in the continuing movement to revise American history.

The history of the United States is not one great success story. And it is not the recounting of deeds of perfect or near-perfect men. Many of the military triumphs were purchased at a fantastically high price: at the price of segregated armies, discrimination in the treatment of black soldiers, insults by white civilians of the black men who were giving their lives to protect those white civilians. Many of its industrial triumphs were purchased at a remarkably high price: at the price of low and discriminatory pay to Negro workers, the inhuman discriminations by labor unions and the exploitation of defenseless Negro labor that was used only in disputes between management and white labor unions. Many of its advances in civilization have been purchased at the price of creating a society that is racially exclusive; where housing, education, and even the means of survival have qualifications of race, rather than of reason or of human capabilities. These triumphs, bought at so dear a price, are not the work of perfect or near-perfect men; they are the work of men bereft of the warmth of humanity and brotherhood.

We ought to have a history worthy of the principles of truth. We must revise our way of looking at our own history—that is, the history of the United States. We must be willing to criticize the past, including our own institutions and the men who made them. We must be willing to re-write our textbooks in the light of the abundance of available materials that deny the exclusive role of one race of Americans. We must be willing to teach a history that is itself revisionist. The search for truth is never-ending, but the way to begin is to be willing to seek it. Only in this way can we arrive at a point in our writings, and in our teachings, and in our study, where what we tell about our past is inspired more by justice than by pride. And where truth, though strange, is more important than fiction. [applause]

13.

SHIRLEY CHISHOLM
(1924–)

"The Black Woman in Contemporary America"

University of Missouri, Kansas City—June 17, 1974

Shirley Chisholm was the first African American woman elected to Congress, where she represented New York's Twelfth Congressional District. In 1972, she became the first black woman to seek a major party nomination for the U.S. presidency. Her threadbare but spirited campaign was viewed as largely symbolic. Chisholm shrugged off the dismissive treatment her candidacy sometimes got, and predicted that later campaigns by women and minorities would find a smoother path "because I helped pave it."[1]

Born in Brooklyn, the oldest of four girls whose parents had emigrated from the West Indies, Chisholm decided to become a teacher while attending Brooklyn College. She graduated in 1946, taught school as she earned a graduate degree from Columbia University, and got involved in Democratic politics. In 1964, Chisholm won a landslide victory for a seat in the New York State Assembly. She built a reputation as an independent and outspoken politician; her 1970 autobiography is titled *Unbought and Unbossed*. She narrowly won the 1968 congressional race, defeating Republican James Farmer.

When Chisholm ran for president in 1972, she proclaimed herself neither the black nor the female candidate—though she was proud to be both black and female—but the candidate of the people.[2] President Richard Nixon was running for reelection, having won the presidency in 1968, in part, through racially divisive campaign tactics.[3] George McGovern easily defeated Chisholm and other contenders for the Democratic nomination, then got slaughtered by Nixon in the general election.

Chisholm served in Congress until 1982. After retiring she taught at Mount Holyoke College and was an energetic supporter of Reverend Jesse Jackson's presidential campaigns.

Chisholm's prominent place in African American culture and mainstream politics made her an authoritative voice for black women in public life. In 1974, she spoke at a conference on black women in America at the University of Missouri in Kansas City. At the time, many women active in the civil rights movement complained of the repressive sexism practiced by their black male counterparts, including conservative clergymen and radical Black Power leaders.[4] Chisholm told her audience of the "twin jeopardies of race and sex" facing black women.

LADIES AND GENTLEMEN, and brothers and sisters all—I'm very glad to be here this evening. I'm very glad that I've had the opportunity to be the first lecturer with respect to the topic of the black woman in contemporary America. This has become a most talked-about topic and has caused a great deal of provocation and misunderstandings and misinterpretations. And I come to you this evening to speak on this topic not as any scholar, not as any academician, but as a person that has been out here for the past twenty years, trying to make my way as a black and a woman, and meeting all *kinds* of obstacles. [laughter and applause]

The black woman's role has not been placed in its proper perspective, particularly in terms of the current economic and political upheaval in America today. Since time immemorial the black man's emasculation resulted in the need of the black woman to assert herself in order to maintain some semblance of a family unit. And as a result of this historical circumstance, the black woman has developed perseverance; the black woman has developed strength; the black woman has developed tenacity of purpose and other attributes which today quite often are being looked upon negatively. She continues to be labeled a matriarch. And this is indeed a played-upon white sociological interpretation of the black woman's role that has been developed and perpetrated by Daniel Moynihan and other sociologists. [applause]

Black women by virtue of the role they have played in our society have much to offer toward the liberation of their people. We know that our men are coming forward, but the black race needs the collective talents and the collective abilities of black men and black women who have vital skills to supplement each other.

It is quite perturbing to divert ourselves on the dividing issue of the alleged fighting that absorbs the energies of black men and black women. Such statements as "the black woman has to step back while her black man steps forward" and "the black woman has kept back the black man" are grossly, historically incorrect and serves as a scapegoating technique to prevent us from coming together as *human* beings—some of whom are black men and some are black women. [applause]

The consuming interests of this type of dialogue abets the enemy in terms of taking our eyes off the ball, so that our collective talents can never redound in a beneficial manner to our ethnic group. The black woman who is educated and has ability cannot be expected to put said talent on the shelf when she can utilize these gifts side-by-side with her man. One does not learn, nor does one assist in the struggle, by standing on the sidelines, constantly complaining and criticizing. [applause] One learns by participating in the situation—listening, observing and then acting.

It is quite understandable why black women in the majority are not interested in walking and picketing a cocktail lounge which historically has refused to open its doors a certain two hours a day when men who have just returned from Wall Street gather in said lounge to exchange bits of business transactions that occurred on the market. This is a middle-class white woman's issue. [applause] This is not a priority of minority women. Another issue that black women are not overly concerned about is the "M-S" versus the "M-R-S" label. [clapping] For many of us this is just the use of another label which does not basically change the fundamental inherent racial attitudes found in both men and women in this society. This is just another label, and black women are not preoccupied with any more label syndromes. [laughter] Black women are desperately concerned with the issue of survival in a society in which the Caucasian group has never really practiced the espousal of equalitarian principles in America.

An aspect of the women's liberation movement that will and does interest many black women is the potential liberation, is the potential nationalization of daycare centers in this country. Black women can accept and understand this agenda item in the women's movement. It is important that black women utilize their brainpower and focus on issues in any movement that will redound to the benefit of their people because we can serve as a vocal and a catalytic pressure group within the so-called humanistic movements, many of whom do not really comprehend the black man and the black woman.

An increasing number of black women are beginning to feel that it is important first to become free as women, in order to contribute more fully to the task of black liberation. Some feel that black men—like all men, or most men—have placed women in the stereotypes of domestics whose duty it is to stay in the background—cook, clean, have babies, and leave all of the glory to men. [laughter] Black women point to the civil rights movement as an example of a subtle type of male oppression, where with few exceptions black women have not had active roles in the forefront of the fight. Some like Coretta King, Katherine Cleaver, and Betty Shabazz have come only to their positions in the shadows of their husbands. Yet, because of the oppression of black women, they are strongest in the fight for liberation. They have led the struggle to fight against white male supremacy, dating from slavery times. And in view of these many facts it is not surprising that black women played a crucial role in the total fight for freedom in this nation. Ida Wells kept her newspaper free by walking the streets of Memphis, Tennessee, in the 1890s with two pistols on her hips. [laughter] And within recent years, this militant condition of black women, who have been stifled because of racism and sexism, has been carried on by Mary McLeod Bethune, Mary Church Terrell, Daisy Bates, and Diane Nash.

The black woman lives in a society that discriminates against her on two counts. The black woman cannot be discussed in the same context as her Caucasian counterpart because of the twin jeopardy of race and sex which operates against her, and the psychological and political consequences which attend them. Black women are crushed by cultural restraints and abused by the legitimate power structure. To date, neither the black movement nor women's liberation succinctly addresses itself to the dilemma confronting the black who is female. And as a consequence of ignoring or being unable to handle the problems facing black women, black women themselves are now becoming socially and politically active.

Undoubtedly black women are cultivating new attitudes, most of which will have political repercussions in the future. They are attempting to change their conditions. The maturation of the civil rights movement by the mid '60s enabled many black women to develop interest in the American political process. From their experiences they learned that the real sources of power lay at the root of the political system. For example, black sororities and pressure groups like the National Council of Negro Women are adept at the methods of participatory politics—particularly in regard to voting and organizing. With the arrival of the '70s, young black women are demanding recognition like the other segments of society who also desire their humanity and their individual talents to be noticed. The tradition of the black woman and the Afro-American subculture and her current interest in the political process indicate the emergence of a new political entity.

Historically she has been discouraged from participating in politics. Thus she is trapped between the walls of the dominant white culture and her own subculture, both of which encourage deference to men. Both races of women have traditionally been limited to performing such tasks as opening envelopes, hanging up posters and giving teas. [laughter and clapping] And the minimal involvement of black women exists because they have been systematically excluded from the political process and they are members of the politically dysfunctional black lower class. Thus, unlike white women, who escape the psychological and sociological handicaps of racism, the black woman's political involvement has been a most marginal role.

But within the last six years, the Afro-American subculture has undergone tremendous social and political transformation and these changes have altered the nature of the black community. They are beginning to realize their capacities not only as blacks, but also as women. They are beginning to understand that their cultural well-being and their social well-being would only be affirmed in connection with the total black struggle. The dominant role black women played in the civil rights movement began to allow them to grasp the significance of political power in America. So obviously black women who helped to spearhead the civil rights movement would also now, at this juncture, join and direct the vanguard which would shape and mold a new kind of political participation.

This has been acutely felt in urban areas, which have been rocked by sporadic rebellions. Nothing better illustrates the need for black women to organize politically than their unusual proximity to the most crucial issues affecting black people today. They have struggled in a wide range of protest movements to eliminate the poverty and injustice that permeates the lives of black people. In New York City, for example, welfare mothers and mothers of schoolchildren have ably demonstrated the commitment of black women to the elimination of the problems that threaten the well-being of the black family. Black women must view the problems of cities such as New York not as urban problems, but as the components of a crisis without whose elimination our family lives will neither survive nor prosper. Deprived of a stable family environment because of poverty and racial injustice, disproportionate numbers of our people must live on minimal welfare allowances that help to perpetuate the breakdown of family life. In the face of the increasing poverty besetting black communities, black women have a responsibility. Black women have a duty to bequeath a legacy to their children. Black women have a duty to move from the periphery of organized political activity into its main arena.

I say this on the basis of many experiences. I travel throughout this country and I've come in contact with thousands of my black sisters in all kinds of conditions in this nation. And I've said to them over and over again: it is not a question of competition against black men or brown men or red men or white men in America. It is a questions of the recognition that, since we have a tremendous responsibility in terms of our own families, that to the best of our ability we have to give everything that is within ourselves to give—in terms of helping to make that future a better future for our little boys and our little girls, and not leave it to anybody. [applause]

Francis Beal describes the black woman as a slave of a slave. Let me quote: "By reducing the black man in America to such abject oppression, the black woman had no protector and she was used—and is still being used—in some cases as the scapegoat for the evils that this horrendous system has perpetrated on black men. Her physical image has been maliciously maligned. She has been sexually molested and abused by the white colonizer. She has suffered the worst kind of economic exploitation, having been forced to serve as the white woman's maid and wet-nurse for white offspring, while her own children were more often starving and neglected. It is the depth of degradation to be socially manipulated, physically raped and used to undermine your own household—and then to be powerless to reverse this syndrome."

However, Susan Johnson notes a bit of optimism. Because Susan, a brilliant young black woman, has said that the recent strides made by the black woman in the political process is a result of the intricacies of her personality. And that is to say that as a political animal, she functions independently of her double jeopardy. Because confronted with a matrifocal past and present, she is often accused of stealing the black male's position in any situation beyond that of housewife and mother. And if that were not enough to burden the black woman, she realizes that her political mobility then threatens the doctrine of white supremacy and male superiority so deeply embedded in the American culture.

So choosing not to be a victim of self-paralysis, the black woman has been able to function in the political spectrum. And more often than not, it is the subconsciousness of the racist mind that perceives her as less harmful than the black man and thus permits her to acquire the necessary leverage for political mobility. This subtle component of racism could prove to be essential to the key question of how the black woman has managed some major advances in the American political process. [laughter and applause]

It is very interesting to note that everyone—with the exception of the black woman herself—has been interpreting the black woman. [applause] It is very interesting to note that the time has come that black women can and must no longer be passive, complacent recipients of whatever the definitions of the sociologists, the psychologists and the psychiatrists will give to us. [applause] Black women have been maligned, misunderstood, misinterpreted—who knows better than Shirley Chisholm? [applause]

And I stand here tonight to tell to you, my sisters, that if you have the courage of your convictions, you must stand up and be counted. I hope that the day will come in America when this business of male versus female does not become such an overriding issue, so that the talents and abilities that the almighty God have given to *people* can be utilized for the benefit of humanity. [applause]

One has to recognize that there are stupid white women and stupid white men, stupid black women and stupid black men, brilliant white women and brilliant white men, and brilliant black women and brilliant black men. Why do we get so hung-up in America on this question of sex? Of course, in terms of the black race, we understand the historical circumstances. We understand, also, some of the subtle maneuverings and machinations behind the scenes in order to prevent black women and black men from coming together as a race of unconquerable men and women. [applause]

And I just want to say to you tonight, if I say nothing else: I would never have been able to make it in America if I had paid attention to all of the doomsday-criers about me. [applause] And I want to say in conclusion that as you have this conference here for the next two weeks, put the cards out on the table and do not be afraid to discuss issues that perhaps you have been sweeping under the rug because of what people might say about you. [applause] You must remember that once we are able to face the truth, the truth shall set all of us free. [applause]

In conclusion, I just want to say to you, black and white, north and east, south and west, men and women: the time has come in America when we should no longer be the passive, complacent recipients of whatever the morals or the politics of a nation may decree for us in this nation. Forget traditions! Forget conventionalisms! Forget what the world will say whether you're *in* your place or *out* of your place. [applause] Stand up and be counted. Do *your* thing, looking only to God—whoever your God is— and to your consciences for approval. I thank you. [applause]

14.

BARBARA JORDAN
(1936–1996)

Statement at the U.S. House Judiciary Committee
Impeachment Hearings

Washington, D.C.—July 25, 1974

Barbara Jordan marked history in a number of ways, using the power of her speech and the clarity of her mind to break down barriers of race and gender. *The New York Times* described her oratory as "Churchillian," and one writer suggested that her deep, Olympian sound could galvanize listeners "as though Winston Churchill had been reincarnated as a black woman from Texas."[1] Jordan was named Best Living Orator by a professional speakers' organization. Texas columnist Molly Ivins said that Jordan would be the obvious choice in a casting call for the voice of God.[2]

The youngest of three daughters of a Baptist minister in a poor Houston neighborhood, Jordan attended segregated schools, graduated from the all-black Texas Southern University, and earned a law degree from Boston University in 1959, where she was deeply affected by Howard Thurman, dean of Marsh Chapel. Jordan was so moved by Thurman's Sunday sermons she would preach them again to her dormitory roommates.[3]

In 1966, Jordan became the first African American elected to the Texas Senate. She went on to become the first black person elected to

Congress from Texas since Reconstruction. On the national scene, Jordan's defining moment came in 1974 when she earned a spot on the House committee considering impeachment charges against President Richard Nixon. The committee was examining whether Nixon's involvement in the cover-up of the Watergate burglary, including possible obstruction of justice, constituted the kind of "high crimes and misdemeanors" meriting impeachment. Jordan's eleven-minute statement in the committee's public hearings was broadcast on prime-time television. She won national acclaim for giving a measured, eloquent lesson on the constitutional principles at stake.

It was a speech she did not initially want to make. In her autobiography, Jordan said she thought the committee should stick to fact-finding instead of speechmaking. "The reaction from the other committee members was: 'You must be out of your head.' It seemed they all wanted that fifteen minutes on television," Jordan wrote.[4]

The night before her statement was scheduled, Jordan sat down to write. More senior committee members had already made their statements, and Jordan was struck by how they all seemed to start by quoting the preamble to the Constitution, "We the people . . ." "It occurred to me that not one of them had mentioned that back then the preamble was not talking about *all* the people," Jordan wrote. "So I said: 'Well, I'll just start with that.' "[5] The next evening, when the camera focused on her, Jordan opened with an African American perspective on the Constitution, then quickly moved her rhetorical position to that of all "the people" covered by that document of protections and promises. Jordan declared she would not be an idle spectator to "the destruction of the Constitution" by Richard Nixon and his administration. In methodical and determined tones, she unfolded the constitutional standards that President Nixon had appeared to have violated. Two days later, on July 27, 1974, Jordan voted to impeach the president (Nixon would resign before the Senate commenced a trial). Telegrams and letters poured into Jordan's office in the days following her speech. A man put up billboards all over Houston thanking Jordan for explaining the Constitution.[6]

Jordan served six years in Congress, then taught at the University of Texas. In 1976, she was the first black woman to deliver the keynote address at a Democratic National Convention. She also gave the keynote address in 1992, this time from a wheelchair; she had been afflicted by multiple sclerosis. Jordan died in 1996 from pneumonia, a complication of leukemia. One writer lamented that Jordan's booming voice, with its thundering call to principles enshrined in the Constitution, was "a song of the past."[7]

MR. CHAIRMAN, I join my colleague Mr. Rangel in thanking you for giving the junior members of this committee the glorious opportunity of sharing the pain of this inquiry. Mr. Chairman, you are a strong man, and it has not been easy but we have tried as best we can to give you as much assistance as possible.

Earlier today, we heard the beginning of the Preamble to the Constitution of the United States, "We, the people." It's a very eloquent beginning. But when that document was completed, on the seventeenth of September in 1787, I was not included in that "We, the people." I felt somehow for many years that George Washington and Alexander Hamilton just left me out by mistake. But through the process of amendment, interpretation, and court decision, I have finally been included in "We, the people."

Today I am an *inquisitor.* An hyperbole would not be fictional and would not overstate the solemnness that I feel right now. My faith in the Constitution is whole; it is complete; it is total. And I am not going to sit here and be an idle spectator to the diminution, the subversion, the destruction, of the Constitution.

"Who can so properly be the inquisitors for the nation as the representatives of the nation themselves? The subjects of its jurisdiction are those offenses which proceed from the misconduct of public men." And that's what we are talking about. In other words, the jurisdiction comes from the abuse or violation of some public trust. It is wrong, I suggest, it is a misreading of the Constitution for any member here to assert that for a member to vote for an article of impeachment means that the member must be convinced that the president should be removed from office. The Constitution doesn't say that. The powers relating to impeachment are an essential check in the hands of the body of the legislature against and upon the encroachments of the executive. The division between the two branches of the legislature, the House and the Senate, assigning to the one the right to accuse and to the other the right to judge, the framers of this Constitution were very astute. They did not make the accusers and the judges the same person.

We know the nature of impeachment. We have been talking about it awhile now. "It is chiefly designed for the president and his high ministers" to somehow be called into account. It is designed to "bridle" the executive if he engages in excesses. "It is designed as a method of national inquest into the conduct of public men." The framers confined in the Congress the power if need be, to remove the president in order to strike a delicate balance between a president swollen with power and grown tyrannical, and preservation of the independence of the executive. The nature of impeachment, is a narrowly channeled exception to the separation-of-powers maxim; the Federal Convention of 1787 said that.

It limited impeachment to high crimes and misdemeanors and discounted and opposed the term "maladministration." "It is to be used only for great misdemeanors," so it was said in the North Carolina ratification convention. And in the Virginia ratification convention: "We do not trust our liberty to a particular branch. We need one branch to check the other."

"No one need be afraid," the North Carolina ratification convention: "No one need be afraid that officers who commit oppression will pass with immunity." "Prosecutions of impeachments will seldom fail to agitate the passions of the whole community," said Hamilton in the *Federalist Papers,* no. 65. "We divide into parties more or less friendly or inimical to the accused." I do not mean political parties in that sense.

The drawing of political lines goes to the motivation behind impeachment; but impeachment must proceed within the confines of the constitutional term "high crimes and misdemeanors." Of the impeachment process, it was Woodrow Wilson who said that "Nothing short of the grossest offenses against the plain law of the land will suffice to give them speed and effectiveness. Indignation so great as to overgrow party interest may secure a conviction; but nothing else can."

Common sense would be revolted if we engaged upon this process for petty reasons. Congress has a lot to do: Appropriations Tax Reform, Health Insurance, Campaign Finance Reform, Housing, Environmental Protection, Energy Sufficiency, Mass Transportation. Pettiness cannot be allowed to stand in the face of such overwhelming problems. So today we are not being petty. We are trying to be big, because the task we have before us is a big one.

This morning, in a discussion of the evidence, we were told that the evidence which purports to support the allegations of misuse of the CIA by the President is thin. We are told that that evidence is insufficient. What that recital of the evidence this morning did not include is what the President *did* know on June the 23rd, 1972.

The President *did* know that it was Republican money, that it was money from the Committee for the Re-Election of the President, which was found in the possession of one of the burglars arrested on June the 17th. What the President *did* know on the 23rd of June was the prior activities of E. Howard Hunt, which included his participation in the break-in of Daniel Ellsberg's psychiatrist, which included Howard Hunt's participation in the Dita Beard ITT affair, which included Howard Hunt's fabrication of cables designed to discredit the Kennedy administration.

We were further cautioned today that perhaps these proceedings ought to be delayed because certainly there would be new evidence forthcoming from the President of the United States. There has not even been an obfuscated indication that this committee would receive any additional materials from the President. The committee subpoena is outstanding, and if the President wants to supply that material, the committee sits here. The fact is that on yesterday, the American people waited with great anxiety for eight hours, not knowing whether their President would obey an order of the Supreme Court of the United States.

At this point, I would like to juxtapose a few of the impeachment criteria with some of the actions the President has engaged in. Impeachment criteria: James Madison, from the Virginia ratification convention. "If the President be connected in any suspicious manner with any person and there be grounds to believe that he will shelter him, he may be impeached."

We have heard time and time again that the evidence reflects the payment to defendants money. The President had knowledge that these funds were being paid and these were *funds* collected for the 1972 presidential campaign. We know that the President met with Mr. Henry Petersen twenty-seven times to discuss matters related to Watergate and immediately thereafter met with the very persons who were implicated in the information Mr. Petersen was receiving. The words are "If the president is connected in any suspicious manner with any person and there be grounds to believe that he will shelter that person, he may be impeached."

Justice Story: "Impeachment is intended for occasional and extraordinary cases where a superior power acting for the whole people is put into operation to protect their rights and rescue their liberties from violations."

We know about the Huston plan. We know about the break-in of the psychiatrist's office. We know that there was absolute complete direction on September 3rd when the president indicated that a surreptitious entry had been made into Dr. Fielding's office, after having met with Mr. Ehrlichman and Mr. Young.

"Protect their rights." "Rescue their liberties from violation."

The Carolina ratification convention impeachment criteria: those are impeachable "who behave amiss or betray their public trust."

Beginning shortly after the Watergate break-in and continuing to the present time, the President has engaged in a series of public statements and actions designed to thwart the lawful investigation by government prosecutors. Moreover, the President has made public announcements and assertions bearing on the Watergate case, which the evidence will show he knew to be false. These assertions, false assertions, impeachable, those who misbehave. Those who "behave amiss or betray the public trust."

James Madison again at the Constitutional Convention: "A President is impeachable if he attempts to subvert the Constitution."

The Constitution charges the President with the task of taking care that the laws be faithfully executed, and yet the President has counseled his aides to commit perjury, willfully disregard the secrecy of grand jury proceedings, conceal surreptitious entry, attempt to compromise a federal judge, while publicly displaying his cooperation with the processes of criminal justice.

"A President is impeachable if he attempts to subvert the Constitution."

If the impeachment provision in the Constitution of the United States will not reach the offenses charged here, then perhaps that 18th-century Constitution should be abandoned to a 20th-century paper shredder.

Has the President committed offenses, and planned, and directed, and acquiesced in a course of conduct which the Constitution will not tolerate? That's the question. We know that. We know the question. We should now forthwith proceed to answer the question. It is reason, and not passion, which must guide our deliberations, guide our debate, and guide our decision.

I yield back the balance of my time, Mr. Chairman.

15.

BENJAMIN L. HOOKS
(1925–)

Speech at Gustavus Adolphus College

St. Peter, Minnesota—April 3, 1978

Attorney and Baptist minister Benjamin L. Hooks led the nation's largest civil rights organization, the National Association for the Advancement of Colored People (NAACP) for fifteen years. His tenure there (1977–93) came after long involvement in law, government, and the civil rights movement. A close associate of the Reverend Martin Luther King Jr., he heard King give his last speech—in Hook's hometown of Memphis, Tennessee—the night before King was assassinated.

Hooks has had a long and varied career, and is well known for his powerful speaking skills. He was an advisor to King and a board member of the Southern Christian Leadership Conference, a group of clergy and activists that organized civil rights marches, boycotts, sit-ins, and freedom rides.

The son of a Memphis photographer and a schoolteacher, Hooks was a shy young man who was drawn to the ministry, but was encouraged by his father to study law. He served stateside in World War II, at one time guarding Italian prisoners of war who were allowed to eat in the segregated restaurants where Hooks would not be served. He attended LeMoyne College and Howard University, and earned his law degree from DePaul University in 1948.[1]

Hooks opened a law practice in Memphis and got involved in local politics and civil rights activity. He became an ordained Baptist minister and began preaching at Middle Baptist Church in Memphis in 1956. (He would later divide his time in the pulpit with a Detroit church, where he would fly twice a month to preach.) In the early 1960s, Hooks became an assistant public defender in Shelby County, Tennessee. He became the first African American criminal court judge in the state in 1965.[2]

In 1972, President Richard Nixon nominated Hooks as the first black commissioner of the Federal Communications Commission. In more than four years on the FCC, Hooks pushed for increased African American ownership of radio and television outlets and more evenhanded representation of blacks in the media.

Hooks took over the top job at the NAACP in 1977. He worked to restore the organization's influence at a time when it drew criticism for being out-of-date and politically inert. As executive director, Hooks pushed the organization to increase its membership and eliminate its debt. He was sixty-seven when he stepped down in 1993. "Despite what is said about the 'old fogeyism' of the association, or about its irrelevance, the NAACP remains the undisputed leader and major force in the civil rights arena," he told reporters.[3]

Since retiring, Hooks has served on the board of several organizations and taught at Fisk University and the University of Memphis.

He made the following speech at Gustavus Adolphus College, a small, Lutheran school in the farmland south of Minneapolis. He was the guest speaker at a conference marking the tenth anniversary of King's death.

[IN MEMPHIS, THE] Mason temple had a tin roof and as I heard the rain pattering tonight on this beautiful place, in this beautiful place, and looked out and saw the flash of the lightning, I was somehow strangely transported back almost ten years. And I remember when Turner and I walked into that Mason temple that night, it was rather late. This is one of those nights when we didn't expect anybody to be present, that place seats perhaps 7,500 or 8,000 people and to our surprise there must have been between 1,500 and 2,000 folk who had turned out on that very, very stormy night.

And Dr. Abernathy presented Martin that night, and Dr. Abernathy can speak quite a long time but that night he spoke even longer than usual. I remember it took him almost 45 minutes to introduce Dr. King. Brought him from 1929, [when] he was born, up until 1968 so that it was providential for me because when I got there, Dr. King had not yet gotten up to speak.

I had worked with Dr. King, I was a member of the Board of Directors of the Southern Christian Leadership Conference; later I was to serve as financial secretary of that organization. I had marched and demonstrated and walked with Dr. King and had been one of his legal counselors and advisors for almost all of his civil rights career. But in all of those years that I heard Dr. King speak, never had I heard him speak with the pathos and the passion and the eloquence which he demonstrated that night. I was literally transfixed in my seat as this prophet of God spoke not only to Memphis, but to the nation and indeed to the world.

I wish I could stand here tonight and say that I had some premonition that that would be his last speech, but I did not. But I shall not forget how, at the conclusion of that speech, Dr. King, who was sort of stoic by nature, I never, in the years that I knew him, saw him exhibit too much joy or sorrow over anything much, he simply took life as it was. He was criticized and abused and vilified, misunderstood and lied on continuously. Would the God that all the folk who follow him now, both black and white, had followed him during his lifetime, we would be closer to the realization of the great American dream.

I remember that night when he finished, he stopped by quoting the words of that song that he loved so well, "Mine eyes have seen the glory of the coming of the Lord." He never finished. He wheeled around and took his seat and to my surprise, when I got a little closer, I saw tears streaming down his face. Grown men were sitting there weeping openly because of the power of this man who spoke on that night.

It's sort of fitting that ten years later I'm here at this great institution as you commemorate the life and the time, the service of one of America's authentic heroes. Today, yesterday, tomorrow, a dream remembered. I suppose that all of you have read now, Langston Hughes's, a beautiful poem, "What Happens to a Dream Deferred?"

Dr. King, as my mind travels back over those years in 1968, spoke rather forcibly on a topic that seemed a little strange that night. For, in 1968, you must recall that Lyndon Johnson was still President and even though we were suffering with the agony of the Vietnamese experience, there were many of us in the black community who felt that finally America had come to grips with the old racial question that had troubled us since our existence as a nation. We had seen, in the mid '60s, the passage of five monumental civil rights bills. In 1954 and 1955 we had witnessed the Supreme Court writing an end—legally and judicially—to the system of separate [but] equal, so-called, but always unequal, education. We'd witnessed Eisenhower calling out the federal troops to ensure that black folk could attend school with whites in Little Rock, Arkansas. So many of us that night we felt that even though there were some little ends to be caught up, that the struggle was all but over. But Dr. King spoke that night so beautifully and forcibly and he kept reminding us that there would be dark and difficult days ahead.

I must confess that I was a little bit surprised because I didn't expect that kind of a speech on April 3, 1968. But as I look back over those years, I must say in all honesty that surely Dr. King spoke prophetically that night. For, in the ten years since he died, we have seen and witnessed in this land and in this country some dark and difficult days.

And I was doing an interview on last Saturday with some reporters from a paper as we talked about Memphis, Tennessee, and even this nation, about the progress. I must sadly confess that as I tried to rack my mind that it looks, except for the escalator effect, that we have not moved very far from '68 to '78. In fact, if I were honest tonight, I would have to say that as I travel the length and breadth of this country, that there seems to be a counter-tide of conservatism sweeping across this nation that threatens to undo all of the progress that we thought we had made. Unless we are very careful, this nation will see a second post-Reconstruction period. And the consequences for the nation will be grim and dreadful, not just for black folk, not just for women, not for Hispanics, Asian-Americans, and Indian-Americans but for *all* of America it will be sad and tragic day if we witness a roll-back of human rights in this nation.

If there is one thing we should have learned by now, if the lessons of Watergate should have taught us anything, it is that liberty is indivisible and that there is no way to roll back the rights of some people in this nation, without all of us inevitably suffering a roll-back in human, spiritual and civil rights.

My mind examines some of the things we face now. In 1968, while Dr. King spoke, we were still celebrating the birth of nationhood of many nations of Africa. But today as we look at that great continent, from Ethiopia on the east all the way back to the west and to South Africa at the tip of the horn, we see a continent that is once again caught up in a struggle to become first-class nations in this world.

Many of the colonial powers, and indeed powers that were not colonial powers, are interfacing in the affairs of Africa. Troops are being landed and all kinds of things are being done to roll back the proud spirit of the '50s and the '60s, when all of these nations unfurled their new flag and started on the road toward nationhood.

Surely, anyone who can read and who can understand the vicious system of apartheid in South Africa, where less than 4 million whites seem determined and bent to utilize the labor, the exploitation, the dehumanization of more than 14 million blacks to build one of the highest standards of living that the world has ever known. It seems nothing will stop them. The seeds of a third world war are being planted now in South Africa and we in America are continuing to send money and our institutions are expanding their industrial economy, they're building property on the backs of people who still work for less than a dollar a day.

There's something un-Christian, something that is alien to our whole Judeo-Christian heritage in what we're doing in South Africa. Unless good people in America rise up and revolt against that type of thing, we will see the seeds of a third world war that might engulf all of us, because of what's happening in South Africa today.

Just two Saturdays ago, the NAACP led a march down in Nashville, Tennessee. It was so strange that we had more than 7,000 people, there were more than 100 people from television and radio and newspaper, reporters from all over the nation and the world. But because the march was nonviolent, because there were no heads busted, because there were no noses bloodied, you saw very little of it. Yet we were there to present our bodies as a witness that we are concerned, we were trying to elevate the level of consciousness in this country that there's something going on. A Nazi regime in South Africa that will threaten to parallel the growth of Hitler and so many of us are satisfied.

I've had an opportunity to talk with Donald Wood, the editor of one of the great white papers in South Africa. He was telling us about how the South African government banned *The World,* which was the largest black newspaper in South Africa, and put Rebozo in jail and then banned him, put him under house arrest, and how he escaped from South Africa. It's difficult to listen to that man without recognizing that here in 1978 we're seeing the most massive deprivation of human rights that this world has known since Hitler held sway in Germany a few years ago. And yet so many of us are unconcerned because it doesn't seem to affect us.

But it seems to me I can still hear the poets saying, "Never seem to know for whom the bells toll, they toll for thee." So all of us tonight, even in this beautiful setting in Minnesota, St. Peter, all of us are involved in what is happening a world away, miles and miles away across 6,000 miles of ocean, somehow we're caught up and we ought begin to pay attention to it and to pay our witness and to do our best to see that the kind of apartheid, the kind of viciousness that exists in South Africa can be brought to a close.

Maybe Dr. King looked in 1968 away from Selma, Alabama, away from Jackson, Mississippi, away from Atlanta and Memphis, Tennessee, and looked down the future and saw Boston, where even today, and just two or three years ago, people would go to church and think of their rosaries and come away from the church saying, "Hail Mary full of grace, blessed art thou and blessed is the fruit of thy womb Jesus," and then having said that, would spit on children and throw bricks through the windows of the school buses and set them on fire, in order that white and black children might not go to school together. Not in Selma, but in Boston, the cradle of liberty, where men first had the tea party and where we first cried out against taxation without representation. In Boston, the symbol of our dreams where the liberty trail begins, in Boston! In this century, in this decade, we found racism raising its ugly head. The whole forces of evil and conservatism come into light.

Maybe Dr. King saw the tragedy of the Bakke case [*University of California v. Bakke*]. As I move across this country, I talk about that case coming out of the University of California Medical School, the Davis Medical College, and I know that all of you perhaps are fed up to your gills with it, but there are still so many facts that people don't understand. I've been asked by so many folk all over this country, what is it that black folk want, what are we looking for? And I would have to say to you again and again that we are not looking for superiority, we are simply looking for some equality, we are simply looking for the fulfillment of the American dream. Because we were not there, we did not participate when the so-called founding fathers in the sweltering heat of a Philadelphia summer wrote those words that "We hold these truths to be self-evident." They need no empirical proof, they needed no recitation to say that men are created equal and they are endowed not by the Magna Carta, not by the parliaments of men, but by *God* with these rights.

I need not stand here tonight and tell you that we didn't really mean it, but when they got to black folks they called us three-fifths of a man instead of a whole man. When they got to women they did not even give them the right to vote until the 1920s. But the fact is they wrote, published, proclaimed those words at a time when they were bright bugle calls to greatness. For almost 202 years now we've been trying to make them come true, a great American dream.

So what black folks are looking for in this nation is for this nation to finally come to the realization and admit honestly that we have not *ever* lived up to it and the time has come that we should. In 1968, in this great country of ours, there were in existence 116 medical schools. In those 116 medical schools, approximately 266 blacks were admitted to first-year medical school, in 1968, ten short years ago. And of those 266, approximately half of them were admitted to Howard and Meharry, which are predominantly black schools. Which means that the other 114 medical schools admitted, between them, hardly 150 black students. If you go back and read 1968's rolls, you'll find that the majority of white, predominantly white, medical schools had less than one black and many of them had none.

Through the use of affirmative action programs we have succeeded in bringing the number of black students admitted to first-year medical schools from less than 300 in 1968 to about 1,100 in 1976. And now come the cries of reverse discrimination. But I also want you to know that in 1968 there were approximately 8,000 white medical students admitted to first-year medical school, but that by 1976 that number had grown to 14,500 whites. So it doesn't look like to me that black folks are taking anybody's place; it looks to me like some folk want to have the bread, the cake, the pie, and all the crumbs that fall from the table and some of us are saying, "Hell no, we won't go!" [applause] The time has come when all of us must enjoy the goodness and the fruit of this American democracy because that's what it's all about.

Now when you talk about qualifications, we're not saying to medical schools, "lower your qualifications." We're simply saying establish your benchmark and then make sure that some blacks and some Asian-Americans and Hispanic-Americans and Indian-Americans and women get admitted along with white males. Because I'm not sure that this business of qualifications is all it's cracked up to be in the first place.

Chief Justice Burger, a very eminent and distinguished jurist, has said publicly on more than one occasion that, in his judgment, 50 percent of all of the lawyers practicing law in this great country are not *competent* to represent people in the courtroom.

Now I was a practicing lawyer for many years. I presided as a trial judge where I had to deal with lawyers every day. I must confess to you I don't quite agree with Chief Justice Burger about 50 percent of all American lawyers being unqualified to represent people in the courtroom. My figure would be closer to 70 percent of all the lawyers being unqualified. I spent many dreary days on the bench. I had to take the cases away from most lawyers to keep them from putting *all* their clients in jail. [laughter]

Now if, in fact, we take Mr. Burger's more conservative figures, remember that less than two percent of all the lawyers who practice in America today are black; 98 percent of all the lawyers who practice in this country are white. So if every black lawyer was unqualified, you've still got 48 percent of all the white lawyers who are not qualified to practice, who are not competent. And if this is what qualifications are all about, then we ought to have a new set of criteria for competence and qualifications.

I look at what the American Medical Association says, even that conservative body, admits that there were more than two million unnecessary cases of surgery performed in America in 1976. *Two million* instances in which people were put on the operating table and operated on, not because they needed it, but because somebody wanted to make money! Is that what qualifications are all about? We say no!

All we're asking in this nation is that you give those of us who have planted your corn and picked your cotton and wet-nursed your babies and fought in every war and been loyal to this nation, all we're saying is that we want equality and parity and an opportunity to demonstrate that we can be a part of the great American dream. We're not asking you to lower your qualifications, because God in heaven knows they're low enough already. All we want is an opportunity. Mr. Bakke talks about sixteen places being reserved for minorities and then the question is asked do we believe in quotas? No, the NAACP has always opposed quotas, because a quota is an artificial ceiling above which one cannot rise. But we do believe in goals and timetables. And if there is to be parity in this nation, goals and timetables must exist.

The classic example, and I sort of changed the figures around a little bit, but this actually happened, you can check it. Judge Johnson, a great federal judge down in Montgomery, Alabama, was dealing with the Alabama highway patrol. In all of their history they had never had a black highway patrolman. So a suit was filed. Under the Title 7 of the Civil Rights laws, the affirmative action section, it says that everybody in this country must be an equal-opportunity employer. So the commissioner of the highway patrol said to Judge Johnson, "We've tried *hard*. But you know how high the standards are for the Alabama highway patrol. Most of our troopers, I suppose, are graduates of great Universities with their PhD degrees—of course most of them couldn't read good, but they were still very well qualified—we haven't found a single Nigra in the whole state of Alabama who'd qualify." Out of one million black folk, he couldn't find one Negro who qualified.

And Judge Johnson wrestled with this dilemma for months and months and months. Now any law in this country which does not have a penalty is no law at all. I came down with one of the most distinguished and law-abiding citizens of this great state. We drove down here at fifty-five miles an hour, because we're patriotic and we love this state and we want to save gas and we want to be loyal to President Carter's program. In addition to that, the highway patrol is always out there to nail the rest of you for going fifty-six. So Isaac, you know, Leon, you know, we believe in obeying the law, but we also think if there's no penalty, I don't know what he would have done because that Lincoln we drove in on seems like it was walking at fifty-five. [laughter] I'm not at all sure what would have happened. So every law in this country has attached to it a penalty.

Judge Johnson, sitting as a federal district judge, was faced with the dilemma of a quota being entered and the highway patrol simply thumbing their noses at him. So Judge Johnson fashioned a remedy and federal

judges all over the nation have fashioned remedies called goals and timetables. One day he suggested to the commission of the highway patrol in
Alabama that "The order for you to integrate the Alabama highway patrol
did not come from the black plaintiffs, it came from the federal district
court. For laws to have any meaning, if we issue an order and it's not carried out, it ceases to have meaning. So Mr. Commissioner, I would suggest
to you, by the first day of September, that's a timetable, you should have
ten, at least ten black highway troopers on duty or you will be held in con-
tempt of court and you will, Mr. Commissioner, go to jail. Is that clear?"

That's not a quota, that's goals and timetables because otherwise the
law loses its majesty, the law loses its meaning, the law loses its ability to
enforce itself and the law becomes a mockery and we may as well disman-
tle the rule of law and have a rule of men and we all do what we want. If
that law does not deserve enforcing, no law deserves enforcing. All laws
ought be equal. And so what happened? Nobody got mad, nobody got
angry, Judge Johnson simply said by the first day of September you will
have ten black troopers or you will go to jail. The highway commissioner is
a reasonable man, he came back on the first of August and said, "Mr.
Judge, I want to report, I'm ahead of time, and I got fifteen instead of ten."
That's what the law can do for you. It may not make you change your heart,
but it can make you change your *conduct!* That's what goals and timetables
are all about.

Somebody asked Dr. King one day, "Dr. King, do you think changing
the law will change men's hearts?" He said, "I'm not particularly concerned
now about changing men's hearts. I want the right to drink from a water
fountain, to use a restroom, and unless you've been up and down these
highways like I have and felt in your own body the sting of discrimination,
you don't really know what it's like. And I don't care what a man thinks
about me as long as I use that restroom and drink from that water fountain. I'll wait until later to change his heart. I want the law changed *now* so
we can enjoy some decency and some parity and some equality now."

And that's all this thing is about. This is to make America a better nation for *all* of us. I saw a recent poll that said that 20 percent of all the
young black people between the ages of eighteen and thirty-five have
given up on this country. They think it will take a revolution to change it.
My brothers and my sisters, that's dangerous to every white and black man

and woman in this nation. *Time* magazine calls it a growing underclass. We surrender our liberties so easily and so quickly.

When I go to the airport tomorrow morning down in St. Paul or Minneapolis, I will go through a buzzing machine and if I set it off I'll hold my hands up and smile while I'm hassled. Today I saw them going through my briefcase, just pulling everything out. I do it gladly and you'd do it. Why? Because I don't want that plane to be bombed in the middle of the air. So little by little we lose the democracy that we have inherited.

Let nobody fool themselves, this is a great land and this is a great country. We do have a marvelous opportunity, those of us who live here now. But if we are to pass on to our children, and to our children's children the type of democracy that we have *inherited,* we must be vigilant about the future. We must make sure that the rights and opportunities that have been guaranteed by the Constitution in these years must be extended to *all* of those who live beneath the sun that rises and sets on America every day. This is our challenge and this is our opportunity.

So I support the concept of affirmative action. When I look at our nation, more than 2,000 cases were filed in 1976 by white males who feel that there is a thing called "reverse discrimination." That is a ludicrous, stupid statement to make because in this nation all we're trying to do is have a *reversal* of discrimination and not reverse discrimination, to open the doors that have been closed.

I never shall forget, just a few days ago, I addressed a meeting of the National Conference of Christians and Jews, and one of my Jewish friends came up to me and told a story of something that happened to him down in Florida many years ago. He had a black chauffeur, and he said they were driving from New York. When they got down to Florida in one of those small towns, there was a big sign up that said, "No dogs and Jews allowed in this town." My Jewish friend said he sat there with tears in his eyes, but then something strange happened. His chauffeur, who was black, turned around and said, "Mr. Bloom," and he said my chauffeur was crying, and he said, "Look, they didn't even think enough of me to put my race on the sign." No dogs, no Jews allowed, and they didn't even think enough of black folks to say "and no blacks." It was understood we were not allowed.

Now we come knocking boldly at the door of Democracy, asking for equal opportunity and a chance. We come not just for ourselves, but we come to make this nation better. For whenever we fence out creativity, whenever we fence out the talent of those who have so much to offer, this nation suffers. That's what Dr. King was about, and I respect and admire his memory. I respect and admire those who can look at this peaceful warrior, so lied on and so criticized, who went to jail thirty-nine times, who had a message not just for black folk, but a message for every man, woman, boy, girl and child who lived in America and, indeed, this world.

He was a man who never gave way to hatred. I've seen him in some moments when I don't understand what it was that kept him moving. I've seen him as he endured the stings and arrows of outrageous fortune. I've seen him as he came to a town and the newspaper would headline his coming with "Here comes a sheep, this wolf, rather, in sheep's clothing trying to destroy the good relations between the Negroes and the whites in our city." That good relation consisted of Negroes in the ditch and white folk with their foot on their necks. Martin King had to endure all of that, his friends lying on him, people talking about him, being threatened. I watched him speak night after night into the floodlights, knowing he had received death threats, never knowing when a bullet would come.

One day that bullet caught up with him, on the fourth day of April 1968. I remember I was on my way to see him that day because we had talked the night before and made an appointment to deal with some things that were of concern to us and to this nation. I remember just a few years before that when he had come to Memphis for a meeting of the Southern Christian Leadership Conference and how he'd come out to our house that night and, in one of the few times that I was privileged to know him, he relaxed, as he was singing some of the songs that you were singing tonight.

One of the greatest heritages ever passed down, passed down from folk who could not read their names in boxcar letters, but who, in the dim and dark night of cruel slavery, looked up and saw stars still shining in the night. I think it was the poet Countee Cullen who said, "And yet do I marvel at this curious thing, to make a poet black and bid him sane." Some of the most profound words ever uttered, some of the most beautiful thoughts ever contained in the hearts of men were written and sent on the air by black folk who were tied up in slavery.

When I was a college student and singing in the choir, I remember singing a song that later on perplexed me because I used to sing it with gusto and with joy, "Before I'd be a slave I'd be buried in my grave, go home and be at peace with my God." It dawned on me that the folk who wrote those words, the folk who were singing them, were indeed the physically tied to chattel slavery, who did not own the shoes on their feet, nor the coats on their back. That little corn-shuck pad on which they slept did not belong to them but they discovered a great and profound truth: that even though their bodies belonged to the master, even though they could be sold like cattle and hogs on the auction block, that there was something that could never belong to the slave master. That was their soul and their spirit. And they discovered what Blind Bunyan discovered and Milton discovered, that there's something about me that can never be taken away. Before I give that *up*, before I become a *slave* in my *mind*, I'd be *buried* in my grave, and go home, be at peace with my God.

It was those people who gave us insightful songs. We thought every time they talked about "Swing Low, Sweet Chariot" they were talking about eschatology and long white robes and some of our less secure and immature minds among black folk fell out with slavery songs. But every time black folk were singing about "Swing Low, Sweet Chariot" they were sometimes talking about Sojourner Truth and Harriet Tubman coming down with the freedom train, not going to heaven in the by-and-by but to Ohio and Pennsylvania in the here and now. God has given to us the gift of song and we have given it to the American nation and to this world. And so I close tonight by saying the one thing that Dr. King stood preeminently for was that we should love everybody, because he taught us that there was a better way than hate.

And so as I move around this country as Executive Director of the NAACP, I say to my brothers and sisters and to my friends everywhere that the time has come when we must not give away to hating. It's a waste of time for black folk to talk about hating the blue-eyed honkies and blue-eyed blonds, that's foolishness. Because if there's any one thing I've learned in fifty years of living, it is that hatred won't destroy the folk you hate, but it will eat you up and kill you graveyard dead and put you in the hospital with high blood pressure and hypertension and strokes. So we have no time to hate. The time has come when we must reach out black and white together and try to build a better nation and thus a better world. We have no message of hate but we have a message of love.

We're telling you now, and I will say it when I'm in the White House, I will say it in the Congress, if I stood up there before the Supreme Court I would say that America now has a date with destiny and that date is to make the great American dream come true. When all of us, whether we got our degrees from Morehouse or no house, from Yale or by mail, can sit down at the welcome table and partake in the fruits of Democracy. When black and white together, male and female, rich and poor, we shall lock arms and join hearts and walk up the King's highway, looking for the coming of the day when our eyes can see the glory of the coming of the Lord.

I know that there are those who are tired of the struggle. As I move around this nation I find some black folk who have gotten tired and they say that they have given so much of their time, but I say we must still struggle on. There are white friends who tell me, "But Brother Hooks you don't understand, I've been ostracized. I go to my country club to have a drink, now they don't want to see me because I keep talking, they call me a nigger-lover, they do all kinds of things." But I simply say to you what I see the sign on the highway saying, "Remember the life you save may be your own."

If we get tired and if we get discouraged, remember that we are the ones who have been given the opportunity by God to make this world a better place. It was at the height of World War II, before we entered it, when Hitler had the very fires of Europe alight with the bodies of those he was burning in concentration camps, that the beleaguered island of Britain stood as the last bastion of hope for the civilized world.

When Winston Churchill, one of the great masters of the English language, got on the radio again and again and sometimes I play those records and the words still come echoing back. When he called on his people to give blood and sweat and toil and tears; when he asked them to fight on the beaches and in the cities but never to surrender; when in one great and memorable address he said, "I want you to so conduct yourselves that if this island empire should endure for a thousand years, historians will look back and say, 'This was your finest hour.' "

Again and again he rallied the British people to the standard of greatness. Then, at a very dark moment, when America stood, as it were, on the sidelines, when the menacing mobs of Hitler seemed about to overtake the civilized world, when only Britain stood in the path of this madman, this tyrant, this cruel dictator, Churchill made one of his most memorable addresses. He recited again what he'd called on his fellow countrymen to do. He reminded them he'd called on them for blood and sweat and toil and tears. He reminded them he'd asked them to fight on the beachheads and on the beaches and in the cities. He reminded them that he'd asked them to so conduct themselves that if the empire should endure for a thousand years, historians would look back and say, "This is your finest hour." And he said that I know that you're tired of me calling you for sacrifices and privations—almost too much for the human spirit to bear. But I close tonight by asking you the question, which I ask of you here gathered at this institution tonight: "If not now, when? If not you, who?" Peace. [applause]

16.

JOSEPH LOWERY
(1924–)

"The Black Presence in America"

Macalester College, St. Paul, Minnesota—March 21, 1980

In the hottest of the civil rights years, few men were closer to the Rev. Martin Luther King Jr. than Rev. Joseph Lowery. As a cofounder of the Southern Christian Leadership Conference (SCLC) and a close advisor to King, Lowery took part in many of the most famous demonstrations, marches, and boycotts of the 1950s and 1960s.

The SCLC was formed in 1957 in the wake of the Montgomery bus boycott, as civil rights activists and African American preachers looked for ways to coordinate their efforts. The SCLC would become one of the most influential civil rights organizations of the century. Using black churches as a hub to rally and organize, the SCLC spread the doctrine of nonviolent protest across the South.

Of the four charismatic preachers who founded the SCLC—King, Lowery, Fred Shuttlesworth, and Ralph Abernathy—Lowery was perhaps the most soft-spoken. His time was often occupied with SCLC tactical issues and staff conflicts. In 1959, Lowery and three others on the staff were named in a libel suit filed by the commissioners of Montgomery, Alabama; their names had appeared in a *New York Times* fundraising ad for a King defense fund. The historic $3 million suit, *Sullivan v. New York Times* would take more than a decade to fight off.[1]

Lowery was an advisor to King in some of King's most difficult situations. In 1964 the FBI mounted a secret campaign to threaten and smear King. The plot included an anonymous package with an audiotape and threatening letter, sent by the FBI. In January 1965, Coretta Scott King, his wife, inadvertently opened the package and listened to the tape. On it, FBI bugs captured the sound of King's extramarital affairs. Lowery was one of four confidants called by King to listen to the tape, read the letter, and plan how to respond.[2]

Lowery was born October 6, 1924, the son of a mortician and a homemaker. He attended Knoxville College, Alabama A&M College, Paine College and Paine Theological Seminary, Garrett Theological Seminary, and the Chicago Ecumenical Institute. A United Methodist minister, he was pastor of churches in Alabama and Georgia.

After King's death, Lowery remained devoted to the civil rights movement and the SCLC. He became the organization's national president, King's initial post, in 1977 and served for twenty years. Upon retirement in 1997, Lowery described the SCLC and, indeed, the movement: "We've been an umbrella in 40 years of rain," Lowery said. "In 1957, we saw a fire burning in the souls of black America. Water hoses couldn't wash it out, billy clubs couldn't beat it out and jails couldn't lock it out."[3]

I HAVE TALKED around the country during the past few weeks on the subject of what the black presence in America has meant to America. I think until the future of blacks is secure in this country, that the celebration of our past, in order to promote understanding and knowledge about our past, is very significant. One of the first things that the slave masters did when they brought slaves from Africa was to try to remove us entirely from our past. Slaves were forbidden to speak in their native tongues. And as much as it was possible, families, members of the same tribe, were separated, in order to *wipe* out the past. Of course, if you can wipe out a person's past, it then facilitates the controlling of his present and the shaping of his future.

So I've chosen that subject—the black presence in America and what it has meant to America—because it gives us an opportunity to look at the broader aspect of the black experience in this country, aside from calling the rolls of the black heroes. I don't need, before such an astute and learned assembly as this, to call the roll of blacks who've made contributions in the development in this country, nor even remind you of those advanced and intelligent ancient civilizations such as Mali, Timbuktu. Don't need to do that with this group—I'd be insulting you if I dealt at that elementary level.

Of course you know that. You know, I don't have to talk about, as we talked in one of the classes today, to tell you that blood plasma was developed by black brains, which has saved white lives, brown lives. I don't have to recite all of that to you; you know all of that. You know that many of our great cities like Chicago and Washington, D.C., were laid out by black urban designers. I ask you not to hold it against them, [laughter] but they did it. I don't have to tell you that the complex railroad signal system, for example in this country, was developed by black minds. I don't need to recite those things because you know that—in an astute academic community such as this, it would be, at best, impertinent for me to suggest calling that kind of roll.

So that's why I've chosen a broader approach to this, in terms of what the black presence has meant to America. I think, the first thing I'd like to suggest is—I understand I'm to speak three hours and discussion two hours, is that right? [laughter] My flight's at 8:15, I'd just as soon keep you up with me all night so I don't miss the flight. The first thing I'd like to suggest is that the black presence in America has reflected, what I think, is the highest, noblest, most authentic form of patriotism. I think the true loyalists, the true patriots of America, have been the black people of America. Not simply because a black man was the first to die at Bull Run; not just because blacks have died in every war to protect America; not just because hardly any blacks have been convicted of treason.

Not just because of that, but because of the more important things, that blacks and the black presence has *challenged* America and has pushed and pulled America up to her tip-toes in terms of what she may become. The black presence has not indulged America at her weaknesses, nor excused her failures, but has challenged her at both, that she might strengthen her weaknesses and correct her mistakes and move on up a little higher. I think real patriotism is not the kind expressed by the self-styled super-patriots, who go around wrapped up in flags and who wear bumperstickers saying "Love it or leave it." I think the true patriotism is expressed by those who love it so much that they will not leave it alone until it lives up to its noble precepts and keeps its lofty promises and commitments to be the land of the free as well as the home of the brave. I think that's authentic patriotism.

Now sometimes authentic patriotism causes discomfort. Just as, you know, a good teacher is not the teacher who indulges the student in the student's weaknesses. The good teacher is the teacher who challenges the student, even causing the student some discomfort and reaping the displeasure of the student. The physician often causes discomfort as he initiates the healing process—I hate to hear my doctor say, "Take off your coat and role up your sleeve," or worse still, "Let down your britches," he's about to injure me and I hate to hear him say that. But it is that discomfort, that temporary discomfort, that initiates the healing process, that permits me to live on in health. I think the black presence in this country, which has sometimes had to fill her streets and jam her jails and take her to court and wrestle with her through the long night of racial crises in order that we might look forward to the dawn of a new day of justice and brotherhood. I think that is authentic patriotism. I think the black presence in America—I have a friend whose son when he was very young was stricken with polio. Carried him to a clinic and they put braces on his leg. My friend says in the middle of the night he would hear his son whimpering. He would go upstairs and say, "What is it son?" And the boy would say, "Daddy, please, loosen the braces." My friend said he said to his son, "My god, son, I'd give my right arm if I could loosen the braces, but they tell me it's the tightness of the braces that stretches the muscles. So all I can do is lie here with you in the bed and weep with you through the long night, so that one day we can walk together." Every Sunday morning, almost every Sunday morning, I see that boy now, young man, walking down the aisle. He has a limp, but he's walking. And he walks because his father wept with him in the night, that they might now enjoy a sunshine day—walking together. I think the black presence in America has been the highest, most authentic form of patriotism that enables America, now, to walk with her head a little higher, because we've challenged her. I think that patriotism has been significant in America's growth. That creative pressure must continue to be exerted on America in the context of love of country because we must complete the task begun a decade or so ago that has not been completed.

And the second thing I'd say, which leads me into some discussion on foreign policy, is that I think the other thing the black presence has meant to America is that, the black presence, black folks have just always been— I know you're gonna accuse me, when I leave you're gonna say that fellow's a black racist. But I don't think so. But you know black folk was almost born with an innate sense of justice. And a sensitivity to human need. It's just; we always know what's right. We don't always *do* what's right. But we know what's right. We just have a sense of justice. And it's been reflected in the black experience. My mother used to whip me and wouldn't tell me what she was whipping me about. And I'd say, "What you whipping me about." And she would say, "You know." And I did. [laughter] It's just an ingrained sense of justice and sensitivity to human need. And it's that sense of justice that has motivated and driven black community. To stand for what was just and what was right even though it was unpopular. Even though it gets you in trouble. I remember the heart of the movement, when white churches were putting young black people in jail for coming to worship, that in the midst of that I don't know a single black church anywhere that *ever* had a white person arrested, or turned a white person away who wanted to come in and praise the Lord. Because we knew it wasn't right. We had a sense of justice. And that sensitivity to human need, that sense of justice helped free not only black people in this country, but helped free white people.

Because a sense of superiority is just as much imprisonment as a sense of inferiority. In order to hold a person in a ditch, a part of you has to remain in the ditch. That sense of justice, that sensitivity of human need is significant now as blacks exercise not simply their *right* to be involved in foreign policy but their *responsibility* to help this country shape its policy toward its neighbors in the world. And this is not new for SCLC. SCLC under the leadership of our first president, Dr. King, was among the first to challenge the morality of the Vietnam conflict. It was Dr. King and SCLC who were severely criticized and rebuked for saying that there was something wrong about the war in Vietnam. It was Dr. King and the SCLC that urged the recognition of red China as an important component of peace in

Southeast Asia. And if the nation had heeded Dr. King and SCLC, we would have saved thousands of lives and billions of dollars. So our foray into foreign policy is not new. Incidentally the same blacks who criticize us today are the successors to the same blacks who criticized Dr. King in that day. But let me not dwell on that. But that wasn't the beginning of black involvement in foreign policy. W.E.B. Du Bois, one of the most outspoken advocates of the most sensitive policy toward Africa Marcus Garvey, Ralph Bunche, a black man, earned a Nobel Peace Prize for his leadership in foreign policy in the Mideast. And if blacks become more involved in foreign policy and the shaping of foreign policy, this country would benefit from that sense of justice and that sensitivity to human need that will characterize our involvement as it has on the domestic scene.

If, for example, blacks had a strong voice in foreign policy, we wouldn't have the hostages in Iran right now. No, no, no, no, no. Black folks would not have dug that dude the Shah, early in our relationship. [laughter] Never would we have been fooled and jived by him. Black folks know shucking and jiving when they sleep [laughter], let alone in the midst of delicate foreign relations. No, the hostages are being held not because they don't like our national anthem. Matter of fact, I don't like our national anthem. [laughter] Matter of fact I don't know anybody who does like our national anthem, I wonder why they don't change it. Nobody sings it, can't sing it. It takes a Lily Pons, or a Leontyne Price to sing it. But they are opposed to America because America's foreign policy supported a despot and a corrupt Shah. Black involvement in foreign policy would have changed that situation. What's happening in Iran is we have sown the wind, and we are reaping the whirlwind. When the Ayatollah released the blacks and the women, some black leaders were offended. I was not offended. I rejoiced at their release and cabled him that I hope tomorrow you release the blue-eyed and the next day the knock-kneed and then the slow-footed, and the pigeon-toed, until they're all released. But seriously, what I think the Ayatollah was trying to say to us was that he released the blacks and the women because he was trying to identify his movement with the movement of the oppressed around the world. Now unfortunately he negates that effort by violating the human rights of the hostages. For we have learned in the movement that you do not use ignoble means to obtain a noble end.

But nevertheless, nevertheless, we—and I am concerned at many instances at the treatment of Iranian students have received in some parts of this country as a result of the holding of the hostages by the militants in Iran. I believe America should respect the human rights of the Iranian students in this country. And by our example show what real respect for human rights can be, and thereby begin the process of reversing the feelings of hostility that exist towards this country in many parts of the world. Because we have identified with those who were oppressors rather than those who were liberators. We have sown the wind, we've reaped the whirlwind.

Blacks must be more involved in the State Department. That tired old wing of government that is tired, insensitive, white, un creative, wishy-washy. Votes one way today, another by nightfall. In the State Department less than 2 percent of the senior level foreign personnel is black. And even where Africa is concerned, you would think that we would have a substantial representation there, less than 6 percent of the senior level foreign officers are black.

Therefore if that sense of justice, that sensitivity to human need, will characterize America's posture to the world on a horizontal level, not the vertical of old, we must have more persons with a sense of justice, with a sensitivity to human need. I am deeply concerned about our reaction to Afghanistan. I'm sorry, and shame on the Russians for invading Afghanistan and they ought to go home and let the Afghanistani—is that what you call them?—people determine their own destiny. But if they stay one hundred years, I'm not willing to see one American die over that issue.

I therefore must take serious opposition to any thought of draft, of drafting of our young people and the interrupting of their lives, and talk of war in that part of the world. As a matter of fact, I don't see the threat to national security that justifies a draft. And if they have to draft, if it comes to that, I have a suggestion. I want them to draft the rich, old, white men, who always making decisions [applause] to send poor young black and white men to war. Truth of the matter is they don't have to draft blacks for a long time. The United States army now is 33 and 1/3 percent black. We who are 11 percent of the population are 33 and 1/3 percent of the army. Not because we so military. But because we like to eat. [laughter] We develop habits of housing and clothes and things. And there's more opportunity there than outside. But even there the same racism exists. But we who are 11 percent of the population and 33 and 1/3 percent of the army, we're only 6 percent of the officers in the army. But more startling than that—we're 47 percent of the *combat* divisions in the army.

So if we go to war, who—they say we're not going to have a nuclear war, we're going to have a conventional war—well then, who will die? No, I think the draft, thoughts of draft is premature. And I'm frightened at what I hear in many conversations and what I heard one presidential candidate say about a limited nuclear war, one that we could survive. And I'm frightened about the debate over whether we're 10 percent behind the Russians or 2 percent in terms of strategic weapons. The truth of the matter is, according to which military expert, they claim we can kill every Russian at least from 20 to 29 times. And that they can kill us at least the same number of times. If that's true, then it seems to me the debate about the number of strategic weapons, whether we're 2 percent or 10 percent behind, becomes extremely irrelevant. I submit that killing every Russian once would suffice [laughter] and I'm satisfied that every American who dies once would be just as dead as he will after the 28th time. [laughter]

So I'm extremely concerned about this kind of talk. We're talking in peculiar ways. We're talking about surviving a nuclear conflict. Somebody had a study recently, they revealed for example that one nuclear weapon dropped on Boston for example, I don't know why they picked Boston as an example. Maybe they were thinking about South Boston, I'm not sure. [laughter] If they dropped a bomb that was 1,000 times as powerful as the bomb dropped on Hiroshima—and that's not the most powerful bomb we have available, that's just an itty-bitty fellow—that bomb would make a crater a half mile in diameter and several hundred feet deep and wipe out completely everything within four miles of the explosion. Forty miles away, people who looked in the direction of the explosion would be blinded. Of the 3 million people in Boston, 2.2 million would be killed at once. With the hospitals, doctors, equipment destroyed, the others would die shortly. How then can we engage in discussions, how can we dare think of nuclear war? And yet the insensitivity of our foreign policy. The growing hawkishness among many of those who spoke eloquently of a new kind of relationship, a new kind of aggressiveness for peace, who now speak emphatically, and hawkishly, and shockingly.

So it is, for example, toward Africa. We've only begun recently to move toward that continent with a sense of justice and a sensitivity to human need. What was so important about Andrew Young's role as ambassador to the United Nations was that it reflected a new kind of sensitivity as we relate to the emerging nations in the world. Emerging nations that are non-white, non-Catholic, non-Protestant, non-Jewish, and non-submissive. To the roar of the lion, or the growl of the bear, or the wingspread of the eagle.

But our self-determinant, proud, and longing for liberty requires a new sensitivity to human need, a new sense of justice that the black involvement must bring to foreign policy. Not simply as a right, but as a responsibility. And finally let me say, that blacks must be involved in shaping foreign policy because it has a direct impact on domestic issues. And those uninformed, head-in-the-sand folks, who say why go to the Mideast, or why go to Africa, you know, I, I, got to say Hallelujah, tonight, because at least the eighties, while the seventies ended on a sad note, at least the eighties have begun on a fairly good note, for my brothers and sisters in Zimbabwe, Rhodesia, can say free at last, [applause] free at last, thank God almighty, they're free at last. But I don't care whether it's Mugabe, Cuomo, or Abel Muzorewa. In fact, I know Abel so well, I guess my head was pulling for Mugabe, and my heart was pulling for Muzorewa. I know him so well, he's a bishop in my church and he and Maggie have been in my home. But he couldn't win, and God knows best. 'Cause if Muzorewa had won we'd a still had war. Now that Mugabe has won I hope we'll have peace, thank God for peace.

But those who say why go to Africa or the Mideast, when you ought to be helping black folks here in the ghetto. Let me help them *understand*. [long pause] That whenever the military and defense budget in this country goes *up*, the programs that will help the ghetto go *down*. And that's as true as if I'm in St. Paul, Minnesota. And I know there ain't that much snow in Atlanta, Georgia. It is undeniably true. In the close of '78, and the black leadership forum met with President Carter. Black unemployment was 11 or 12 percent when President Carter took office. Black unemployment is still 11 or 12 percent. That's officially, and we know it's twice that high realistically.

We said to Mr. Carter, you're not keeping your commitment. You promised to tackle black unemployment problem with vigor and a sense of urgency but you put it on the back burner. Mr. Carter said well, I'm sorry.

But we said you've got to increase those programs designed to provide job training, and jobs, and health care, and housing, more quality education. The President said I'm sorry, but we've got to fight inflation. And in order to fight inflation I not only can't increase the budget for those programs, I've got to reduce it. Mr. President, don't you realize you're making the people who are the least able bear the burden of fighting inflation? But then, in his next breath, while he must reduce programs that speak to the needs of the *poor*, he adds 11.6 *billion* dollars to the defense budget.

And anybody who can't see the correlation between domestic issues and foreign policy is simply not being realistic. And right now the budget he is suggesting, in spite of his talk about two billion dollars for hard-core unemployed, which won't go into effect for another two years, he's proposing even now to reduce that by twenty million dollars. Not one red penny will come out of the military defense budget. So then where will it come from? It'll come from CETA, it will come from housing, it'll come from education, it'll come from health care. It's our foreign policy that determines the intensity with which we grapple with our domestic problems. So, yes, black folks must be involved.

Not only do we have a right, but we have a responsibility to take that sense of justice, that sensitivity to human need into the world of striped-pants diplomacy and change it to jeans, which reflect the sense of equity among the children of God. When the national crises negatively impact this country, it has its worst effect on black folk. See, America as a whole is suffering a repression; black folks are suffering a depression. When America has a bad cold, black folks have pneumonia. So don't tell me we're not concerned—we cannot afford to be anything less than urgently concerned, urgently involved. It's our country. What right do I have to not offer a sense of justice, and sensitivity to human need to our country?

I notice black folks every now and then say let us stand and sing the Negro national anthem. They're referring to a great hymn by James Weldon Johnson that begins, "Lift every voice and sing." I reject that—it's not my national anthem. It's my national *hymn*. I love it—we sing it every Sunday at my church for doxology. But I'm going along with the Star Spangled Banner. What is it—"Oh say can you see"—as I said earlier, it's a terrible song. [laughter] It cannot be sung melodically, the words don't represent what America ought to represent—the bombs bursting in air—that's a bad song. Congress ought to change it. Why don't Minnesota start it? But as long as the country says that's it, it's mine. Because I'm not going to abdicate my ownership of this country. I'll let no one else abrogate nor abridge my privileges and my opportunities. It's my country. It ain't yours—it's us's. And we have to learn that. It ain't white folks' country—they just act like it. [laughter] It's *our* country. [applause]

17.

LOUIS FARRAKHAN
(1933–)

Address to the National Press Club

Washington, D.C.—July 30, 1984

Minister Louis Farrakhan, head of the black nationalist Nation of Islam, is a controversial figure on America's racial landscape. While he has been denounced as a hate-monger and a demagogue, Farrakhan's critics have also recognized that his words echo the abiding anger many blacks feel in America as issues of race and inequality fade from the political agenda.

Born Louis Eugene Walcott in 1933, Farrakhan was reared in a tightly knit, West Indian enclave of Boston. He was a talented student and gifted musician. As a traveling calypso singer in the early 1950s, he called himself "The Charmer." Farrakhan says his first bitter taste of racism came in the mid 1950s when he couldn't buy a ticket to a movie in Washington, D.C., because he was black. "A very close friend of mine had just been killed in Korea, and I walked down the street with a twenty-dollar bill in one hand, my wallet in the other, and at that point I was very, very angry with America," he recalled. Farrakhan began to write a calypso song called, "Why America Is No Democracy."[1]

Malcolm X recruited Farrakhan to the Nation of Islam (NOI) in the late 1950s. Farrakhan was riveted by Malcolm's speeches. "I'd never heard any man talk like that," he said. "I was convinced that this was where I wanted to be."[2] Farrakhan learned to emulate Malcolm X's speaking style and by the early 1960s was head of the NOI's mosque in Boston. When Malcolm X broke with the NOI in 1964, Farrakhan repudiated him and eventually took over Malcolm's role as spokesman for the Nation of Islam.

Before his death in 1975, NOI leader Elijah Muhammad named his son, Wallace, as his successor. Wallace began to reshape the Nation of Islam according to more traditional Muslim principles and eventually dissolved the organization. In 1979, Farrakhan resuscitated the Nation of Islam, purchasing a funeral home in Chicago for its new headquarters and starting a weekly paper, *The Final Call*.[3] From this base, Farrakhan solidified his national reputation.

There was tight security and a capacity crowd the day Louis Farrakhan spoke at the National Press Club in 1984. Farrakhan's security guards used their own metal detector to search cameramen, reporters, and other visitors for weapons. When someone booed Farrakhan at the end of his speech, four bodyguards advanced toward him until the Press Club manager shooed them away.[4]

In early 1984 Minister Farrakhan made headlines by supporting the Reverend Jesse Jackson's presidential bid. But in a June radio address Farrakhan denounced Israel, calling Judaism a dirty religion. Political leaders and activists insisted Jackson denounce Farrakhan or lose the chance to speak at the upcoming Democratic National Convention. Jackson complied.[5]

The Press Club's decision to invite Farrakhan to speak at the nationally broadcast luncheon was controversial. The director of the Anti-Defamation League, Nathan Perlmutter, said, "By providing Farrakhan with a bull horn for his ravings, the press is magnifying his significance. The result is print pollution and a disservice to the large majority of black Muslims, to Jews, and in the guise of reportage, a distortion of black-Jewish relations."[6]

However, the *Washington Post* observed that, despite his anti-Semitism, people generally clamored to hear Farrakhan speak.[7] Journalist Tamar Jacoby wrote in *Commentary* that Farrakhan's appeal "lies largely in his ability to speak for the alienation of his community. As an expressive voice and gadfly, he is without peer."[8] For poor African

Americans, Roger Wilkins wrote, "Their plight is not on anyone's agenda anymore. Farrakhan supplies an answer, and an emotional discharge."[9]

In October 1995, Farrakhan organized the Million Man March in Washington, D.C., which was attended by more African Americans than any march in history. National Urban League president Hugh Price called it "the largest family-values rally in the history of the United States." Activist and author Randall Robinson wrote of Farrakhan: "He has made himself the steward of the teeming black forgotten."[10]

IN THE NAME of Allah the beneficent, the merciful, and in the name of his true servant, our beloved leader, teacher and guide, the most honorable Elijah Muhammad, I greet you with the greeting words of peace in the Arabic language, *a'salaam alaikum*. [crowd responds: *wa'alaikum a'salaam*] To Mister Fogarty, to the members of the National Press Club, distinguished head table, members of the press, visitors, friends, brothers and sisters: I'm highly honored and greatly privileged as a representative of the honorable Elijah Muhammad and his great work of redeeming, reforming, and saving black people in this country and throughout the world, to have been invited by this august body to address you—even though I have the distinction of being the most openly censured and repudiated black man in the history of this country.

I represent the honorable Elijah Muhammad, a messenger and warner from almighty God Allah to black people, to America, and the world. I do not speak to you from mere personal desire, but I speak in the name of the God who raised up the honorable Elijah Muhammad, and I am backed by them both.

This statement that I just made should be given careful study and weight. Whenever warners or messengers appear, this represents God's intervention in the affairs of that nation, because in God's sight, neither the people nor their affairs are in a right state. The gravity of the situation and God's own integrity demands his intervention to warn us of the consequences of our deeds, that we may take a better course. This course of action demonstrates God's great mercy and his desire to redeem over his right to punish and destroy.

In the case of the United States of America, God's warning must be sounded regardless to how painful it is to the ears and no matter what the

consequences may be to the warner. The spirit of the warner is not that of
hate or malice. His spirit is the spirit of Allah, which is divine love. The
warning of the warner is given out of a deep concern and compassion for
human life. He works that the life of his people and others may be saved or
spared by his urging the people to act on the principles of truth and justice.
However, if we mistreat the warner and discard the warning as a lie, stick-
ing our fingers in our ears as though we heard nothing, then the consequences of the rejection of good council is violence and bloodshed. In this
case, it will lead to the destruction and death of this republic and the
tremendous loss of life, which could have been spared if only the leaders
had listened.

The responsibility of the well-being of the people of this nation rests
primarily on the shoulders of the leadership. The honorable Elijah
Muhammad said to us that neither justice nor peace shall come to the nations of earth, until the four-hundred-year-old problem of black people in
America has been solved with justice. The reason why no other nation can
have justice or peace until the problem of the black people in America is
properly solved is because almighty God himself is championing our
cause. No solution to this grave problem can be considered proper, nor
will any solution work, unless that solution is in accord with the nature of
the problem and in harmony with the demands of the time. That solution
and the time is given by the Prophet and is found written in the Bible and
in the Holy Koran. I repeat: America can have no peace, no joy in liberty,
and the deprived nations can have no justice until the black man's problem
is solved with justice, as the nations are tied to America in such a way that
her problems make problems for them. So what truly helps America helps
the nations of the earth.

Little did those who brought our fathers and our mothers into slavery
realize that they were creating a problem that it would take the almighty
God and his guidance to the nations to solve. Little did those who brought
us into slavery realize that out of this wretched people, almighty God
would lift up a criterion to measure the worthiness of the nations to escape
the fall and destruction of this world and qualify them to enter into his new
world order. Arabs, Jews, Africans, Europeans, and Americans were involved in bringing the black people in this country to this wretched and
shameful condition and position at the foot of the nations of the earth. So
it is natural that these people particularly are being offered the wonderful

and merciful chance to escape the chastisement that each is justly due by their being asked to help in solving the problem of the black people of America.

They that brought black people into slavery or participated in the slave trade were not aware of the Prophet's predictions. Nevertheless, their actions and our suffering are well documented in the writings of the Bible and the Holy Koran and in the written history of the nations. The history of our suffering and fall, written in symbols, signs and parables, formed the basis of the secret societies in America—particularly the Masons and Shriners, who are studying thirty-three degrees of the circle of the wisdom of Islam. However, these students of divine light are not permitted to make public what they know or what they are studying. The three million or more Muslim sons or Muslim Shriners in America are now charged with the responsibility of helping America or helping the black people in America out of this dilemma. Remember, it is written in the scriptures, "To whom much is given, much is required."

America has never really addressed the problem of justice for black people. America knew that when we were so-called "freed" by the Emancipation Proclamation, America had a duty to perform by us. Since America robbed us of all knowledge of self, in freeing us, we needed to be taught self-knowledge—the arts and sciences of civilized people, that we might be able to make an independent existence for ourselves. This America did not do. Thus, we were left in a state of ignorance, where we have been a continual prey in the hands of the people of America.

The first President of these United States, George Washington, said and I quote, "I fear that before too many years have passed over our heads, the Negro will become a most troublesome species of property." Thomas Jefferson said, quote, "I tremble for my country when I reflect that God is just, that his justice cannot sleep forever." Abraham Lincoln addressed a contingent of black leaders in the first White House conference attended by black leaders. And that conference was on the propriety of separation between white and black. Honest Abe said in part, "You and we are different races. We have a broader difference than exists between almost any other two races. Whether it is right or wrong I need not discuss." He continued, "I think your race suffer very greatly. Many of them by living among us, while ours suffers from your presence. In a word, we suffer on each side. If this is admitted, it affords a reason, at least, why we should be separated." Abraham Lincoln wanted separation. These black intellectuals disagreed. Mister Lincoln regarded their rejection as extremely selfish.

And so in recent years, government sponsored integration, busing and affirmative action have all been advanced and tried half-heartedly as solutions. We must be honest. Social integration is not a serious attempt to solve the problem of the masses of black people. In fact, at its root, were insincere government officials and others who knew better. Now the Supreme Court, in effect, has rejected affirmative action. Busing is a failure, and integration as a solution is causing blacks to be further and further behind whites. These meager, improper, and insincere attempts at a solution have failed miserably. And at best, they have only satisfied the longing of a certain class of black people who have always wanted to be included in the mainstream of American life. But the masses of black people remain unaffected, disillusioned, dissatisfied, distraught, angry and impatient. The light of hope in America's ability and will to do justice by us is flickering and dying.

So in 1984, the problem of giving justice to thirty or more million children of slaves is still with us. The problem will not vanish; it will not go away. Genocide is not the answer. A few token blacks in positions of responsibility is not yet the answer. We need a solution that considers the masses. We need a solution that considers the unborn generations. We need a solution that will allow all of our people to bring forth their genius and justify their existence on this earth. Jesse Jackson's bid for the presidency was not the solution. But it gave hope to millions whose hope had died. It gave time to America to think and rethink her position.

Almighty God used Jesse Jackson to create movement again in the masses of black people. His was a call not to violence and extremism; his was a call not to hate and intolerance; his was a call to the unregistered blacks to register to vote to make a difference. His was a call to use the ballot and not the bullet to bring about meaningful change in this society. His was a call to organize to gain power politically to change the conditions under which we live. Jesse Jackson was rebuffed and mistreated at the convention. And all that he and others concerned for the suffering masses of the locked-out advanced in the form of planks of the Democratic platform was rejected. Reverend Jackson is still seeking a signal from Mr. Mondale that will increase his enthusiasm and the enthusiasm of the masses of black Democratic voters to work hard for Mr. Mondale's election in the fall.

In my judgment, Mr. Mondale has already sent his signal. We must not be oblivious to the signal that Mr. Mondale has already given, and that is, that he does not intend to honor his debt to black people who helped him get the nomination and whom he needs to get elected to the presidency of the United States. When Mr. Mondale's campaign was floundering and he was about to be written off as the nominee of his party, on Super Tuesday, it was blacks in Georgia, Alabama and Florida that gave him the margin of victory to keep his campaign afloat. The unwritten law in politics is that those who give should get. How much more should we give before get what we are justly due? Mr. Mondale slapped Jesse Jackson and all black people in the face, because he feels that black people, beleaguered and withered under Mr. Reagan and Reaganomics, have no other alternative but to go along with Mondale and the Democratic Party.

However, there is another way: God's way. And only through his way can all of us get out of this dilemma. The honorable Elijah Muhammad, during the election of 1968, because of the critical internal condition of America and the external condition of the world, asked black people to use their vote wisely. My advice to black people is the same today: black people, if we vote at all, must use our vote carefully, cautiously and judiciously.

This election is so important, because it is not just deciding who shall sit as President. For the next four years, whoever is President must have the vision, the wisdom and the will to save this country from the wrath of God and the nations. And in my humble judgment, after listening to the words of both Mr. Reagan and Mr. Mondale, at this time, neither of them have displayed the vision necessary to take America safely through these next four years. America does need a change of direction and that change of direction cannot come unless there is a change of vision. It is written in the scripture, "Where there is no vision, the people perish." We are here today with that vision from almighty God Allah, through the honorable Elijah Muhammad, which includes the welfare of America.

The government of America and the heads of both political parties, who say they want black people included in the mainstream of this society, must realize that if blacks are going to be successful within this society, blacks must organize to achieve unity and power. Jesse Jackson's candidacy was a bid for unity, to achieve power. This frightened those who have power and refuse to share power with black people. So immediately schemes were hatched by those in power to break the budding unity that Jesse Jackson and those whom he represents might not achieve power. Jesse Jackson and Louis Farrakhan stood as the symbol of this budding unity to black people.

In New York City in April, according to a report that appeared first in the *Boston Globe* and a few days later in the *Washington Post,* powerful Jewish leaders met. And out of that meeting, according to the *Globe,* a threat was sent to the leaders of the Democratic Party and to Mr. Mondale and Mr. Hart, that if they caved in to Jackson's demands—particularly where Middle Eastern policy was concerned—the Jews would leave the Democratic Party en masse, take their money, join Reagan and the Republicans. This kind of threat was kept over the head of Mr. Mondale and the officials of the Democratic Party. So when I made the statement that Israel had not had any peace in forty years, and that she will never have any peace because there can be no peace structured on injustice, lying, thievery and deceit, using God's name to shield your dirty religion or dirty practices under his holy and righteous name—this was termed to be an attempt on my part to discredit Judaism as a religion.

Then tremendous pressure was exerted on Mr. Mondale, the leaders of the Democratic Party, on the President and the Vice President, on Jesse Jackson's staff, then on Jesse Jackson, members of the Congress, pressure was put on certain black religious, civic and political leaders to repudiate Louis Farrakhan. There seems to be an unwritten law that Israel and Jews cannot be criticized, particularly by blacks. For anyone who does so must bear the burden of being called an anti-Semite. But how could Reverend Jackson be considered a serious candidate for the presidency of the United States and not touch on the critical issue of America's Middle East policy? Particularly since the scholars and scientists agree that the Middle East is the flashpoint or the trigger of the war of Armageddon will result in a clash between America and Russia.

What kind of power does this small minority of Jewish people hold over the government that the Senate would call an emergency session to denounce me? Ted Kennedy and the leaders of the Democratic Party felt compelled to denounce me without ever hearing or reading my words completely, despite the fact that they have access to all my words. Larry

Speakes, the White House press secretary, was defensive in saying that the President was not timid or afraid to come out forthrightly against Farrakhan. This abnormal show of the power of Jewish leadership demonstrates that the American people are losing, or have lost a grip, over their political process and over their elected officials. For whenever a powerful lobby can force an emergency session of the Senate just to repudiate me, something is gravely wrong. [applause]

The American people must rise up and gain better control of their political process and their political leaders again. Black political, civic and religious leaders who repudiated me on the basis of a lie, without ever contacting me or getting my words to find out what I actually said, run the risk of being looked upon as pawns of Jewish leaders and Jewish interests and therefore cannot lead in the best interests of black people.

The religious scholars and scientists who advise presidents and politicians have gravely misunderstood the scriptures where Israel is concerned. And have misapplied these scriptures to justify the taking of land from the Palestinians by force. And they use these same scriptures to justify America's continued support of Israel with the taxpayer's money. But is this really justified? We can prove that the Israel that is the creation of the Zionists, with the help of England and America, is *not* the fulfillment of divine prophecy. It has no divine power behind it. And before too many days pass, it will prove to be the destruction of the power of the Western world. The Israel mentioned in the Bible and the Holy Koran as the People of the Book, or the Chosen of God, was to serve as a type to give us a picture of the people that God would choose for his glory in the last days of the rule of the wicked. The prototype Israel is pictured as a people of bondage—despised, rejected and lost. Yet God, out of the abundance of his mercy, would choose a people like this to make a nation out of them for his glory. But that people that God would choose would be hidden under the name "Israel." And this people is the black people of America—the real Israel and the true choice of God. Truth hurts, but it hurts only the guilty. [applause]

It hurts only the guilty who have practiced deceit. If America showed concern for the *real* Israel—black people—and the solution to our problems, America could save herself. For the fate that religious and political leaders believe will befall America if she abandons the false Israel is now befalling America because she has abandoned justice for the real Israel—

the black people of America, the chosen of almighty God. America now faces divine judgment.

According to the Prophet's predictions, the people of God would be in bondage and affliction in a strange land for over four hundred years. This is a prophetic, symbolic picture found in the Bible and the Holy Koran of our sojourn and suffering in America. The word of Allah to the honorable Elijah Muhammad and the Congressional Library here in Washington bears witness that the first slaves were brought to these shores on a ship named *Jesus* captained by an English slave trader, Sir John Hawkins, in the year 1555. It is written in the scriptures that the exodus took place in the four hundred and thirtieth year of Israel's sojourn. 1985 marks the four hundred and thirtieth year of our sojourn and affliction in America.

And now, black people are making our exodus, spiritually and mentally, out from the power of the slave-master's children over our lives. It is time that black people go free. We cannot ever again tolerate a master-slave relationship. If this is not recognized, there will be constant and increasing clashing between the two people. America is saying to black people, the Republicans and the Democratic parties are saying to black people, that they don't care for us. You don't want us. You do not care that we who helped to build your country, who fought, bled and died to keep it free for you, get no justice within your social, economic and political system.

So if you will not give us justice, then you must let us go, that we may do something for ourselves in a state or territory of our own. You should help us to maintain ourselves in a separate territory, either here or elsewhere, for the next twenty or twenty-five years and as the honorable Elijah Muhammad said, if we are unable to be self-independent after twenty or twenty-five years of your help, then you can bring your armies and shoot us down. You can take this advice if you will and God will have mercy upon you and save your country; but you say, "How can we do this? This is impossible." However, you found a way to aid in taking land away from the Palestinians and giving it to the Jewish people, contrary to God's will. You have found a way to subsidize Israel for nearly forty years and forty years later, Israel is not able to go for herself; nor does she even seem willing to become a self-independent nation. But she is becoming an increasing burden on the taxpayers of America. [applause]

If the American economy continues to falter, how can America continue to subsidize Israel at this rate? If Israel is trying as hard as she can to develop herself to the point where she is economically independent and is yet unable, then this should cause you to see that God is against her. But here we are, the *real* Israel of your Bible, the *real* chosen people of the almighty God, suffering in your midst for four hundred years. We have no land that we can call our own. The acreage that we have owned is quickly being taken away from us by fraudulent schemes and tax schemes and neglect, due to our own ignorance of the value of the land. At the rate that we are losing land, by the year 2000, we will be completely landless.

You refuse to give us justice. You refuse to create jobs to ease the burden of unemployment. Black people live in fear of tomorrow because we have no security today. It seems to me that America is in the valley of decision. Allah God, is now lashing America with the same ten plagues that Egypt was lashed with. The neighboring nations are turning against America because of her wicked policies in Central and South America, even as was done against Babylon.

The corruption in the legion of Rome's armies are now seen in the armed forces of America and the unwillingness of the real American citizens to fight for this country is evident, for it is the foreigners coming to these shores, who see the benefits of this nation and who are the most willing to defend the values of America. Why should we, who only represent twelve percent of the population, bear the burden of thirty-five percent of the casualties in Vietnam? Why should we today be thirty-five percent of the armed forces of America? And America refuses to create jobs for our jobless that will give us stability and security in this society. And now black men and women are looking to the armed forces as our employer. Is this justice? We who are underrepresented and have no part in the making of foreign policy must fight and die, not to make the world safe for democracy, but to make the world safer for the multi-national corporations, the greedy, the selfish, and the rich. And to think that the president and the Senate has said there is no room in this society for hate and no place for the haters. We the victims of America's hatred and bigotry are now being charged with her crime.

What I represent is truth. What America is saying to Farrakhan is what is written that the Jews said to Jesus when they rejected him. And Jesus responded, "You cannot understand my words because my words have no place in you." The Jews in that day wanted no truth to be told if it conflicted with their selfish desires. They did not care for the truth. They only wanted to hear that which made them comfortable in their web of lies and deceit.

What crime have I committed that warrants the censure and repudiation of the entire government, religious and civic leadership? I don't smoke, I don't drink. [shouts] I don't use drugs, I've never been arrested. I don't chase women nor do I chase men. [laughter and applause] I have been a doer of good. I have been a doer of good among black people for three decades, doing a duty of civilizing and reforming black people, a duty which America failed to do. For which of the good works that I do in the name of my father, the honorable Elijah Muhammad, do you stone or repudiate me?

Poor Jesse, poor Jesse. You hated our love and friendship and our mutual desire to defend and protect one another. You prevailed upon my brother to repudiate me on the basis of your lies. You frightened his staff to urge this upon him. You threatened that you would not let him speak at the convention unless he repudiated me. You forced him to apologize again to a people to whom he owes no apology, so that he might have a place [applause] of honor and respect among Democratic leadership. But did you give him such a place? No. You mistreated him and now you have him and those whom he represents out in the cold, waiting for a signal that they may enthusiastically work for the Democratic ticket. You were not satisfied with his repudiation of my words. You want him to repudiate me personally. You don't want him to be seen with me in the public, or even shaking the hand of his own brother. You desire to destroy our unity and our friendship completely, but why? It is because you fear the unity of the children of the slaves because you know that our unity will give us the power to throw off the yoke of slavery, and you will have to relate to us as men and women. [applause]

But America, how do you treat your friends, which others dislike? You don't repudiate them. Look at the friendship you have with South Africa. [applause] We and many of the nations do not like this. You admit that the government of South Africa deprives millions of black people of life, liberty and the pursuit of happiness. But you have not repudiated them. Why has not the Senate, which cannot tolerate hatred and bigotry, not repudiated South Africa, but instead has rewarded South Africa with nearly fifteen billion dollars in trade, huh? And America's involvement with her is steadily on the increase. The President hypocritically says there's no room in this society for haters. Yet there's room in his heart to embrace South Africa.

Two years ago, Mr. Menachem Begin and his government invaded Lebanon, reportedly against the wishes of Mr. Reagan and his administration. American weapons, which were given to Israel to be used defensively, were used aggressively to maim and kill thousands of innocent people, leaving many more thousands homeless. Did not this violation of the sovereignty of another nation merit the repudiation of the Begin government by the American government? Yet there was no repudiation, even though some argued that America must do something to bring the Begin government in line. Neither was there a threat to lessen America's commitment to Israel, unless these acts were stopped. America, instead of repudiating Israel, rewarded her by increasing her grants and aid—from two point four-six billion to nearly three billion dollars. Mr. Begin could sit in Israel and defy the American president, while the powerful Jewish lobby went to work on the Congress to increase America's aid to Israel. America's increasing support of Israel is paying for more Israeli settlements on the West Bank, which America says she's against. Again this American support finances Israel's continued unlawful occupation of Lebanon.

What will it take for America to repudiate this expansionist ally/friend? And who is brave, bold, and courageous enough in the Senate or in the Congress or in the government to call for such repudiation? I respectfully say that the Jewish leadership is spiritually blind. And if the American government and the Reagan administration allow such a lobby, which is spiritually blind, to have the great power to influence the guidance of this nation, then they will guide this nation to its total destruction.

In my conclusion I say that Reverend Jackson and other black leaders should pay no attention whatsoever to the attempts of the wicked to divide us. Reverend Jackson, come on with your brother! And let us seek justice for our people *in* America! And if America refuses to give us justice, since you have experience in negotiating the release of captured persons, then let us negotiate the release of this captured nation, that we may go free to build a nation for ourselves.

Abraham Lincoln was faced with the problem of saving this union, which was his paramount concern. And at the root of that problem was the question of slavery and what to do with us. President Reagan, or whoever will be elected president, will have on his shoulders the awesome responsibility of saving this nation and again, at the root of the problem, is what to do with thirty million black people. Reagan said within the covers of that single book, the Bible, are all the answers to the problems that face us today—if we'd only look there. If the president truly believes this, then we urge the president to look at this that has been offered by almighty God, through the honorable Elijah Muhammad, for it fulfills all that has been written as guidance in the book as the solution to this grave problem. America should act to correct the wrong while she has time and do so before judgment is taken out of her hands and her ability to rectify the problem is taken away from her by the supreme judge. It is written, "All who bless Israel, God will bless. All who curse Israel, God will curse." We say to you, all who work to bless this black people in America, God will bless you; and all who continue to curse the black man are already cursed by God.

Thank you for listening. [applause]

18.

JESSE JACKSON
(1941–)

"Keep Hope Alive"

Democratic National Convention, Atlanta, Georgia—July 19, 1988

Jesse Jackson wasn't born preaching, but it wasn't long before he began speaking the Word. Jackson's father, Noah Robinson, told a journalist: "Even when he was learning to talk . . . he would say he's going to be a preacher. He would say, 'I'm going to lead people through the rivers of water.' "[1] Jackson is one of the most celebrated American orators of the past century, a full-throated Baptist preacher with an uncanny gift for off-the-cuff sermonizing.

The two-time presidential candidate has also gotten closer to the White House than any black politician in history. Jackson's 1984 and 1988 campaigns made him, for a time, a powerful figure in Democratic politics. Since then, Jackson's fortunes have fluctuated. Personal scandal and the country's political shift rightward have affected his clout. But Jackson still makes himself heard. Conservative columnist William F. Buckley Jr. wrote of Jackson in 2003: "Say what you will about the wilting Jesse, he still has the power to bring listless partisans to their feet."[2]

Jackson was born in 1941 in Greenville, South Carolina, a place as segregated as most Southern towns. His mother was a high school student, his father the thirty-three-year-old married man next door. Jackson was a diligent high school student and an exceptional athlete. When he graduated in 1959, Jackson turned down a chance to play baseball for the Chicago White Sox to go to college, where he became active in the civil rights movement. He graduated from North Carolina Agricultural and Technical College in 1964 and went on to study at Chicago Theological Seminary at the University of Chicago, but left before finishing his degree to devote himself to the civil rights movement. In 1966, he joined the Southern Christian Leadership Conference (SCLC) and worked with Martin Luther King Jr.[3]

Jackson became known as an ambitious young organizer and a talented public speaker. He could hold his own among heavyweight orators, like Reverend King, Benjamin Hooks, and Ralph Abernathy.

Three years after King's assassination in 1968, Jackson left the SCLC and formed Operation PUSH (People United to Save Humanity). Over the years, Jackson won praise for his efforts to promote the social and political welfare of African Americans. He worked and traveled relentlessly to promote his causes. Critics sometimes charged that Jackson's management was undisciplined and that his inspiring words were not met with equivalent deeds. To this Jackson retorted, "I'm a tree shaker, not a jam maker."[4]

From 1991 to 1996, Jackson served as the non-voting "shadow senator" for the District of Columbia. He continues his activist work in the U.S. and internationally. He also hosts TV and radio programs, writes columns and books, and remains an ever-quotable figure in public affairs.

Tonight, we pause and give praise and honor to God for being good enough to allow us to be at this place at this time. When I look out at this convention, I see the face of America: red, yellow, brown, black and white. We are all precious in God's sight—the real rainbow coalition. [applause]

All of us, all of us who are here think that we are seated. But we're really standing on someone's shoulders. Ladies and gentlemen, Mrs. Rosa Parks—[applause] the mother of the civil rights movement.

[Mrs. Rosa Parks is brought to the podium.]

I want to express my deep love and appreciation for the support my family has given me over these past months. They have endured pain, anxiety, threat, and fear. But they have been strengthened and made secure by our faith in God, in America, and in you. Your love has protected us and made us strong. To my wife, Jackie, the foundation of our family; to our five children whom you met tonight; to my mother, Mrs. Helen Jackson, who is present tonight; and to our grandmother, Mrs. Matilda Burns; to my brother Chuck and his family; to my mother-in-law, Mrs. Gertrude Brown, who just last month at age sixty-one graduated from Hampton Institute—a marvelous achievement. [applause]

I offer my appreciation to Mayor Andrew Young, who has provided such gracious hospitality to all of us this week. [applause]

And a special salute to President Jimmy Carter. [applause] President Carter restored honor to the White House after Watergate. He gave many of us a special opportunity to grow. For his kind words, for his unwavering commitment to peace in the world, and for the voters that came from his family, every member of his family, led by Billy and Amy, I offer my special thanks to the Carter family. [applause]

My right and my privilege to stand here before you has been won. Won in my lifetime, by the blood and the sweat of the innocent.

Twenty-four years ago, the late Fannie Lou Hamer and Aaron Henry—who sits here tonight, from Mississippi—were locked out on the streets in Atlantic City—the head of the Mississippi Freedom Democratic Party. But tonight, a black and white delegation from Mississippi is headed by Ed Cole, a black man from Mississippi—twenty-four years later.

Many were lost in the struggle for the right to vote. Jimmy Lee Jackson, a young student, gave his life; Viola Liuzzo, a White mother from Detroit, called "nigger lover," and brains blown out at point-blank range; [Michael] Schwerner, [Andrew] Goodman and [James] Chaney—two Jews and a black—found in a common grave, bodies riddled with bullets in Mississippi; the four darling little girls in a church in Birmingham, Alabama. They died that we might have a right to live.

Dr. Martin Luther King Jr. lies only a few miles from us tonight. Tonight he must feel good as he looks down upon us. We sit here together, a rainbow, a coalition—the sons and daughters of slave masters and the sons and daughters of slaves, sitting together around a common table, to decide the direction of our party and our country. His heart would be full tonight.

As a testament to the struggles of those who have gone before; as a legacy for those who will come after; as a tribute to the endurance, the patience, the courage of our forefathers and mothers; as an assurance that their prayers are being answered, that their work has not been in vain, and, that hope is eternal—tomorrow night my name will go into nomination for the presidency of the United States of America. [applause]

We meet tonight at the crossroads, a point of decision. Shall we expand, be inclusive, find unity and power; or suffer division and impotence?

We've come to Atlanta, the cradle of the Old South, the crucible of the New South. Tonight, there is a sense of celebration because we are moved, fundamentally moved, from racial battlegrounds by law, to economic common ground. Tomorrow we'll challenge to move to higher ground.

Common ground. Think of Jerusalem, the intersection where many trails met. A small village that became the birthplace for three great religions—Judaism, Christianity, and Islam. Why was this village so blessed? Because it provided a crossroads where different people met—different cultures, different civilizations could meet and find common ground. When people come together, flowers always flourish—the air is rich with the aroma of a new spring.

Take New York, the dynamic metropolis. What makes New York so special? It's the invitation at the Statue of Liberty: "Give me your tired, your poor, your huddled masses who yearn to breathe free." Not restricted to English only. [applause] Many people, many cultures, many languages with one thing in common: they yearn to breathe free. Common ground.

Tonight in Atlanta, for the first time in this century, we convene in the South. A state where governors once stood in schoolhouse doors; where Julian Bond was denied a seat in the state legislature because of his conscientious objection to the Vietnam war; a city that, through its five black universities, has graduated more black students than any city in the world. Atlanta, now a modern intersection of the New South.

Common ground. That's the challenge of our party tonight—left wing, right wing. Progress will not come through boundless liberalism, nor static conservatism, but at the critical mass of mutual survival. It takes two wings to fly. Whether you're a hawk or a dove, you're just a bird living in the same environment, in the same world.

The Bible teaches that when lions and lambs lie down together, none will be afraid and there will be peace in the valley. It sounds impossible.

Lions eat lambs. Lambs sensibly flee from lions. Yet even lions and lambs find common ground. Why? Because neither lions nor lambs want the forest to catch on fire. Neither lions nor lambs want acid rain to fall. Neither lions nor lambs can survive nuclear war. If lions and lambs can find common ground, surely we can as well—as civilized people. [applause]

The only time that we win is when we come together. In 1960, John Kennedy, the late John Kennedy, beat Richard Nixon by only a hundred and twelve thousand votes—less than one vote per precinct. He won by the margin of our hope. He brought us together. He reached out. He had the courage to defy his advisors and inquire about Dr. King's jailing in Albany, Georgia. We won by the margin of our hope, inspired by courageous leadership. In 1964, Lyndon Johnson brought both wings together—the thesis, the antithesis, and the creative synthesis—and together we won. In 1976, Jimmy Carter unified us again, and we won. When we do not come together, we never win. In 1968, the vision and despair in July led to our defeat in November. In 1980, rancor in the spring and the summer led to Reagan in the fall. When we divide, we cannot win. We must find common ground as the basis for survival and development and change and growth. [applause]

Today when we debated, differed, deliberated, agreed to agree, agreed to disagree, when we had the good judgment to argue a case and then not self-destruct, George Bush was just a little further away from the White House and a little closer to private life. [applause]

Tonight, I salute Governor Michael Dukakis. He has run, [applause] he has run a well-managed and a dignified campaign. No matter how tired or how tried, he always resisted the temptation to stoop to demagoguery.

I've watched a good mind fast at work, with steel nerves, guiding his campaign out of the crowded field without appeal to the worst in us. I've watched his perspective grow as his environment has expanded. I've seen his toughness and tenacity close up. I know his commitment to public service. Mike Dukakis's parents were a doctor and a teacher; my parents a maid, a beautician, and a janitor. There's a great gap between Brookline, Massachusetts, and Haney Street, the Fieldcrest Village housing projects in Greenville, South Carolina.

He studied law. I studied theology. There are differences of religion, region, and race, differences in experiences and perspectives. But the genius of America is that out of the many we become one.

Providence has enabled our paths to intersect. His foreparents came to America on immigrant ships. My foreparents came to America on slave ships. But whatever the original ships, we're in the same boat tonight. [applause]

Our ships could pass in the night—if we have a false sense of independence—or they could collide and crash. We would lose our passengers. Or we can seek a higher reality and a greater good. Apart, we can drift on the broken pieces of Reaganomics, satisfy our baser instincts, and exploit the fears of our people. At our highest, we can call upon noble instincts and navigate this vessel to safety. The greater good is the common good.

As Jesus said, "Not my will, but thine be done." It was his way of saying there's a higher good beyond personal comfort or position. The good of our nation is at stake. Its commitment to working men and women, to the poor and the vulnerable, to the many in the world.

With so many guided missiles, and so much misguided leadership, the stakes are exceedingly high. Our choice? Full participation in a democratic government, or more abandonment and neglect. And so this night, we choose not a false sense of independence, not our capacity to survive and endure. Tonight we choose interdependency and our capacity to act and unite for the greater good.

Common good is finding commitment to new priorities, to expansion and inclusion. A commitment to expanded participation in the Democratic Party at every level. A commitment to a shared national campaign strategy and involvement at every level. A commitment to new priorities that ensure that hope will be kept alive. A common-ground commitment to a legislative agenda for empowerment. For the John Conyers bill—universal, on-site, same-day registration everywhere. [applause] A commitment to D.C. statehood and empowerment—D.C. deserves statehood. [applause] A commitment to economic set-asides, a commitment to the Dellums bill for comprehensive sanctions against South Africa. [applause] A shared commitment to a common direction.

Common ground. Easier said than done. Where do you find common ground? At the point of challenge. This campaign has shown that politics need not be marketed by politicians, packaged by pollsters and pundits. Politics can be a moral arena where people come together to find common ground.

We find common ground at the plant gate that closes on workers without notice. We find common ground at the farm auction, where a good farmer loses his or her land to bad loans or diminishing markets. Common ground at the schoolyard, where teachers cannot get adequate pay, and students cannot get a scholarship and can't make a loan. [applause] Common ground at the hospital admitting room, where somebody tonight is dying because they cannot afford to go upstairs to a bed that's empty waiting for someone with insurance to get sick. We are a better nation than that. We must do better. [applause]

Common ground. What is leadership if not present help in a time of crisis? And so I met you at the point of challenge in Jay, Maine, where paper workers were striking for fair wages; in Greenville, Iowa, where family farmers struggle for a fair price; in Cleveland, Ohio, where working women seek comparable worth; in McFarland, California, where the children of Hispanic farmworkers may be dying from poisoned land, dying in clusters with cancer; in an AIDS hospice in Houston, Texas, where the sick support one another, too often rejected by their own parents and friends.

Common ground. America is not a blanket woven from one thread, one color, one cloth. When I was a child growing up in Greenville, South Carolina, and Grandmama could not afford a blanket, she didn't complain and we did not freeze. Instead she took pieces of old cloth—patches, wool, silk, gabardine, crockersack—only patches, barely good enough to wipe off your shoes with. But they didn't stay that way very long. With sturdy hands and a strong cord, she sewed them together into a quilt, a thing of beauty and power and culture. Now, Democrats, we must build such a quilt.

Farmers, you seek fair prices and you are right—but you cannot stand alone. Your patch is not big enough. Workers, you fight for fair wages, you are right—but your patch, labor, is not big enough. Women, you seek comparable worth and pay equity, you are right—but your patch is not big enough. [applause] Women, mothers, who seek Head Start and day care and prenatal care on the front side of life, rather than jail care and welfare on the back side of life, you are right—but your patch is not big enough. [applause] Students, you seek scholarships, you are right—but your patch is not big enough. Blacks and Hispanics, when we fight for civil rights, we are right—but our patch is not big enough. [applause] Gays and lesbians, when you fight against discrimination and [for] a cure for AIDS, you are right—but your patch is not big enough. [applause] Conservatives and progressives, when you fight for what you believe—right wing, left wing, hawk, dove—you are right, from your point of view, but your point of view is not enough.

But don't despair. Be as wise as my grandmama. Pull the patches and the pieces together, bound by a common thread. When we form a great quilt of unity and common ground, we'll have the power to bring about health care and housing and jobs and education and hope to our nation. [applause]

We, the people, can win. [applause and chanting]

We stand at the end of a long, dark night of reaction. We stand tonight united in the commitment to a new direction. For almost eight years, we've been led by those who view social good coming from private interest. Who view public life as a means to increase private wealth. They have been prepared to sacrifice the common good of the many to satisfy the private interests and the wealth of a few.

We believe in a government that's a tool of our democracy in service to the public, not an instrument of the aristocracy in search of private wealth. We believe in government with the consent of the governed. Of, for and by the people. We must now emerge into a new day with a new direction.

Reaganomics—based on the belief that the rich had too little money and the poor had too much. That's classic Reaganomics. They believe that the poor had too much money and the rich had too little money. So they engaged in reverse Robin Hood—took from the poor, gave to the rich, paid for by the middle class. We cannot stand four more years of Reaganomics in any version, in any disguise. [applause]

How do I document that case? Seven years later, the richest one percent of our society pays twenty percent less in taxes. The poorest ten percent pay twenty percent more. Reaganomics.

Reagan gave the rich and the powerful a multibillion-dollar party. Now the party is over. He expects the people to pay for the damage. I take this principled position, convention: let us not raise taxes on the poor and the middle class, but those who had the party, the rich and the powerful, must pay for the party. [applause]

I just want to take common sense to high places. We're spending one hundred and fifty billion dollars a year defending Europe and Japan forty-three years after the war is over. We have more troops in Europe tonight than we had seven years ago. Yet the threat of war is ever more remote.

Germany and Japan are now creditor nations. That means they've got a surplus. We are a debtor nation—means we are in debt. Let them share more of the burden of their own defense. Use some of that money to build decent housing. [applause] Use some of that money to educate our children. Use some of that money for long-term health care. Use some of that money to wipe out these slums and put America back to work! [applause]

I just want to take common sense to high places. If we can bail out Europe and Japan; if we can bail out Continental Bank and Chrysler—and Mr. Iacocca make eight thousand dollars an hour—we can bail out the family farmer. [applause]

I just want to make common sense. It does not make sense to close down six hundred and fifty thousand family farms in this country while importing food from abroad subsidized by the U.S. government. Let's make sense. [applause]

It does not make sense to be escorting all our tankers up and down the Persian Gulf paying two-fifty for every one dollar worth of oil we bring out, while oil wells are capped in Texas, Oklahoma, and Louisiana. I just want to make sense. [applause]

Leadership must meet the moral challenge of its day. What's the moral challenge of our day? We have public accommodations. We have the right to vote. We have open housing. What's the fundamental challenge of our day? It is to end economic violence. Plant closings without notice—economic violence. Even the greedy do not profit long from greed—economic violence. Most poor people are not lazy. They are not black. They are not brown. They are mostly white and female and young. But whether white, black or brown, a hungry baby's belly turned inside out is the same color—color it pain; color it hurt; color it agony. [applause]

Most poor people are not on welfare. Some of them are illiterate and can't read the want-ad sections. And when they can, they can't find a job that matches the address. They work hard every day. I know. I live amongst them. I'm one of them. I know they work. I'm a witness. They catch the early bus. They work every day. They raise other people's children. They work every day. They clean the streets. They work every day. They drive dangerous cabs. They work every day. They change the beds you slept in in these hotels last night and can't get a union contract. They work every day. [applause]

No, no, they are not lazy! Someone must defend them because it's right, and they cannot speak for themselves. They work in hospitals. I know they do. They wipe the bodies of those who are sick with fever and pain. They empty their bedpans. They clean out their commodes. No job is beneath them, and yet when they get sick they cannot lie in the bed they made up every day. America, that is not right. [applause] We are a better nation than that. We are a better nation than that. [applause]

We need a real war on drugs. You can't "just say no." It's deeper than that. You can't just get a palm reader or an astrologer. It's more profound than that. [applause] We are spending a hundred and fifty billion dollars on drugs a year. We've gone from ignoring it to focusing on the children. Children cannot buy a hundred and fifty billion dollars worth of drugs a year; a few high-profile athletes—athletes are not laundering a hundred and fifty billion dollars a year—bankers are.

I met the children in Watts, who, unfortunately, in their despair—their grapes of hope have become raisins of despair—and they're turning on each other and they're self-destructing. But I stayed with them all night long. I wanted to hear their case.

They said, "Jesse Jackson, as you challenge us to say no to drugs, you're right; and to not sell them, you're right; and not use these guns, you're right." By the way, the promise of CETA [Comprehensive Employment and Training Act]—they *dis*placed CETA, they did not *re*place CETA.

"We have neither jobs nor houses nor services nor training—no way out. Some of us take drugs as anesthesia for our pain. Some take drugs as a way of pleasure, good short-term pleasure and long-term pain. Some sell drugs to make money. It's wrong, we know, but you need to know that we know. We can go and buy the drugs by the boxes at the port. If we can buy the drugs at the port, don't you believe the federal government can stop it if they want to?" [applause]

They say, "We don't have Saturday night specials anymore." They say, "We buy AK-47s and Uzis, the latest make of weapons. We buy them across the counter along these boulevards." You cannot fight a war on drugs unless and until you're going to challenge the bankers and the gun sellers and those who grow them. Don't just focus on the children. Let's stop drugs at the level of supply and demand. We must end the scourge on the American culture. [applause]

Leadership. What difference will we make? Leadership cannot just go along to get along. We must do more than change presidents. We must change direction.

Leadership must face the moral challenge of our day. The nuclear war build-up is irrational. Strong leadership cannot desire to look tough and let that stand in the way of the pursuit of peace. Leadership must reverse the arms race. At least we should pledge no first use. Why? Because first use begets first retaliation, and that's mutual annihilation. That's not a rational way out. No use at all. Let's think it out and not fight it out, because it's an unwinnable fight. Why hold a card that you can never drop? Let's give peace a chance.

Leadership. We now have this marvelous opportunity to have a break-through with the Soviets. Last year two hundred thousand Americans visited the Soviet Union. There's a chance for joint ventures into space—not Star Wars and the war arms escalation but a space defense initiative. Let's build in the space together and demilitarize the heavens. There's a way out. [applause]

America, let us expand. When Mr. Reagan and Mr. Gorbachev met there was a big meeting. They represented together one-eighth of the human race. Seven-eights of the human race was locked out of that room. Most people in the world tonight—half are Asian, one-half of them are Chinese. There are twenty-two nations in the Middle East. There's Europe. Forty million Latin Americans next door to us; the Caribbean; Africa—a half-billion people.

Most people in the world today are yellow or brown or black, non-Christian, poor, female, young and don't speak English in the real world.

This generation must offer leadership to the real world. We're losing ground in Latin America, Middle East, South Africa because we're not focusing on the real world. That's the real world. We must use basic principles—support international law. We stand the most to gain from it. Support human rights—we believe in that. Support self-determination—we're built on that. Support economic development—you know it's right. Be consistent and gain our moral authority in the world. I challenge you tonight, my friends, let's be bigger and better as a nation and as a party. [applause]

We have basic challenges—freedom in South Africa. We've already agreed as Democrats to declare South Africa to be a terrorist state. But don't just stop there. Get South Africa out of Angola. Free Namibia. Support the frontline states. We must have a new, humane, human rights–consistent policy in Africa.

I'm often asked, "Jesse, why do you take on these tough issues? They're not very political. We can't win that way." If an issue is morally right, it will eventually be political. It may be political and never be right. Fannie Lou Hamer didn't have the most votes in Atlantic City, but her principles have outlasted every delegate who voted to lock her out. Rosa Parks did not have the most votes, but she was morally right. Dr. King didn't have the most votes about the Vietnam War, but he was morally right. If we are principled first, our politics will fall in place.

"Jesse, why do you take these big, bold initiatives?" A poem by an unknown author went something like this: "We mastered the air, we conquered the sea, annihilated distance and prolonged life, but we're not wise enough to live on this earth without war and without hate." As for Jesse Jackson: "I'm tired of sailing my little boat, far inside the harbor bar. I want to go out where the big ships float. Out on the deep where the great ones are. And should my frail craft prove too slight for waves that sweep those billows o'er, I'd rather go down in the stirring fight than drown to death at the sheltered shore." We've got to go out, my friends, where the big boats are! [applause]

And then for our children. Young America, hold your head high now. We can win. We must not lose you to drugs and violence, premature pregnancy, suicide, cynicism, pessimism and despair. We can win. Wherever you are tonight, I challenge you to hope and to dream. Don't submerge your dreams. Exercise, above all else, even on drugs, dream of the day you are drug free. Even in the gutter, dream of the day that you will be up on your feet again.

You must never stop dreaming. Face reality, yes, but don't stop with the way things are. Dream of things as they ought to be. Dream. Face pain, but love, hope, faith and dreams will help you rise above the pain. Use hope and imagination as weapons of survival and progress, but you keep on dreaming, young America. Dream of peace. Peace is rational and reasonable. War is irrationable in this age and unwinnable. Dream of teachers who teach for life and not for a living. Dream of doctors who are concerned more about public health than private wealth. Dream of lawyers more concerned about justice than a judgeship. Dream of preachers who are concerned more about prophecy than profiteering. Dream on the high road with sound values.

And then America, as we go forth to September, October, November and then beyond, America must never surrender to a high moral challenge. Do not surrender to drugs. The best drug policy is a "no first use." Don't surrender with needles and cynicism. [applause] Let's have "no first use" on the one hand or clinics on the other.

Never surrender, young America. Go forward. America must never surrender to malnutrition. We can feed the hungry and clothe the naked. We must never surrender. We must go forward. We must never surrender to illiteracy. Invest in our children. Never surrender; and go forward. We must never surrender to inequality. Women cannot compromise ERA or comparable worth. Women are making sixty cents on the dollar to what a man makes. [applause] Women cannot buy meat cheaper. Women cannot buy bread cheaper. Women cannot buy milk cheaper. Women deserve to get paid for the work that you do. It's right! And it's fair. [applause]

Don't surrender, my friends. Those who have AIDS tonight, you deserve our compassion. Even with AIDS you must not surrender. In your wheelchairs. I see you sitting here tonight in those wheelchairs. I've stayed with you. I've reached out to you across our nation and don't you give up. I know it's tough sometimes. People look down on you. It took you a little more effort to get here tonight. And no one should look down on you, but sometimes mean people do. The only justification we have for looking down on someone is that we're going to stop and pick them up.

But even in your wheelchairs, don't you give up. We cannot forget fifty years ago when our backs were against the wall—Roosevelt was in a wheelchair. I would rather have Roosevelt in a wheelchair than Reagan and Bush on a horse. [applause] Don't you surrender and don't you give up. Don't surrender and don't give up! [applause]

Why can I challenge you this way? "Jesse Jackson, you don't understand my situation. You be on television. [laughter] You don't understand. I see you with the big people. You don't understand my situation."

I understand. You see me on TV, but you don't know the me that makes me, me. They wonder, "Why does Jesse run?" Because they see me running for the White House. They don't see the house I'm running from. [applause]

I have a story. I wasn't always on television. Writers were not always outside my door. When I was born late one afternoon, October 8th, in Greenville, South Carolina, no writers asked my mother her name. Nobody chose to write down our address. My mama was not supposed to make it, and I was not supposed to make it. You see, I was born to a teenage mother who was born to a teenage mother. I understand. I know abandonment, and people being mean to you and saying you're nothing and nobody and can never be anything.

I understand. Jesse Jackson is my third name. I'm adopted. When I had no name, my grandmother gave me her name. My name was Jesse Burns 'til I was twelve. So I wouldn't have a blank space, she gave me a name to hold me over. I understand when nobody knows your name. I understand when you have no name.

I understand. I wasn't born in the hospital. Mama didn't have insurance. I was born in the bed at home. I really do understand. Born in a three-room house, bathroom in the backyard, slop jar by the bed, no hot and cold running water. I understand. Wallpaper used for decoration? No. For a windbreaker. I understand. I'm a working person's person. That's why I understand you whether you're black or white. I understand work. I was not born with a silver spoon in my mouth. I had a shovel programmed for my hand.

My mother, a working woman. So many of the days she went to work early, with runs in her stockings. She knew better, but she wore runs in her stockings so that my brother and I could have matching socks and not be laughed at at school. I understand.

At three o'clock on Thanksgiving Day, we couldn't eat turkey because Mama was preparing somebody else's turkey at three o'clock. We had to play football to entertain ourselves. And then around six o'clock she would get off the Alta Vista bus and we would bring up the leftovers and eat our turkey—leftovers, the carcass, the cranberries—around eight o'clock at night. I really do understand.

Every one of these funny labels they put on you, those of you who are watching this broadcast tonight in the projects, on the corners, I understand. Call you outcast, low down, you can't make it, you're nothing, you're from nobody, subclass, underclass. When you see Jesse Jackson, when my name goes in nomination, your name goes in nomination. [applause]

I was born in the slum, but the slum was not born in me. And it wasn't born in you, and you can make it. [applause]

Wherever you are tonight, you can make it. Hold your head high; stick your chest out. [applause] You can make it. It gets dark sometimes, but the morning comes. Don't you surrender! Suffering breeds character, character breeds faith. In the end faith will not disappoint.

You must not surrender! You may or may not get there but just know that you're qualified! And you hold on and hold out! We must never surrender!! America will get better and better.

Keep hope alive. Keep hope alive! Keep hope alive! [applause] On to-morrow night and beyond, keep hope alive! I love you very much. I love you very much. [applause]

19.

JOHNETTA B. COLE
(1936–)

"Defending Our Name"

Massachusetts Institute of Technology, Cambridge,
Massachusetts—January 13, 1994

Known as America's "Sister President," Johnetta Cole was the first African American woman appointed president of Spelman College, the historically black women's college in Atlanta. Cole took the job in 1987; her inauguration was accompanied by a $20 million gift to the school from comedian Bill Cosby and his wife, Camille. Cole spent a decade at the helm of Spelman, increasing the college's endowment by more than $100 million and significantly boosting its visibility and prestige.

Cole once said in an interview that she hadn't wanted to be a college president, but Spelman offered an irresistible challenge. "What kept standing out," she said, "was that this is a place that dares to say it will educate African American women well. No matter where I turned, I saw a reflection of myself. I saw black women, women in leadership, women professors, women intellectuals—words we rarely put together. And one of my tasks was to make us so at ease with being black women that we could reach out to the rest of the world."[1]

Cole has spent a lifetime reaching out to the rest of the world. She fell in love with cultural anthropology while an undergraduate at Oberlin College and earned a Ph.D. in anthropology from Northwestern University in 1964. She has carried out research in Africa and the Caribbean, as well as in the United States. Before joining Spelman, Cole taught at Washington State University, where she struggled in the 1960s to establish a Black Studies program. In 1970, she joined the faculty of the Afro-American Studies Department of the University of Massachusetts at Amherst, expanding her research in women's studies and navigating the controversial work of overhauling the general curriculum. Cole spent the early 1980s teaching at Hunter College in New York City. In 1998, Cole left Spelman for a teaching job at nearby Emory University, where she was appointed Presidential Distinguished Professor in Anthropology, Women's Studies, and African American studies. The triple appointment united Cole's abiding interests in race, gender, and class—interests formed growing up in the Jim Crow era.

Johnetta Cole was born to a prosperous family in Jacksonville, Florida. Her great-grandfather, the son of slaves, founded the first insurance company in the state, and her mother and father, both college graduates, helped run the highly successful family business.

One of Cole's great early influences was Mary McLeod Bethune. Her great-grandfather was friends with Bethune and was a benefactor of Bethune-Cookman College. Cole's elders encouraged young Johnetta to grow up to be just like Bethune. Cole says, "It would make great folklore to say that I remember receiving words of wisdom and my calling to education while sitting on the lap of Mary McLeod Bethune. But as a young girl, what I remember most is being mesmerized by the wonderful hats she wore."[2] As she matured, Cole's appreciation for Bethune's pioneering work in African American education superseded her awe of the hats.

Cole left Emory in 2001, announcing her retirement from academia. She was pulled back from retirement in 2002, taking the job of president at Bennett College, a small, predominantly black women's college in Greensboro, North Carolina. Asked in a radio interview if she regretted her return to work, Cole said, "I don't at all. You know, there's something so sacred about the kind of work I do. It's a work of helping young people, and sometimes not such young people, to use education as a means to transform their lives."[3]

———

WELL, when I walked out here, I knew that whatever it said on the first page of this speech was not what I was going to say first. [laughter] The first thing that I must say to you, my sisters, was of course said by one of the most extraordinary *SHEroes* in our history. You know that that extraordinary abolitionist and feminist Sojourner Truth once said, "If the world was really turned upside down once by one woman, I don't understand why all of these women can't turn it right side up again." [applause]

I don't know that I have ever sensed, as I do at this moment, the unbelievable power that we have. To tell you the truth, it'll give you chill bumps. But before I try to say all of those things that I feel very, very deeply in my heart and that are running around in my mind and that I think my soul wants released, I have to say it is a thing of beauty what these women have done to organize this conference. [applause] I must tell you that when I first heard of this from Spelman alumna Evelyn Hammond it seemed of course not impossible. Black women *do* when *don't* wants to prevail. But it did seem difficult. But we are here, somewhere, 1,800, 19, 2,000 women strong. Yes we can take a moment from Sterling Brown's poem, and we can put it in our own image and say, "Strong women who just keep on a-comin'." So, my sisters, good evening.

I want you to know that it is an extraordinary joy for me to come within this circle; to be of this great gathering of womenfolk, womenfolk of the darker race, women prepared to stand in defense of our righteous and proper name. What an honor it is to have been asked to be in the company of sister professors Angela Davis and Lani Guinier. [applause] When I was asked to give one of the three keynote addresses, I could just say "hmm." Actually I said, "Mmm, mmm, *mmm!*" [laughter] Because to be asked to give a keynote address when my sister professors Lani and Angela will have, and will tomorrow do so, says to me that if a woman is known by the company she keeps, I'm doing alright. [applause]

I want to tell you, my sisters, I want to tell you that it was a considerable struggle to try to determine what I could possibly say that would be meaningful. I needed to find something meaningful to say at a gathering where a good percentage of the serious sisters of the academy would have come together and many times over would have presented the sharpest of analyses on how we have been shut out of the academy. What is it, then, that we know and feel so deeply about black women in the academy? If we know anything, or as the old folk would say in the part of the country that I just came from, "If I know my name, I know this!" If I know my name, I know this: that the academy is an intensely accurate mirror of the society in which we live. And so if I know my name, I know that in the academy, like in America—and it is our America—the sister is caught between a mighty rock of racism and an unbelievably hard place of sexism. Now there are a multitude of ways of saying quite simply that things are not well by the sisters, that we black women have got a hard row to hoe. Yet, just as in the larger society, it could well be that it is we, African American women, who have the best chance of being change agents, the greatest possibility of transforming the academy and in some long-term and ultimate sense, even transforming America.

Come with me now my sisters and let me stretch out on these points. Each and every one of us ain't the *same* black woman, found in exactly the same place, doing exactly the same thing. And so I must ask, when we speak of black women in the academy, who you talking 'bout? Do you mean the black women—fewer than you can count on one hand—who serve as presidents of so-called majority institutions? Or do you mean the substantial number of black women who can be found in majority *and* minority institutions, cleaning the bathrooms in the dormitories, [applause] cooking food for campus dining halls? Now, I don't know what you mean, but when I say "black women in the academy," I mean *all* these sisters. [applause]

When we gather, my sisters, when we gather here, when we gather here to defend *her* name, is it the name of sister professor so-and-so of such-and-such history department? Or is it the sister's secretary who word-processes all day long for the professors, all of them, in that history department? I have the feeling—I just got here—but I have the feeling that we will insist on defending both of their names. [applause]

So I am asking a very basic yet important question. When we refer to black women in the academy, do we remember to take into account the considerable—no, the *extraordinary* diversity among us, as well as the shared experiences that bind us one to the other? Precisely because we African American women are the victims of racism and sexism that turns all of us into homogenized globs of racial and gender stereotypes, precisely because we are the victims of those two systems of inequality, we dare not ignore the diversity among ourselves. For within the academy, as in American society at large, we will never fully comprehend who we are, nor can we effectively struggle against the totality of our oppressions, until we confront the reality that all black women are not of the same class, are not of the same sexual orientation, are not of the same religious faiths, are not of the same age groups or physical abilities.

I insist on this point. And yes, I made it in the textbook *All-American Women*. But you know, when you get a good point, it's worth making it again and again and again. Somebody told me the other day, as I feared that I was going to talk once again about issues of diversity, the sister said, "Don't worry, it's alright, when it comes to education," she said, "repetition is good for the soul." [laughter]

So, being repetitive, I insist on this point quite simply. Because should I ignore the specificities of who my sister is; or, as we more frequently do, should I simply assume "she's just like me; she's a sister." If I do that, at best I can actually become an instrument of her discomfort. At worst I can become an instrument of her oppression. As the president of Spelman College, I need to be sensitive to the fact that the sister who works in the physical plant division of the college and who, every night during the week, cleans my office, I need to be very aware that we are indeed sisters, but that I have access to opportunities and resources that she does not have access to, and that if I am a president worth her salt, that a part of my agenda must be to make her life and her work better. [applause] We as black women must know our sisterhood and understand that within it we can indeed love each other even when we are not each other.

At Spelman, when faculty or students or staff speak and pray in public, as if everyone at Spelman is a Christian, it is surely a source of discomfort for the Muslim students on our campus, for the women on our campus of other faiths. I don't think that this is done out of any sense of intended maliciousness. And yet, an insensitivity to differences among us can nevertheless hurt the women that we love. At Spelman, the assumption among many at the college that homosexuality and bisexuality are somehow not *normal* sexual orientations has to be unusually painful to lesbian and bisexual women who are, after all, a part of a community of women at a women's college. It is my view that any expression of homophobia oppresses all of us. [applause]

There are still other ways in which some of us in the academy express insensitivity to other black women. For example, on campuses such as mine and ours—it's called Spelman, actually it's yours, it *belongs* to every black woman—on a campus that has a tradition of welcoming and educating and empowering African American women roughly between the ages of 18 and 22, do we really present a welcoming for older women? Are we really sensitive to what it is like for women *with* children who *passionately* want an education? On your campus, in what ways do you reach out to women who are differently-abled? We're discovering at Spelman now just how rewarding and how complicated it is to welcome to our campus African American women who are visually impaired, African American women who are deaf, African American women with a range of different abilities. What is clear is that we must not only make sure that the ramps are up and that the paths are friendly to those who cannot see them but must walk them, we must make sure to engage in a kind of education among those of us who see and hear and walk well—so that the sisterhood becomes large enough to embrace all.

Now I turn to ways in which we, as black women in the academy, are indeed bound together by our shared experiences. You remember Brother Malcolm's query, "What do you call a black person with a PhD?" Well, it ain't "Doctor." But we must ask by what name will *she* with a PhD be called? Of course we African American women are not the only folks in the academy to experience racism and sexism. With our African American brothers in particular, but with all men and women of color, we know that look that says, "Hello, I guess you're the affirmative action person." [applause]

We have in the academy, then, women who, after the end of a full day, go home to the second shift. That means, my sister, it is time—and you ought to move rather rapidly—to cook the food, throw in the wash, put the child to the table and give a hand with the math problems, tidy up the place, "No these socks don't belong to you, and this doesn't belong to you either," but somehow folk don't seem in charge of their own. You are to call and check on the sick relative, and you know, there's a particular chapter in *his* article, it would be awfully nice if you could word-process it up. [laughter and applause]

My sisters, without any intention to set up a contest on oppression, to see which of us can claim that we have the hardest row to hoe, without engaging, then, in that contest on oppression, it is clear that in the academy, as in our nation as a whole, black women know, black women know what it means to be the victims of racism and sexism. For many of us there are those other jeopardies based on our class and our age, our sexual orientation, our physical abilities. In the American academy, life, then, for black women clearly ain't been no crystal stair.

I want to turn now to the final point that I want to make—actually, make it [the] next two—the possibility that we African American women could become a major force in helping to transform the academy. But how could it be that individuals who are among the most discriminated against might become a major force in helping to address that very discrimination? The core course at Spelman College is no longer Western Civilization. [applause] The core course at Spelman College—struggled for, fought over, indeed some of the major participants, my colleagues, are here, sister professors, I know you are here: Beverly Guy-Sheftall, Gloria Wade Gales, and Mona Phillips, and our provost, Glenda D. Price—the core course at Spelman College is entitled Africa: The Diaspora and the World.

I want to close now on a particular note. Alvin Singleton, a brother who served for two years as a composer-in-residence at Spelman, traveled all over our nation and all over the world, really, during the period of his stay with us. He was often asked—no doubt with something of an anticipation of "ain't easy being there"—he was often asked, "How are things at Spelman?" Alvin tells me, with the same ingenuity with which he composes, he says he always said, "Things are just fine—you see at Spelman, the sisters are in charge." [applause]

I must ask—isn't that what we all work toward? We work for the day when the sisters are in charge of their own intellectual and personal development. And in taking charge, how different it will be, because we will not violate the rights of any others. What a day that will be! What a great gettin'-up morning, when each of us—each and every one of us—has been truly empowered within a community of teacher, scholar, activist. It's just that wishing it won't make it so; unfortunately, we've got some work to do. My sisters, I am convinced that that work rests unusually heavily upon us. I want to thank you, really very much, for the honor of simply coming to acknowledge what we know about us black women in the academy. I really am grateful for this opportunity to simply reaffirm that which we feel most deeply. And how good it was to have the chance to dream with you of a better academy for each and every one of us. Thank you so much. [applause]

20.

LANI GUINIER
(1950–)

"Different Voices, Common Talk:
Why We Need a National Conversation About Race"

National Press Club, Washington, D.C.—November 29, 1994

On April 29, 1993, newly elected President Bill Clinton nominated Lani Guinier to be assistant attorney general for civil rights. The job of the assistant attorney general is to enforce civil rights laws, and Guinier was a relatively unknown law professor at the University of Pennsylvania. A *Wall Street Journal* opinion piece the next day dubbed Guinier a "Quota Queen" for her views on voting reform. A slew of other caricatures were soon flying through the press. As Guinier recounted, "I was pigeonholed in a litany of alliteration: 'Loony Lani,' the 'Czarina of Czeparatism,' the 'Princess of Proportionality,' 'Real America's Madwoman.' "[1]

Guinier had published several articles in academic law journals on voting reform in the 1980s. Her ideas drew on the work of one of the nation's founding fathers, James Madison. Guinier's theories sought to remedy violations of the 1965 Voting Rights Act and broaden voter participation. Conservatives savaged her ideas as racially divisive and politically polarizing. President Clinton, sensing defeat, distanced himself from his nominee. On June 3, 1993, the president withdrew Guinier's nomination. Clinton called her ideas "anti-democratic."[2]

The hardest part of the debacle for Guinier was that it ended before she could explain herself in a Senate confirmation hearing. In the weeks leading up to what she called her "dis-appointment," Guinier tried to meet with senators in person. "[They] had to be pushed past stereo-types just like other Americans—black and white," Guinier wrote. "I was confident that I could, through direct eye contact and the unflinching candor for which I was known, take advantage of a personal encounter to become more than a cartoon character."[3]

Guinier also wanted to explain her views to the American public, to show that her personal background, legal work, and academic writing were devoted to building consensus, not conflict, in the democratic process. In a way, she finally got her wish: the controversy made her greatly in demand on the speaking circuit.

Guinier was born in New York City in 1950, the daughter of a black man and a Jewish woman. She attended Radcliffe College and earned her law degree from Yale University in 1974. Bill and Hillary Clinton, friends from law school, attended Guinier's wedding. She worked as a civil rights lawyer in the Carter administration, then spent most of the 1980s as a civil rights attorney for the NAACP Legal Defense Fund. In 1988, Guinier joined the law faculty at the University of Pennsylvania. In 1998, she became the first tenured black female law professor at Harvard.[4]

The controversy over Guinier's nomination forged her belief that Americans need a neutral space where they can talk about race. So she set up a nonprofit organization called Commonplace, where peo-ple with competing interests and differing viewpoints could talk. In her National Press Club speech, Guinier described the program and called for a national conversation on race. Her proposal would be echoed in 1997 when President Clinton appointed a seven-person panel to travel the country holding town hall meetings on race.

As you can all imagine, this has been a most interesting year and a half for me. I have gone from relative obscurity to being someone that people stop in the street and introduce themselves to. I was trying to catch a taxi-cab not too long ago right outside the University of Pennsylvania Law School. It was raining, and there were a number of other people who were also trying to catch taxicabs. So I was on my way to the airport, and I put my bags down on the corner and waited my turn, and all of a sudden a cab pulled up and stopped right in front of me. And the driver got out and he said, "The man inside wants to take you to the airport." [laughter]

Now, as I said, I knew that people thought they could recognize me, but I did not realize they could also read my mind. [laughter] So I was skeptical. I didn't move, but the driver, seeing that I was hesitating, he tried to reassure me. He picked up by bags and started to load them into the trunk of the cab, and he said, "Well, the man inside says he knows you." So I looked inside the cab, and I saw a well-dressed businessman, but not someone that I thought I had ever met before. I managed a very weak grin, and he smiled broadly and said, "Zoe Baird." [laughter] And I said, "No, I'm Lani Guinier, but I'd still like a ride to the airport." [laughter]

So, as you can imagine, it's been an interesting year and a half for a disappointed nominee. But I am not here today to speak to you about the past. I'm really here to talk about the future. The title of my talk is, "Different Voices, Common Talk: Why We Need a National Conversation About Race."

No matter who won the recent mid-term elections, the voters all lost. People voted their fears, not their hopes, they voted against candidates not for solutions; sound bites eroded deliberation; hate-mongering seemed to count for more than ever before. In the rush to take sides, candidates and commentators alike sliced complex issues into noisy bits of sound and fury signifying nothing. Quote: "It's intellectual violence," said a Virginia bookstore owner. "There's so much hatred," she continued, "it scares me. This campaign appealed to people's lowest emotions," end quote.

In response, voters have become angry, disillusioned and apathetic. They have developed a negative view of all political candidates, and they stayed home from the polls in disgust. Fewer than four in ten eligible Americans voted November 8th. Two-thirds of the Republican seats were won with fewer votes than were polled by unsuccessful Republicans in 1992 in those same districts.

Typical is the clerk in an athletic store in Los Angeles who declared, and I quote, "I'm not going to vote. It's a no-win situation. They're all losers." End quote. Many voters are angry, including those who did not vote. Those candidates who won often did so by mobilizing the discontent of

some voters and demobilizing others whose anger could not be directed at
easy scapegoats. This has been called the politics of exclusion or the cult of
otherness. "They"—"they" are not like us. "They" are blameworthy.

If we simply name and then blame our problems on "them," we can, we
are told, sleep well, like the normal Americans we are. But our discourse of
blame is failing Americans of all races. We will all lose if we allow negative
campaigns with their racial coding about "them" to dominate the conversation of democracy. As Kathleen Hall Jamieson counsels, and I quote,
"We have now devised a means of campaigning that creates an angry electorate which then vents its anger by voting no, no, no, no. But," she continues, "if you go in and just vote no, you're not really licensing someone to
govern."

Moreover, negative campaigns breed low voter turnout. They polarize
the electorate. But negative campaigns are a symptom of a deeper problem. They are the visible sores of a poisoned, winner-take-all political discourse. They are the most obvious examples of what is wrong with our
winner-take-all politics.

Winner-take-all election formats raise the stakes. They disproportionately reward winners and punish losers. Since losers get nothing and the
winners get it all, competition to win is fierce. The struggle to win at all
costs turns language into public relations; words become bullets in the
struggle for advantage. Citizens are buried in the onslaught of negative
political messages and conflict-driven news coverage. The public is immobilized and demobilized. Elections as spectator sport means that when the
fans turn off, we have a democracy without citizens.

Governance itself has become one seamless election contest in which
voters are invited through constant public opinion surveys to vote for or
against the antagonist of the day. No one thinks about the issues; they simply choose sides. Inspired by a winner-take-all mentality, institutions designed to foster communication of fact now operate to pervert and distort
it. In the mass media, the focus is on controversy and conflicts between extreme points of view. Within the academic community and among intellectual elites, there is little or no conversation across racial or ideological
lines.

At the highest levels of decision-making, we see disdain for genuine
conversation as a way of resolving or mediating conflict. We distort the
views of those with whom we disagree and then we attack them for the car-

icatures we have drawn. We reward each other for simple-minded solutions and slogans when legitimate conflict arises—in crime, three strikes and you're out; on welfare, two years and you're off.

And candidates desperate to win all use race to whip voters into a frenzy to get them excited enough about something so that they will vote, rather than changing the nature of the debate to justify better, more accountable government or to show how protecting the interests of racial minorities and the urban poor are integral to our collective self-interest.

Instead, politicians of all stripes have been pandering to white fears of blacks, coating the racial subtext in the language of welfare reform and tough-on-crime policies. Many liberals now seem overwhelmed by the magnitude of the problems, convinced that the problems defy solution or that the solutions are the problem. Others are in deep denial about the need for collective action and community responsibility to solve the problems. Still others openly accept the formulations of personal responsibility and individual behavior modification that characterize the conservative assault on black people and poor people, who are made out to be victims of their own so-called maladaptive behavior or character flaws. No one offers an approach that gives working-class whites and blacks, poor people of all hues and other political orphans a reason or a way to make common ground.

Think of the code words whites have for blacks—and these code words come from an AP wire story out of New Haven, they're not mine: minority, urban, criminal, crime rate, social program participant, inner city, qualified candidate, welfare mother, them. Same article then lists the black codes for whites: suburban type, Republican, conservative, them.

Notice, both groups see each other as "them." And many whites express their resentment at "them" in the language of less government—meaning no more subsidies for "them." According to a Times-Mirror poll of September 21st, 1994, fifty-one percent of whites now agree—and I quote—"We have gone too far in pushing for equal rights in this country"—equal rights—we have gone too far in pushing for equal rights for "them" in this country.

The American people have learned to see race as an issue of blame and punishment. Who is guilty and who is innocent? Who is at fault for the breakdown of our moral compass on this and other controversial issues? Individual bigots or race-obsessed blacks? Right-wing zealots or left-wing black nationalists? Individual incumbents or their individual opponents? The media? The Congress? The American people? In this polarized, winner-take-all climate, our so-called leaders have lost the political will to do more than simply condemn our problems.

Even worse, they have lost the political imagination to do more than censure the victims or blame the victimizers. Concerns about excess welfare dependency and random violence are certainly real, but our elected officials have failed to cast the debate over the country's future in terms of new or compelling ideas. We are stuck in a 1960s paradigm where government specially dispenses to deserving individuals the formal opportunity to overcome barriers erected by individual bigots. This kind of rights talk also assumes a winner-take-all positioning. It reinforces the notion that the government has taken sides in a zero-sum competition between us and them. It encourages the idea that "me and my interests" are incompatible with "you and your rights." It promotes an approach in which we justify in the name of winning all the total disparagement of those who then lose all.

But the answer is not to stay home and worry about how to allocate or apportion blame among "them." The answer is to find democratic public spaces where we can communicate with "them" about us. The answer is to move away from the discourse of naming and blaming, and to move toward a conversion of asking, telling, and listening. We need new democratic spaces to develop and implement new strategies for thinking and talking about race, about welfare reform, about crime. We need to identify ways to talk about controversial issues such as race among people who are deeply divided experientially and ideologically. We need to focus on dialogue and conversation as a way to begin communicating across difference. We need to remove the discussion of race from the culture of conflict, deception and hypocrisy, which characterizes contemporary public discourse. We need to replace an "I'm right, you're wrong" adversarial model of truth detection in favor of an approach where participants are encouraged to identify points of agreement, understand the basis for disagreement, and then cooperate in collective brainstorming and task-oriented problem solving.

Changing demographics, the globalization of our economy and the transformation of information technology make it imperative that we utilize all—all—of America's resources to meet the challenges of the twenty-first century. If within the notion of global competition is the concept of

"us against them," then we the American people should all be pulling together as a single team. But we shall be permanently disabled from adapt-
ing as a noble and caring society to a more diverse, complex world if we do
not first address America's race problem in the context of a more engaged,
more participatory democratic conversation. After all, race is the great
taboo. It is like a giant pothole: If we do not fix it but deny it is there, or
simply try to drive around it, it does not go away.

Its presence preoccupies us and distorts our thinking. We start to believe that "they" have taken our money, our freedom, and our country.
"They" take our money in the form of welfare. "They," we start to believe,
take our freedom in a slow-motion riot called crime, and "they" take our
country as black and brown immigrants or recipients of foreign aid. But
the Pentagon and Social Security together account for almost forty percent of federal spending. Aid to Families with Dependent Children accounts for just over one percent of federal outlays. When informed of the
actual budget figures, and when given a chance to learn the facts about the
efficiency of front-loading money on crime by paying for prevention as opposed to waiting for a victim in order to back-end punishment, most voters
opt for [front-loading] efficiency. Indeed, a survey of twelve hundred voters on election night found that voters had powerful misconceptions about
where their money went. When asked for specific programs to cut, a majority actually supported decreasing military spending as a way to balance
the budget.

So I say we must find alternative democratic spaces that ensure the
representation of a range of viewpoints in all forms of public discourse.
And as part of that project, I have started the process of incorporating this
nonprofit center, Commonplace, in Philadelphia in order to try to develop
a new consensus, in order to try to influence both the content and approach to public debate. And toward this goal, Commonplace, in con-
junction with the University of Pennsylvania Annenberg School, is going
to hold a national conversation on race next fall. A national conversation
on race as a place, a first place, a beginning of a series of conversations to
address that pothole whose subtext is driving so much of current debate.

We will have a national conversation to bring together media, decision-
makers, academics, civil rights advocates, and public policy experts. We
will have a national conversation that brings people of different perspectives to the table, provides a common set of readings, trains participants in

a less conflict-driven form of public dialogue, and then seeks their assistance and collaboration in developing a more inclusive, non-adversarial public discourse on race, justice, and America's future.

One of the arguments I was given for the decision to withdraw my nomination without even a hearing was that confirmation hearings would be divisive and polarizing. But I do not believe that talking about race invariably leads to an "us versus them" debate. Talking, especially if structured to assure reasonable representation of relevant perspectives and the need not just to talk but to listen, may instead reveal points of commonality.

Talking can be cathartic, not just chaotic. It can vent and relieve pressure and help identify positive-sum solutions, solutions in which we all win something. But whatever it accomplishes, we do need to talk.

The goal is to move beyond the polarizing discourse about race that characterized the 1980s, beyond the claims of formal racial equality that rallied the movement in the 1960s and beyond the notion that racial preferences are the only or best way to remedy racial inequality. We need a new approach to race and racism that moves beyond notions of intentional acts of bigotry and prejudice, away from claims based on individual guilt and individual innocence, and disavows—an approach that disavows the drama of divide and polarize, in which everyone is made to feel comfortable with their prejudices and uncomfortable about "them." We need to move forward to the concept of societal discrimination and collective responsibility for overcoming racial disadvantage. And one of the ways Commonplace will try to do this is to use racial inequity as a window on the larger unfairness of distribution of resources.

Let me give you an example. Lowell High School in San Francisco is a magnet public school which boasts distinguished alumni such as Supreme Court Justice Stephen Breyer. As a result of court proceedings to desegregate the San Francisco public schools, admission to the school is supervised by a court consent decree. No one ethnic group can be more than forty percent of the population of any magnet school in San Francisco. Consequently, a 1993 admission to Lowell High School proceeded on a sliding scale. Chinese Americans were required to score sixty-six out of a perfect sixty-nine to gain admittance. Other whites and Asian Americans—but not Chinese Americans—could qualify with a fifty-nine, blacks and Latinos a fifty-six.

As a result of pressure from the Chinese-American community, these cut-off scores were modified somewhat and the entry credentials changed, but the school still employs race-based quotas to protect diversity. A group of Chinese Americans are now challenging the consent decree and a group of African Americans are defending it. Both groups are proceeding within a winner-take-all frame that pits minority groups into competing factions.

When I have presented this problem to a class I teach that very much models the process approach of Commonplace, I have urged my students to buck the hypo. I've urged them to try to escape the false choice of winner-take-all decision-making, and we have come up together, collaboratively, with a different way of thinking about admission to Lowell High School.

My students suggested using a lottery that allows anyone with a score over fifty-six, the lowest the school now uses, to compete for admission by a random selection. On the other hand, they have said, if the school can demonstrate that those with a perfect sixty-nine or close to it are more likely to do something that the school values, such as achieve a seat on the Supreme Court, or win recognition as a Westinghouse Science Finalist, or become a successful candidate to a competitive college, something that will reflect well on the school's reputation, then my students have said, well, put their names in the lottery twice or even three times.

Now, this alternative approach is not perfect, but it might lead to a re-examination of the school's admissions policy, not just for Chinese Americans or blacks, but for everyone. No one would feel entitled to admission but no one would feel unjustly excluded, either. This approach recognizes that claims of merit and diversity are each legitimate. This approach does not proceed as "us against them." It does not assume that only one group wins and only one group who wins, wins all. It avoids a zero-sum solution in favor of a positive-sum solution—a win-win solution that accommodates the goals of diversity and genuine merit more broadly.

Well, in our national conversation on race, we will look for remedies that do not separate working Americans of all hues into warring factions. We will look for remedies that instead demonstrate ways in which the status quo is unfair and is treating many people, not just African Americans or Chinese Americans arbitrarily.

Alternative remedies, such as admission lotteries with a base index score threshold, might accomplish a broader consensus. Similarly, I have advocated cumulative voting as something that may be a more palatable and ultimately more transformative remedy for voting discrimination than separate racially homogenous districts.

But the point is not that I have the answers. The point is not that there is a single answer. The point is not to identify one answer to a complex set of problems but to locate each problem and its solution within a context that unites or links "us" to "them." This is not about more or less government. It is about better, more accountable government. It is about taking the legitimate concerns of people on all sides of the debate and forging a new, transformative approach.

Some argue that to govern is to choose, but to govern is also to deliberate. Voting in a winner-take-all paradigm forces complex issues into simple choices; it should be the last, not the first, resort. Voting for a winner who wins all should be secondary to debate and genuine discussion within a representative body. And only if that body gathers people from all walks of life, is representative of all viewpoints, and encourages genuine honest talk will democracy achieve the collective wisdom of its people. Ultimately, governance must be first and foremost about a well-conducted conversation, a conversation in which we all get a chance to speak, to listen, to be heard, and to collaborate to solve *our* problems.

Participatory democracy is not just insider talk about or among winners. To be part of a genuine democracy we *all* must be encouraged, actively, to partake in its conversation.

Thank you very much. [applause]

21.

CLARENCE THOMAS
(1948–)

"Be Not Afraid"

American Enterprise Institute, Washington, D.C.—February 13, 2001

U.S. Supreme Court Justice Clarence Thomas has been one of the most controversial African American figures of the past century. Thomas is a political conservative and his 1991 nomination to the Court by President George Bush outraged many civil rights leaders, liberals, and African Americans. Thomas's outspoken critique of affirmative action and welfare programs, among other positions, appalled his opponents, especially given that Thomas was chosen to fill the seat vacated by civil rights legend Thurgood Marshall.

Thomas's Senate confirmation hearings were further roiled by law professor Anita Hill's accusation that Thomas sexually harassed her when she worked for him at the Equal Employment Opportunity Commission (EEOC) in the 1980s. Thomas steadfastly denied the charges, calling the nationally televised hearings a "high-tech lynching."[1] Thomas was ultimately confirmed. He was sworn in as an Associate Justice of the Supreme Court in November 1991.

Thomas was one of three children born in a dirt-floor house in Pin Point, Georgia, a tiny coastal community named for the plantation that once stood there. When Thomas was a toddler, his father abandoned the family. When he was six, Thomas went to live with his maternal grandparents in Savannah. He would credit his grandfather Meyers Anderson as the most influential person in his life. Anderson was a small businessman, and his example of individual initiative in the face of racial segregation, along with his devout Catholicism, framed Thomas's young life.[2] "The most compassionate thing [our grandparents] did for us was to teach us to fend for ourselves and to do that in an openly hostile environment," Thomas said in a 1987 speech.[3]

After graduating from a Catholic private school, Thomas attended a Catholic seminary in Missouri and then Holy Cross College in Massachusetts. These were the late 1960s and for a time Thomas was attracted to black radicalism. He owned almost all the recorded speeches of Malcolm X.[4]

Thomas earned his law degree from Yale University in 1974. He worked for the attorney general of Missouri and for Monsanto Corporation before joining the Reagan administration in 1980 as head of the EEOC. President Bush nominated him to the U.S. Court of Appeals in 1990, and by the time Bush nominated him to the Supreme Court, Thomas had become a popular speaker at law schools and in conservative circles.[5] He also sparked controversy when he told the *Washington Post* in 1984 that black leaders who failed to collaborate with the Reagan administration on race problems chose instead to "bitch, bitch, bitch, moan and moan, whine and whine."[6]

In the years since his appointment to the Supreme Court, Justice Thomas has continued to draw fire from liberal opponents and prominent African American figures. He also has continued to complain publicly—as he did in this speech—that conservative blacks face intense ostracism for expressing views contrary to the "orthodoxy" of mainstream African American politics.

IT IS VERY TEMPTING tonight to confine my talk to a subject that I am most familiar with: the law and my years at the Court. But even though straying from that narrow ground may be hazardous, I am going to speak more broadly tonight—as a citizen who believes in a civil society, and who is deeply concerned because too many show timidity today precisely when courage is demanded.

Judges do not cease to be human beings when they go on the bench. In important cases, it is my humble opinion that finding the right answer is often the least difficult problem. Having the courage to assert that answer and stand firm in the face of the constant winds of protest and criticism is often much more difficult.

As Alexander Hamilton wrote in *Federalist,* no. 78, "It would require an uncommon portion of fortitude in the judges to do their duty as faithful guardians of the Constitution, where legislative invasions of it have been instigated by the major voice of the community." This point is rarely stressed.

The trait that Hamilton singles out—fortitude—is fundamental to my philosophy of life, both as a judge and, more fundamentally, as a citizen of this great nation.

I've heard that the great UCLA basketball coach John Wooden taught his players how to play the game by first teaching them how to lace up their shoes. Making the right decisions as a judge requires a similar focus on fundamentals. Long before walking onto the court, one must be clear about how to conduct oneself as a human being and as a citizen. One must be clear and confident about one's judicial philosophy, and have the courage to stand by the decisions that an honest adherence to the law requires.

On July 1, 1991, when I arrived at President Bush's home in Kennebunkport, he invited me to join him in the sitting area of his bedroom. During that brief meeting, he asked me only two questions. First, could my family and I endure the confirmation process? Not knowing what was in store for us, I answered yes. [laughter]

The second question was simply whether I could "call it as I saw it" when I became a member of the Court—whether I could rule on the *law,* and not my personal opinions. To that, I also answered yes.

In a perfect world, the second question would be the only one members of the Court should ever have to answer, [applause] either to a President or to the legislators who confirm their appointments. Judges can be buffeted by strong winds that tear them away from the basic principles they have sworn to safeguard. Fulfillment of our oath requires us to have both a clear understanding of the principles that allow us to "call it as we see it," and the fortitude to stand by those principles and the decisions that rest upon them.

I'd like to reflect tonight upon those two questions: judicial principles and the question of courage in American political life. If we are to be a nation of laws and not of men, judges must be impartial referees who defend the Constitutional principles from attempts by particular interests, or even the people as a whole, to overwhelm them. By insulating judges from external retaliation and from the internal temptations of ambition, the framers hoped that the judiciary would be free of pressure not only from the government, but also from the people.

Life tenure and an irreducible salary exist only to help judges maintain their independence and, hence, their impartiality. Impartiality is central to judging and to being a judge. When deciding cases, a judge's race, sex, religion are all irrelevant. A judge must push these factors to one side, in order to render a fair, reasoned judgment on the meaning of the law. A judge must attempt to keep at bay those passions, interests, and emotions that beset every frail human being. A judge is not a legislator, for whom it is entirely appropriate to consider personal and group interests. The ideal of justice is to be blind to such things.

In addition to these personal challenges, judging is difficult because the Constitution itself is written in broad, sometimes ambiguous terms. And unfortunately, the Constitution does not come with Cliffs Notes or a glossary. When it comes time to interpret the Constitutional provisions— such as, for instance, the Speech or Press Clauses—reasonable minds often differ on their exact meaning. But that does not mean that there is no correct answer, that there are no clear, eternal principles recognized and put into motion by our founding documents. These principles do exist. The law is not a matter of purely personal opinion. The law is a distinct, independent discipline, with certain principles and modes of analysis that yield what we can discern to be correct and incorrect answers to certain problems.

When struggling to find the right answer to a case, judges should adopt principles of interpretation and methods of analysis that reduce judicial discretion. Reducing discretion is the key to fostering judicial impartiality. The greater the room for judicial discretion, the greater the temptation to write one's personal opinions into the law. This is especially important at the Supreme Court, where many of the usual limitations on judicial discretion, such as authority from a superior court or *stare decisis,* either do not exist, or do not exist with the same strength as with other courts. Hence, other doctrines and principles designed to narrow discretion and to bolster impartiality assume greater significance for the Court.

When interpreting the Constitution and statutes, judges should seek the original understanding of the provision's text if the meaning of that text is not readily apparent. This approach works in several ways to reduce judicial discretion and to maintain judicial impartiality. First, by tethering their analysis to the understanding of those who drafted and ratified the text, modern judges are prevented from substituting their own preferences for the Constitution.

Second, it places the authority for creating the legal rules in the hands of the people and their representatives, rather than in the hands of the judiciary. [applause] The Constitution means what the delegates of the Philadelphia Convention and of the state-ratifying conventions understood it to mean, not what we judges think it should mean.

Third, this approach recognizes the basic principle of a *written* Constitution. "We the people" adopted a written Constitution precisely because it has a fixed meaning, a meaning that does not change. Otherwise we would have adopted the British approach of an unwritten, evolving Constitution. Aside from amendment, according to Article V, the Constitution's meaning cannot be updated, or changed, or altered by the Supreme Court, the Congress, or the President. [applause]

Of course, even when strictly interpreted as I believe it should be, the Constitution remains a modern, "breathing" document, as some like to call it, in the strict sense that the Court is constantly required to interpret how its provisions apply to the Constitutional questions of modern life. Nevertheless, strict interpretation must never surrender to the understandably attractive impulse towards creative but unwarranted alterations of the first principles.

Another principle of self-restraint derives from the nature of the legal analysis we employ. It is always tempting to adopt *balancing* tests, or to rest one's decision on the presence of several factors. Judges can then say that they decided the case on its facts, thereby preserving some degree of flexibility for the next case. While this may be appropriate for trial courts or for state courts, it is seldom the best approach for the Supreme Court or a federal appellate court. Whenever possible, the Court and judges generally should adopt clear, bright-line rules that, as I like to say to my law clerks, you can explain to the gas station attendant as easily as to a law professor—or is that the other way around? [laughter and applause]

Rules not only provide private parties with notice, but also limit judicial discretion by narrowing the ability of judges in the future to alter the law to fit their policy preferences. Broader rules are more likely to be impartial as to how they affect specific parties. Thus, clear rules, along with life tenure and an irreducible salary, encourage judges to maintain their impartiality.

A judge who strictly adheres to the rules of impartiality and judicial restraint is likely to reach sound conclusions. But as I've said, reaching the correct decision itself is only half the battle. Having the courage of your convictions can be the harder part.

My beliefs about personal fortitude and the importance of defending timeless principles of justice grew out of the wonderful years I spent with my grandparents in Georgia; the years I have spent here in Washington, and my interest in world history—especially the history of countries in which the rule of law was surrendered to the rule of fear, such as during the rise of Nazism in what was one of the most educated and cultured countries in Europe at the time.

I have now been in Washington, D.C., for more than two decades. When I first arrived here in 1979, I thought that there would be great debates about principles and policies in this city. I worked as a legislative assistant for Senator John C. Danforth. I expected these great debates to occur in the Senate. Like so many of you, I was surprised to see soliloquies spoken in almost empty chambers, and unspoken statements included in the Congressional Record as though spoken.

For some reason that now eludes me, I expected citizens to feel passionately about what was happening in our country, to candidly and passionately debate the policies that had been implemented and suggest new ones. I was disabused of this heretical notion in December of 1980, when I was unwittingly candid with a young *Washington Post* reporter. He fairly and thoroughly displayed my naive openness in his op-ed about our discussion, in which I had raised what I thought were legitimate objections to a number of sacred policies, such as affirmative action, welfare, school busing—policies that I felt were not well serving their intended beneficiaries. In my innocence, I was shocked at the public reaction. I had never been called such names in my entire life.

Why were these policies beyond question? What or who placed them off limits? Would it not be useful for those who felt strongly about these matters, and who wanted to solve the same problems, to have a point of view and to be heard? Sadly, in most forums of public dialogue in this country, the answer is no.

It became clear in rather short order that on the very difficult issues such as race there was no real debate or honest discussion. Those who raised questions that suggested doubt about popular policies were subjected to intimidation. Debate was not permitted. Orthodoxy was enforced. When whites questioned the conventional wisdom on these issues, it was considered bad form; when blacks did so, it was treason.

These "rules of orthodoxy" still apply. You had better not engage in serious debate or discussion unless you are willing to endure attacks that range from mere hostile bluster to libel. Often the temptation is to retreat to complaining about the unfairness of it all. But this is a plaintive admission of defeat. It is a unilateral withdrawal from the field of combat.

Today, no one can honestly claim surprise at the venomous attacks against those who take positions that are contrary to the canon laid down by those who claim to shape opinions. Such attacks have been standard fare for some time. Complaining about this obvious state of affairs does not elevate one's moral standing. And it is hardly a substitute for the courage that we badly need. [applause]

If you trim your sails, you appease those who lack the honesty and decency to disagree on the merits, but prefer to engage in personal attacks. [applause] A good argument diluted to avoid criticism is not nearly as good as the undiluted argument because we best arrive at truth through a process of honest and vigorous debate. Arguments should not sneak around in disguise, as if dissent were somehow sinister or clandestine. One should not be cowed by criticism. [applause]

In my humble opinion, those who come to engage in debates of consequence and who challenge accepted wisdom should expect to be treated badly. Nonetheless, they must stand undaunted. That is required. And that should be expected. For it is bravery that is required to secure freedom. [applause]

On matters of consequence, reasons and arguments must be of consequence. Therefore, those who choose to engage in such debates must themselves be of consequence. Much emphasis these days is placed on who has the quickest tongue and who looks best on television. There seems to be an obsession with how one looks to others; hence, a proliferation of public relations professionals and spin doctors. As I was counseled some years ago, perceptions are more important than reality. But this is madness. No car has ever crashed into a mirage. [applause] No imaginary army has ever invaded a country.

It is sometimes thought that we must all have some great insight into life and the intellect of the great philosophers. Obviously, it is quite important that we have people of ideas and great intellect. It is awe inspiring to me to read the works of Gertrude ["Bea"] Himmelfarb, Michael Novak, Michael Ledeen, James Q. Wilson, and, of course, Judge Bork and others in this audience. But as much as great works of genius are necessary, they are insufficient. This is particularly so when the responses are not of the intellect. It does no good to argue ideas with those who will respond as brutes. Works of genius have often been smashed and burned, and geniuses have sometimes been treated no better.

But there is much wisdom that requires no genius. It takes no education and no great intellect to know that it is best for children to be raised in two-parent families. [applause]

Yet those who dare say this are often accused of trying to impose their values on others. This condemnation does not rest on some great body of counterevidence; it is purely and simply an in-your-face response. It is, in short, intimidation. For brutes, the most effective tactic is to intimidate an opponent into the silence of self-censorship.

In September of 1975, the *Wall Street Journal* published a book review by Michael Novak of Thomas Sowell's book *Race and Economics.* At the time, I lived in Jefferson City, Missouri. The opening paragraph changed my life. It reads:

> Honesty on questions of race is rare in the United States. So many and unrecognized have been the injustices committed against blacks that no one wishes to be unkind, or subject himself to intimidating charges. Hence, even simple truths are commonly evaded.

This insight applies with equal force to very many conversations of consequence today. Who wants to be denounced as a heartless monster? On important matters, crucial matters, silence is enforced.

Some years ago, I wrote a dissenting opinion which argued that a prisoner who had been beaten but only received minor injuries could not, in this case, base a claim on the "cruel and unusual punishment" clause of the Eighth Amendment. Now, there are obviously different, legitimate points of view on this case. If not, I would not have been in dissent. But what is striking is that I was widely denounced for advocating the beating of prisoners, which is ridiculous. When a wrong is done, justice requires that it be weighed impartially. The critics weren't content to argue that I was analytically wrong—that I had misinterpreted the law in making my decision. Rather, they sought my conformity, or, in the alternative, my silence.

Even if one has a valid position and is intellectually honest, he has to anticipate nasty responses aimed at the messenger rather than the argument. The aim is to limit the range of the debate, the number of messengers, and the size of the audience. The objective is to pressure dissenters to sanitize their message, so as to avoid being subjected to hurtful *ad hominem* criticisms. Who wants to be calumniated? It's not worth the trouble.

But is it worth it? Just what is worth it, and what is not? If one wants to be popular, it is counterproductive to disagree with the majority. If one just wants to tread water until the next vacation, it isn't worth the agony. If one just wants to muddle through, it's not worth it. In my office, I have a little sign that reads: "To avoid criticism, say nothing, do nothing, be nothing."

None of us really believes the things we fear discussing honestly and openly these days are really trivial—and the reaction of our critics shows that we are right. If our dissents are so trivial, why are their reactions so intense? If our ideas are trivial, why the headhunting? Like you, I do not want to waste my time on the trivial. I certainly have no desire to be browbeaten and intimidated for the trivial.

What makes it all worthwhile? What makes it worthwhile is something greater than all of us. There are those things that at one time we all accepted as more important than our comfort or our discomfort—if not our very lives: duty, honor, country. There was a time when all was to be set aside for these. The plow was left idle, the hearth without fire, the homestead abandoned.

We all share a reasonable and, in many ways, admirable, reluctance to leave the safety and peacefulness of private life to take up the larger burdens and challenges of active citizenship. The price is high, and it is easier and more enjoyable to remain within the shelter of our personal lives and our local communities, rather than the larger state. To enter public life is to step outside our more confined, comfortable sphere of life and to face the broader, national sphere of citizenship. What makes it all worthwhile is to devote ourselves to the common good.

When one observes the pitched battles that rage around persons of strong convictions who do not accept the prevailing beliefs of others, it is no wonder that those who might otherwise wish to participate find more hospitable outlets for their civic interests. When one of my friends began feeling the urge to get involved, his spouse glared at him and said, "Don't even think about it. We love our life the way it is." And that is not an unreasonable perspective—not at all. But is reasonableness always our standard of review of this question? I hope not.

During my youth there were many wonderful sayings, now considered perhaps trite, that provided cryptic, yet prescient guidance for my life. Among them was one based on Luke 12:48: "To whom much is given, of him much is required." Perhaps such sentiments are embarrassing in sophisticated company these days, but I continue to believe that this is right for me, and I believe it in my heart.

I do believe that we are required to wade into those things that matter to our country and our culture, no matter what the disincentives are, and no matter the personal cost. [applause] There is not one among us who wants to be set upon, or obligated to do and say difficult things. Yet there is not one of us who could in good conscience stand by and watch a loved one or a defenseless person or a vital national principle perish alone, undefended, when our intervention would make all the difference. This may well be too dramatic an example. But nevertheless, put most simply: if we think that something is dreadfully wrong, then someone has to do something.

In the spring of 1980, I received a call asking if I had any interest in going to the Office for Civil Rights in the Department of Education. Until then, for the good of my career, I had assiduously avoided any work that was related to civil rights and frankly I had no interest in such a position. Then a dear friend of mine, Jay Parker, spoke to me about it, insisting that these issues were of great importance to me, and that I had a point of view that should be a part of the policy process and the continuing debate.

I had to admit that what happened in this area did mean a lot to me.

But I didn't want to be the one arguing publicly for policies that would raise the ire of the civil rights establishment. I had just gotten a taste of the penalty for candor and honesty as a result of the *Washington Post* op-ed, and I had no interest in a repeat performance. There is, of course, such a thing as self-preservation. Also, I was insulted that I was being offered the job for no reason other than my race.

I hesitated, unsure of how to proceed. But Jay Parker's final words of advice to me were compelling: "Put up or shut up." [applause] What a choice that is. But he was right. Even with all the complications, in the end the choice is just that stark. One might shut up when it doesn't matter; but when it really counts, we are required to put up.

It goes without saying that we must participate in the affairs of our country if we think they are important and have an impact on our lives. But how are we to do that? In what manner should we participate?

Today, there is much talk about moderation. It reminds me of a former colleague of mine at the EEOC [Equal Employment Opportunity Commission] who often joked that he was a "gun-toting moderate"—a curiously oxymoronic perspective. Just think of that: dying over half a loaf. [laughter and applause]

I do not believe that one should fight over things that don't really matter. But what about those things that *do* matter? It is not comforting to think that the natural tendency inside us is to settle for the bottom, or even the middle, of the stream. This tendency in large part results from an overemphasis on civility. None of us should be uncivil in our manner as we debate issues of consequence. No matter how difficult it is, good manners should be routine. However, in the effort to be civil in conduct, many who know better actually dilute firmly held views to avoid appearing "judgmental." They curb their tongues not only in form but also in substance. The insistence on civility in the form of our debates has the perverse effect of cannibalizing our principles, the very essence of a civil society.

That is why civility cannot be the governing principle of citizenship or leadership. As Bea Himmelfarb observed in her book *One Nation, Two Cultures,* "To reduce citizenship to the modern idea of civility, the good-neighbor idea, is to belittle not only the political role of the citizen but also the virtues expected of the citizen—the 'civic virtues,' as they were known in antiquity and in early republican thought."

These are the virtues that Aristotle thought were necessary to govern oneself like a "free man"; that Montesquieu referred to as the "spring which sets the republican government in motion"; and that the Founding Fathers thought provided the dynamic combination of conviction and self-discipline necessary for self-government.

Bea Himmelfarb refers to two kinds of virtues. The first are the "caring" virtues. They include "respect, trustworthiness, compassion, fairness, decency." These are the virtues that make daily life pleasant with our families and with those we come in contact.

The second are the vigorous virtues. These heroic virtues "transcend family and community and may even, on occasion, violate the conventions of civility." "These are the virtues that characterize great leaders, although not necessarily good friends"—courage, ambition, creativity.

She notes that the vigorous virtues have been supplanted by the caring ones. Though they are not mutually exclusive or necessarily incompatible, active citizens and leaders must be governed by the vigorous rather than the caring virtues. We must not allow our desire to be decent and well-mannered people to overwhelm the substance of our principles or our determination to fight for their success. Ultimately, we should seek both caring and vigorous virtues—but above all, we must not allow the former to dominate the latter.

Again, by yielding to a false form of civility, we sometimes allow our critics to intimidate us. As I have said, active citizens are often subjected to truly vile attacks; they are branded as mean-spirited, racist, Uncle Tom, homophobic, sexist, etc. To this we often respond, if not succumb, so as not to be constantly fighting, by trying to be tolerant and nonjudgmental—that is, we censor ourselves. This is not civility. It is cowardice, or well-intentioned self-deception at best.

Immanuel Kant pointed out that to escape shame and self-contempt we must learn to lie to ourselves. These lies create a formidable obstacle to action on behalf of truth, and one of the greatest human accomplishments is to find a way to shatter those lies.

We've learned how easy it is to deceive ourselves even when the truth is luminously clear. The little-known story of Dimitar Pešev shows both the power of self-deception and the explosive effect of telling the truth, and the dangers inherent in allowing the rule of law and the truth to succumb to political movements of the moment.

Pešev was the vice president of the Bulgarian parliament during World War II. He was a man like many, simple and straightforward, not a great intellect, not a military hero—just a civil servant, doing his job as best he could, raising his family, struggling through a terrible moment in European if not world history.

Bulgaria was pretty lucky, because she managed to stay out of the fighting, even though the Nazis had placed the Bulgarian government, and the king, under enormous pressure to enter the war on the side of the Axis, or at a minimum to permit the destruction of the Bulgarian Jews. Bulgaria had no tradition of widespread anti-Semitism, and the leaders of the country were generally unwilling to turn over their own citizens to certain death. But like all the other European countries, Bulgaria moved toward the Holocaust in small steps.

Pešev was one of many Bulgarian officials who heard rumors of the new policy and constantly queried the ministers. They lied to him, and for a time he believed their lies. Perhaps the ministers somehow believed the lies themselves. But, in the final hours, a handful of citizens from Pešev's hometown raced to Sofia to tell him the truth: the Jews were being rounded up, the trains were waiting.

According to the law such actions were illegal. Pešev forced his way into the office of the interior minister, demanding to know the truth. The minister repeated the official line, but Pešev didn't believe him. He demanded that the minister place a telephone call to the local authorities, and remind them of their legal obligations. This brave act saved the lives of the Bulgarian Jews. Pešev then circulated a letter to members of Parliament, condemning the violation of the law, and demanding that the government ensure that no such thing take place.

According to his biographer, Pešev's words moved all those "who until that moment had not imagined what could happen but who now could not accept what they had discovered." He had broken through the wall of self-deception and forced his colleagues to face the truth.

There is no monument to this brave man, quite the opposite. The ministers were embarrassed and made him pay the price for *their* wickedness. He was removed from the position of vice president, publicly chastised for breaking ranks, and politically isolated. But he had won nonetheless: the king henceforth found ways to stall the Nazis; the leader of the Bulgarian

Orthodox Church publicly defended the country's Jews; and even the most convinced anti-Semite in the Bulgarian government dared not advocate active cooperation with the Third Reich.

After the war, when the Communists took over Bulgaria, they rewrote the wartime history to give the Communist Party credit for saving the Jews. Pešev was sent to the Gulag, and his story was only rediscovered after the collapse of the Soviet Union.

Though this is a dramatic case, examples of this sort are not as rare as one might imagine, nor should they be. Pope John Paul II has traveled the entire world challenging tyrants and murderers of all sorts, speaking to millions of people, bringing them a simple, single message: "Be not afraid."

He preached this message to the people living under Communist tyranny in Poland, in Czechoslovakia, in Nicaragua and in China—"Be not afraid." He preached it to the Africans facing death from marauding tribes and murderous disease—"Be not afraid." And he preached it to us, warning us how easy it is to be trapped in a "culture of death" even in our comfortable, luxurious country—"Be not afraid."

Listen to the truths that lie within your hearts and be not afraid to follow them wherever they may lead. Those three little words hold the power to transform individuals and change the world. They supply the quiet resolve and unvoiced courage necessary to endure the inevitable intimidation.

Today we are not called upon to risk our lives against some monstrous tyranny. America is not a barbarous country. Our people are not oppressed and we face no pressing international threat to our way of life, such as the Soviet Union once posed. Though the war in which we are engaged is cultural, not civil, it tests whether this "nation: conceived in liberty . . . can long endure." President Lincoln's words do endure:

> It is for us, the living . . . to be here dedicated to the great task remaining before us—that from these honored dead we take increased devotion to the cause for which they gave the last full measure of devotion—that we here highly resolve that these dead shall not have died in vain—that this nation, under God, shall have a new birth of freedom—and that government of the people, by the people, for the people, shall not perish from the earth.

The Founders warned us that freedom requires constant vigilance and repeated action. It is said that when asked what sort of government the Founders had created, Benjamin Franklin replied that they had given us "a Republic, if you can keep it." Today, as in the past, we will need a brave "civic virtue," not a timid civility, to keep our republic. So, this evening, I leave you with the simple exhortation: "Be not afraid."

God bless you. [applause]

22.

RANDALL ROBINSON
(1942–)

"The Debt and the Reckoning"

University of Minnesota, Minneapolis, MN—May 2, 2002

Randall Robinson's widely read book *The Debt* argues that American blacks deserve monetary reparations from their government for the continuing psychic and economic injuries wrought by slavery. In his frequent speeches and media appearances, Robinson drives home the message: "At long last, let America contemplate the scope of its enduring human-rights wrong against the whole of a people."[1]

Robinson was born in the segregated capital of the Confederacy, Richmond, Virginia. His parents were schoolteachers, and his brother, Max, would become the first African American news anchor on national television. One of Robinson's boyhood buddies was the future black tennis champion Arthur Ashe. Robinson attended public schools, and earned a B.A. in sociology at Virginia Union University in 1967. He then attended Harvard Law School, where he took part in protests against South African apartheid.

After working for a social services agency, Robinson moved to Washington, D.C., where he worked as a congressional staffer and a civil rights lawyer. In 1977, he founded TransAfrica, a lobbying and research organization on African and Caribbean policy issues. Robinson was central in bringing the plight of blacks in South Africa and Haiti to American attention. In the 1980s, he helped coordinate a year-long protest at the South African embassy in Washington. Thousands of people protested peacefully and got arrested, including celebrities, politicians, and, repeatedly, Robinson. He later went on a twenty-seven-day hunger strike to draw attention to the Haitian refugee crisis. Both strategies succeeded in changing U.S. policy.

Robinson's call for slavery reparations has won strong support from some in the political left and from some African Americans (meanwhile, other activists and politicians have made similar, independent proposals). But the concept has also generated considerable criticism. Economist Glenn C. Loury called reparations a noble but mistaken idea, one that would allow Americans to wash their hands of slavery's legacy without directly facing the issue.[2]

Robinson has been lauded for his savvy and effective use of the media as "the chief weapon" in his activism.[3] Robinson is a compelling public speaker with extensive experience before crowds, cameras, and microphones. But he claims to hate the spotlight, describing himself as a "shy extrovert" who is uncomfortable in crowds and can't remember names. Robinson wrote in a 1998 memoir: "Were I not paid to do it, I would never again make a public speech. I loathe it. Not so much the speaking, but the time just before."[4]

The message he delivers on American racism is often blunt and harsh, one that can be uncomfortable for whites to hear. That's the point. But Robinson has also been praised for the "exquisite politeness" he employs while delivering intensely challenging news. "He's not a demagogue or a separatist. He urges people's morality to cross racial lines," according to civil rights historian Taylor Branch.[5]

An introspective student of human power and weakness, Robinson growls at the stupefying effect of the publicity platform he so regularly climbs atop to speak his views. He condemns the incessant media buzzing of politicians and experts, writing: "Damn the mesmerizers and the drug of oratory. Damn all of us who, lost in battle, obfuscate and distort. Damn the millions who believe dogmas without a clue as to why. Damn the demagogues who cast us all on the road to hell."[6]

———

I WANT TO TALK TONIGHT about the issues that join these two books, *The Debt* and *The Reckoning*, because I think we are in something of a crisis. Social crisis is so difficult to see, and what I think is a very complacent and essentially narcissistic society. You almost need to live outside of America to appreciate the depth of those two descriptions because we are so satisfied with ourselves in this country. We are, as well, a country essentially without memory, without any capacity to attribute, to ascribe, to remember, and thus, without any capacity or need to explain or to understand. And so our insights largely are very flat and banal as a society.

I was living, I had moved to St. Kitts in August and I didn't return to the U.S. for the first time since moving there until November. So I was out of the country when 9/11 happened and I had hoped that that tragic event might cause our country to ask a simple question, and one really expected it of journalists. And the question was *why?* [applause] What would cause any people, inasmuch as any of us are essentially alike in our needs and attitudes and basic humanity, what would cause any people to do so extreme a thing? Why? The question was never asked. Instead of taking a discussion in what might have been a constructive direction, I fear we have taken it in another unconstructive direction altogether.

African Americans should understand this terribly well. Many years ago, the great Southern author William Faulkner wrote that, "The past is never dead, it is not even past." It is impossible to understand the present without understanding the past. No society should ever, and particularly a democratic society, be afraid to explore the question, What happened? And what were the consequences? And what does the past have to do with any present condition?

When I wrote *The Reckoning*, I spent a great deal of time with young men who have lived the gangster life in New York City. And in many ways their experience is so typical of millions of young black men who people their generation. And I was embarrassed to learn that their experience was, in many ways, so foreign to me. It caused me to believe that the civil rights struggle benefited some of us, but it really was not to benefit all of us. With that, families like mine—stable, together, hopeful, expectant, demanding, having survived slavery and the 20th century miraculously more or less unscathed in their basic structure—were in a position to move up and out with the success of the civil rights movement. Failure for people like me would have been, not just difficult but, given my father's attitudes, dangerous. [laughter]

People like us take, sometimes, too much credit for Martin's success. It was so predictable, that given the conditions under which I grew up, that it would have been hard for me to fail colossally. The young men that I have been working with, who have described *their* lives to me, had no chance to succeed. None. One is embarrassed to discover that they are as able as you. They are perhaps even smarter than you. These young men who have sold drugs, dealt dope, defrauded, bopped people in the head and doing all of these things because every other road was closed to them, have turned their lives around, left with what could be called even the miracle of an incurable grammar. Meaning that there's some success they're never going to have. When they might have been microbiologists; they might have been physicists; they might have been a lot of things.

So our society is not a fair society. But I am saddened to understand that with the end of the civil rights movement, I believe that the black community cleaved into two parts. Some of us went up and out, the rest of us remained bottom-stuck since the Emancipation Proclamation. I feel further strongly that those of us who went up and out largely forgot about those who could not. And so it saddens me further to see that during the last presidential campaign, our leadership organizations invited national leaders to our meetings and we talked about things like racial profiling as if racial profiling were essentially about driving while black. We talked about that because that is the racial profiling that affects *all* blacks. But we did not talk about private prisons. We did not talk about the prison-industrial complex. We did not talk about the contemporary and modern slavery that is claiming the better part of the whole generation of our youth, the future of black men in America.

The state of New York, under the leadership of Governor Rockefeller, many years ago, a Republican liberal governor, passed the Rockefeller drug laws. I was a flat reader of news, I worked in the Congress, had a little booklet we used to pass out to you all when you came to Washington, *How Our Laws Are Made.* You'd come in the office and I'd give you the booklet, this is *How Our Laws Are Made;* if you believe that you'd believe anything. [laughter] You read your little newspapers and you see what was legislated and what was not. And I've come to learn in public policy work that you can understand nothing about public policy unless you can ask and answer the question, with every public policy decision, Who benefits? Unless you can puzzle out how to follow the money, it is never in the paper and it will never be explained to you. Rockefeller passes the Rockefeller drug laws, criminalizing virtually everything including non-violent drug offenses. Why would he do that? Because drugs are bad, unholy and un-Christian and not nice and people who do them should go to prison. But it created an enormous population of new criminals. Who were these people and where were you going to put them? Then Governor Cuomo began to build the prisons to house these people. The state of New York from the 1700s until 1980 built 33 prisons. From 1981 until 1999 it built 38 more.

There's a little town in upstate New York called Malone. Malone was a dying city. Malone [was] down on its heels, Malone reached its zenith with the trial of Dutch Schultz in the late 1930s. Those of you who are anywhere near my age would remember that Dutch Schultz was a crony of Al Capone. They moved the trial to Malone. For some strange reason Malone went into a nose-dive right after that trial. [It was] an all-white town, the Sears closed, the hotel closed, everything closed, town collapses. With the passage of the Rockefeller drug laws and Cuomo's prison-building juggernaut, Malone saw its chance. It applied for one of these prisons; it got two. With it Malone got 18 new holes for their golf course. They got 1,400 new jobs for the white citizens of Malone. They got a raise in their federal subsidy because they had more people. They got more power in the Congress because they had more constituents. But the political leaders of Malone didn't have to worry about the people who made it possible because they were inmates and they had lost their right to vote. The all-white city of Malone had been restored to economic health by an inmate population that was and is 84 percent black and Hispanic. It is happening across America. It is the new slavery.

Sometimes the hardest things to see are the things that are right in front of you. The reason we don't beat our heads against the wall on this is largely that it has little to do with me. That's somebody else's problem, "you commit a crime, you should do the time." Black people commit 12 percent of the non-violent drug offenses in America. But we comprise 35 percent of the arrests for non-violent offenses, 55 percent of convictions for non-violent offenses, 75 percent of prison admissions for non-violent offenses. A young white male has one chance in fifteen of being convicted of a crime in America, a young Hispanic male, one in ten, a young black male, one in three.

We loved Bill Clinton. No community loved him like ours. [laughter] It was the most *mystifying* thing to me. I really couldn't understand it. We were so bedeviled by symbolism: he could play the saxophone, he could sing the hymns in our churches without use of the hymnal, Lordy! [laughter] Bill Clinton added more people to the federal prison rolls than Bush and Reagan combined, and refused to remove the distinction between powder and crack-cocaine as a sentencing judgment and guideline. On so many scores, one is hard-put to find, with the exception of the appointment of federal judges and other people in the administration, anything that this president in eight years did for the black community. So we're complicit in our own dilemma without any good sense of what is happening to those people, as we speak tonight, being ground-up by our criminal justice system.

Now how does this all happen? And how does one come to call for reparations? I used to think, before I began to write this book, *The Debt,* that this business of reparations was really a radical notion indeed. It just shows you how little of my mind I had under my own control, because it's a relatively simple and straightforward proposition. When a government commits a crime against humanity, against sections of its own population, as a notion of international law, that government is responsible for making the victims whole. Nazi Germany committed a terrible crime for a period of 12 years in Europe before and during World War II. After the war, a democratic German government, not responsible for the crimes directly, but nonetheless a German government, understanding that there is no statute of limitations on the crimes that governments commit, a German government committed itself to reparations for the Jewish people. And we supported that. For we have said to Germany then and since that you must never forget your crime against humanity, you must never forget your past.

As recently as a year or so ago President Clinton named Stuart Eisenstadt, the Deputy Secretary of Treasury, to lead the American effort, with the support of the Congress, to compel 16 German corporations, Volkswagen included, that had used Jews as slave laborers to compensate them. The compensation ran upwards of $5 billion, with American support. Nobody at Volkswagen now, atoning, compensating, was *alive* when

Volkswagen did these awful things—but the corporation was alive. One is not talking about individual culpability. We're talking about the responsibility of a government to compensate a people. A better word to use is *repair* the damage, because that's what reparations means, for a crime that ran 346 years from the arrival at Jamestown of the first group of slaves until in 1965, at least until the Voting Rights Act was passed, before which African Americans could not be said to have accomplished full citizenship. See, with the Emancipation Proclamation we were simply told to "run along, run along." [laughter] No 40 acres, no mule, no nothing.

Now I'm going to get to the part of the material consequence. It's easy to line item what happened, what got built, how the value of the labor of this group was appropriated by another group that ran ahead in the race and now you find almost in every area of economic measure this enormous disparity that will never even itself without intervention and restitution. But you see there is a larger part of the crime that we seldom think about because the crime occurred over such along period of time and was so massive that we've been conditioned not to even begin to understand what happened to us. There is no worse crime you can commit against a people than to strip them of their memory of themselves. [applause]

I used to think when I was a child that history teachers taught history because they were just mean, sadistic people. [laughter] Teachers were old and old people just don't like young people. [laughter] I know how that feels because now that I'm old I don't like them either. [laughter] You know, because they're young! You know [they say] we have our lives to live, you've lived yours. I asked my mother, my mother's 88. I said, "Mother you feel old? You don't want to live anymore?" She said, "Boy I want to live as long as I can go on with this thing." You're never ready if you feel good, you know?

But I really misunderstood why our society invests so much in history. I'm not just talking about textbooks and courses. I'm talking about ephemeral literature. I'm talking about statuary. I'm talking about museums and parks. I'm talking about symbolism in all of this. You see, if you are caused to measure the significance of your life only between the date of your birth and the date of your death, disconnected from a past, blind to a future, unknowing of a continuum, you would have to measure your life as insignificant. But if you can stand knowledgeably before a tapestry of enormous achievement and connect yourself to it, even a hillbilly from

Idaho can feel *big*. History causes us to cohere as a society. It gives people a notion of their collective greatness. Once one is free in here, anything is possible. That's why I say if we got 11 billion dollars, trillion dollars tomorrow in reparations, but we could not fix ourselves in here, the money would do us no good. [applause] But if we can get well in here, even were we not to get a cent, just maybe we could do all right. You could knock down Hiroshima and Nagasaki, but as long as the victims can remember—remember their mores, remember their culture, remember their language, remember their religion, remember their history, remember who they are—they can put the buildings back up again.

But you see, slavery stripped us of everything. It took our languages, it took our religions, it took our mores. Culture is the matrix in which fragile human beings remain hopeful and on-marching. Without culture, you have nothing. Of course, we were caused to invent a culture. As Duke Ellington says, it's no accident that jazz is improvisational. [laughter] Because slavery caused us to *be,* in the remaking of ourselves, improvisational. But our country says to other countries, we say to the Turks, "What you did in 1915 and 1912 just can't be stood for." We say it to the Japanese in their treatment of Korean women during World War II. We've said it to a number of countries: you must face your past. When I was writing this book, Hazel told me, "I want you to walk down to the Capitol and I want you to walk into the Rotunda. When you get there, I want you to look up." This was in the summer. So I said, "Why do I have to go down there, I used to work down there?" I worked there for five years and you walk through there every day. I said, "Why do I have to do that?"

Now, I'm lying to you, I didn't say anything of the kind. [laughter] This is what I like to tell young men—you'll understand this—what young men can't understand, you can't *get it,* Mr. Hudleston, until you go past 40. [laughter] It's because of some male chemical imbalance or something, you can't get it. The secret to a happy marriage is very simple: just do what you're told. [laughter] But you won't listen to me. Your wife'll tell you, "Are we lost, darling, should we ask for directions?" You'll say, "No, I've got it." Better to be lost. [laughter]

But in any case, I went down to the Capitol. I took my little girl with me, who was 11 at a time, so that she could prove to my wife that I had been there. [laughter] We started walking on the Mall first. I had always seen the Mall as just a space. You never sort of figure out that the Mall is

America's first park. This is America's big ad to the world. This is where people from all over the world come to see symbolic America, symbolic democracy, symbolic freedom. So we were on the Mall, and Washington city is 60 percent black. And we were at the Vietnam War memorial and my daughter said, "I thought you said black people fought in Vietnam." I said, "Not only did we fight, we died disproportionately." She said, "Well why aren't there any black people at this Vietnam War memorial?" Then we walked over to where Lincoln sits on that stone chair and I saw a couple, they're from Idaho I think; [laughter] I can just tell you know. [laughter] They kind of had that Idaho air. And they were just leaning against each other. You know, they wore these vacation clothes that they will never, ever wear again in public. They're leaning and they're swaying and they're looking up at Lincoln transfixed and they're practicing what we ridicule elsewhere in the world: ancestor worship. Because he helps them to define their own greatness, their identification with him is complete. That's why our nation put him in the chair. That's why we build monuments.

So we started to walk the Mall, there must have been 6,000 people there that day. We decided, let's count the black people. We counted six black people! [laughter] There was one black man who was with a white woman; there was a black woman with a white man; there was a black schoolchild with a white school-class; there was me and my daughter; and one black we did not get a chance to interview, we don't know why he was there, his presence was not explained. [laughter] Sixty percent black and it dawned on me that we do not go to the Mall because there is nothing there that has anything to do with us. [applause]

The reason I'm making this point is not just as a moral matter and what is *right*. I don't want to sound religious on you, because people who are just right and only right invariably fail. But when you consider that in fewer than 60 years, blacks, Latinos, Asian Americans, Native Americans, will comprise the new American majority, and that we can't lock up everybody, and that we have a combustible situation in our country if we don't address it with vision. It is a sad thing to walk on the Mall from Lincoln to the Capitol and not see a statue, not a monument, not a museum, not a tablet, not a name of a single one of the 30 million Africans who died making their way into the American holocaust.

So I walked into the Rotunda, as Hazel told me to do, and I looked up, and on the dome is installed a painting, painted by Remedi, an Italian artist, and installed there as the Civil War was drawing to a close. It's called the *Apotheosis of George Washington*. It was painted to extol the virtues of our first President. In it, you see George Washington surrounded by 60 robed figures, in front of whom, you see the banner *e pluribus unum,* "out of many, one." But all 60 of the figures are white. Then you drop down to the hatband, a gray frieze running around the interior of the dome. You see this frieze depicting the stages of American history from the age of exploration to the dawn of aviation. No Douglass, no Truth, no Tubman. It is as if slavery never happened. Then you get down to ground level and you see these huge auricle sandstone blocks, into which are inserted these enormous paintings. The only person with even a suggestion of melanin is Pocahontas and she is only there, one thinks, because she is receiving the sacraments in a Christian English chapel.

But what you're not told is that the sandstone blocks of which the Capitol is constructed were mined in Stafford Country, Virginia, by slaves; brought up the Potomac River by slaves, they were put in place and fixed there with mortar mixed by slaves; the forest between the White House and the Capitol, cleared by slaves. Atop the Capitol there is a statue—ironically enough named Freedom—of an Indian maiden, cast in Bladensburg, Maryland, by slaves. Brought to the east grounds of the U.S. Capitol, reassembled, hoisted to the top of the dome by slaves. They were never paid. The early buildings of Georgetown University—erected by slaves, who were later sold by Jesuit priests to a plantation in Louisiana. You see we've repressed so much history, there's so much you don't know, and can't know. But it is beginning to come out now because we have provoked the discussion.

In 1967 I went to Harvard Law School. I was coming from Virginia Union University in Richmond, Virginia. I may have been the first Virginia Union graduate to go to Harvard Law School. I was scared and proud at the same time: scared that I would flunk out and you couldn't tell anybody that you were just bored, nobody was going to believe it. I was scared, but I was proud to be there. I remember having my briefcase and you got these decals, "Harvard" and *"Veritas"* on the decal. I must have had one on each side of my briefcase, swinging the thing high [laughter], oh yes. "You go to Harvard?" "Oh that, oh." [laughter] I was so happy about the thing. When you walk the halls, you just get the feeling of *oozing* money. You know, wainscoting and oil paintings of bewigged old white men on the walls and all this stuff—just money, old 1636 money. [laughter]

We all have the impression that if people are poor, they've always been poor; if people are rich, they've always been rich. Because Americans take a snapshot and they freeze everything in the present because they don't know any [better]. Martin Luther King said we've got a two-week memory as a nation. So nobody told me anything about the provenance of Harvard Law School. Harvard University has an endowment worth more than $19 billion. Was it always so? Well on that decal were three baskets of sugar-cane. The word *veritas*—truth!—under that, against a field of red, may have suggested blood. Harvard Law School was founded by a man named Isaac Royale, who endowed that place from the proceeds he had gotten from the sale of slaves on his Antiguan sugar plantation in 1865.

This nation had become powerful largely because cotton added more to the federal coffers in taxes than all other American exports combined. Everybody associated with the industry got rich. Slavery was not a Southern industry alone. It ran from Maine to Mississippi. The people who built the ships, the people who made the ropes to outfit the ships, the people who made the caulk to caulk the ships, the jobbers, the middle-people, all of it involved in an industry that made them wealthy because the employees were not *paid*. This gap between us and the rest, in 1865, was enormous. Lincoln calls Frederick Douglass and others to the White House to suggest a plan that would cause us all to return to Haiti or Liberia. It turned out to be unworkable. But although the Congress passed "40 acres and a mule," it never went anywhere—it was vetoed by President Andrew Johnson. So we were told to run along, illiterate and without prospect. You don't close that gap; you will *never* close that gap. It was not *intended* that you close that gap. [applause]

By 1910, 70 percent of the lynchings in the South were the lynchings of black businessmen. By the same time, the state of Georgia hadn't built a classroom for a black child. They were still going to school in the backs of churches. Until 1950, when I was a little boy, we had restrictive covenants—you couldn't buy homes. My parents were both college graduates. My father worked three jobs, he never made more than $9,000 a year. We were poor. We used to cage rats and drown them in the bathtub, run the water up to a high level to drown them in the morning. My father worked himself to death. My parents were talented, principled and decent people. They never talked about a will because they had nothing to will. The principle wealth-building tool for middle-class Americans is home ownership. It is estimated that because of red-lining and restrictive covenants, the loss to the black community per generation is over $30 billion. Berkeley did a study that showed that from 1929 to 1969, in wage discrimination alone, the consequence runs to $1.6 trillion. This gap doesn't close because it was not supposed to close. Like you're running a race, a 100-yard dash, you sound the gun for this group over here and they're off running. You tell this group, you have to stay back. When they hit the 50-yard mark, you take the gun and shoot these runners in the knee [laughter] and then you tell them, "Run along! You can make it; Oprah made it!" [laughter]

It is really very straightforward. It is not complicated. On the memory side, we've been doing this thing every year, in February. [laughter] Dick Gregory said they even gave us the month with some of the days missing. [laughter] The notion of Black History Month is ludicrous on its face, but it is so telling. You can't segregate history. The story of America is the story of America. It begins with the story of the first Americans—left untold. It involves the story of Hispanic Americans, who would explain to us why Texas, New Mexico and Arizona are not a part of Mexico. It goes to tell us the contributions of Asian Americans. And it involves, in some central wealth-building way, a significant, indispensable contribution of African Americans. To have Black History Month is tantamount to a confession that American history is a lie, and not wholly told. What is worst of all, is that it suggests that our history started with slavery. For those of us who hear it, they think that the story they hear is the only story there is to be told. I don't know how many seasons more I can weather how many things George Washington Carver did with that peanut. [laughter] And even that is trivialized! As we have trivialized King as a civil rights leader—and not a man who supported reparations and economic democracy, but who failed on those points because America wasn't ready for that. But Dr. Carver had so many applications for the peanut because he was looking for ways to put nitrogen back into the soil, to restore it. It saved Southern agriculture. But that was not the truncated version we got.

But the crime was much bigger than that. My mother used to tell me, she'd come into my room and she'd say, "Boy your room looks like the wreck of the *Hesperus*." And I'd say, "What the hell is the *Hesperus*?" We used to say a lot of stuff we didn't know what it meant. Everybody used to say, "From here to Timbuktu." What was Timbuktu? Nobody told me it was one of the greatest centers of learning and literature the world had known in the middle centuries. It was in Mali, West Africa, but nobody told me. We all know who Moses was. I knew who Moses was *in utero*. [laughter] Jews have been able to survive all of the hardships because they can remember 4,000 years back. That gives them strength and so they can go to Abraham and come forward to Moses. But what about Zipporah, the wife of Moses, who was Ethiopian and black. Nobody told me anything about that—and I *needed* to know that. I was told in college—a black school!—that civilization began in Greece. Now I knew I played basketball, but I shouldn't have been that stupid to think that civilization can begin somewhere. [laughter] Like there were two Greek guys a long time ago in downtown Athens, near the Acropolis before the Parthenon were put there, it's hot in August and they're bored and they say, "What can we do?" [laughter] One of them says to the other one, "I know, we can start a civilization!" [laughter] So on Monday you didn't have a civilization, on Tuesday it was in all of our classrooms at Virginia Union University.

Herodotus, the great Greek historian, wrote 500 years before the birth of Christ, that everything that ancient Greece was—its calendar, its division of the year into 12 parts, its language, its math, its science, its gods, its mythology, its practice of carving figures of stone, all of it, according to Herodotus, 500 years before the birth of Christ—had been derived from older civilizations to the south, the civilizations of Egypt and Ethiopia. But I didn't know anything about it, and I needed to know. But I was taught that George Washington and Thomas Jefferson, who started with Sally when she was 14, who never freed her—for if you cannot deny consent, you cannot give it, which makes him a rapist. But I was told that he was a great man and I had somehow to cobble my story from that.

There's no worse crime you could commit against a people than to strip them of their story of themselves. So I am hoping that as we approach a new America, a new demographic America, we can have a discussion not just about inclusiveness, from my point of view. But I was short-changed in my education, because I don't know enough about Hispanic Americans; I don't know enough about the first Americans, Native Americans, who contributed so much to our society, with their wonderful music and their culture of humanitarianism and sharing and their relationship to nature; I don't know enough about Asian Americans; I don't know enough about all of the parts that comprise this society. For we were all fitted with one story—and that can no longer work.

So it seems to me as I close the book that that is in large part what this debate is about. It is not essentially about money. It is about the restoration of a people who were distinguished and proud. It is about remembering an Africa before slavery, when Africa was grand. It's about knowing the Caribbean. It's about knowing what happened to Haiti as punishment for their successful revolution against Napoleon Bonaparte. It's about knowing what Thomas Jefferson did to cripple Haiti in a way that cripples it still. It's about knowing how Haiti made possible the Louisiana Purchase by weakening France, so that France was caused to sell it. It's about knowing who we are. I think the last sentence of that books says that, in the last analysis, if we accomplish nothing else from this discussion, from this struggle, from this conversation, from this self-examination, we will at least, in the last analysis, have discovered ourselves. Thank you. [applause]

23.

JULIAN BOND
(1940–)

"The Broken Promise of *Brown*"

*Miller Center of Public Affairs, University of Virginia,
Charlottesville, VA—June 5, 2004*

Julian Bond has defied expectations all his life. His father, the revered scholar Horace Mann Bond, once drank a champagne toast with his friend W.E.B. Du Bois to the three-year-old Julian. He decreed "in a tongue-in-cheek ceremony" that the boy "would follow in their prominent footsteps."[1] Bond has enjoyed an illustrious career, but not exactly in the path his father mapped.

In the winter of 1960, Julian Bond co-founded the Atlanta Committee on Appeal for Human Rights (COHAR), a nonviolent civil rights protest organization. The group set out to desegregate Atlanta's all-white lunch counters. On March 15, Bond—a student at Morehouse College—led a sit-in at the lunch counter in Atlanta's city hall cafeteria. He was arrested for the first and only time in his life, but in that moment an activist was born.

Over the Easter weekend of 1960, Bond and other student leaders met with Martin Luther King Jr. and formed what became a key protest group of the 1960s: the Student Nonviolent Coordinating Committee (SNCC). According to Bond, the Atlanta chapter was exceptionally well organized. "We had nearly $6,000 in the bank," he recalled, "and we had almost 4,000 people picketing in downtown Atlanta, a masterpiece of precision. Oh, man, we had waterproof picket signs and football parkas for the girls to wear to keep the spitballs off. Martin Luther King Jr. got arrested with us one time—and the lunch counters were integrated."[2]

Bond's political activism and work editing a newspaper he started with friends left him little time for college. He dropped out midway through his senior year at Morehouse to become SNCC's director of communications. In 1964, he launched his first political campaign, easily winning a seat in the Georgia legislature. But the Georgia House of Representatives tried to bar Bond from taking his seat in 1966, after he voiced public opposition to the Vietnam War.[3] He refused to rescind his statements and pressed his case all the way to the U.S. Supreme Court. On December 5, 1966, the Court ruled unanimously in his favor, finding that the Georgia House had violated Bond's right to free speech.[4]

Bond served in the Georgia House of Representatives until 1975; he was a member of the Georgia Senate from 1975 to 1987. As the decades unfolded, Bond's career took new directions. He narrated a PBS documentary series on the civil rights movement, *Eyes on the Prize,* hosted the public affairs program *America's Black Forum,* and wrote a nationally syndicated column called "Viewpoint." He also moved into his father's old domain: academia. In 1990, Bond began teaching history at the University of Virginia (he finished his B.A. at Morehouse in 1971) and has been a distinguished scholar in residence at American University for more than a decade. He has also chaired the board of directors of the NAACP since 1998.[5] In this speech, Bond surveys the history of American race relations in the latter half of the twentieth century, a history in which he himself played a crucial role.

WE'RE HERE, OF COURSE, because it was fifty years ago on May 17th, 1954, that the Supreme Court in *Brown v. Board* unanimously declared that segregated schools violated the Constitution's promise of equal protection. And two months later, on July 17th, construction began at Disneyland. Sadly, today much of *Brown's* promise is lost in fantasyland. The Magic Kingdom remains closed to many children of color across America.

But there can be no mistake—these fifty years have seen the fortunes of black America advance and retreat, and the decision is always cause for sober celebration, not for impotent dismay.

We celebrate the brilliant legal minds who were the architects; we celebrate the brave families who were its plaintiffs; and we celebrate the legal principle that remains *Brown's* enduring legacy—that, in the words of Chief Justice Earl Warren, "the doctrine of separate but equal has no place." That the quest for meaningful equality—political and economic equity—that that quest remains unfulfilled today is no indictment of past efforts. Instead it is testament to our challenge.

And as we commemorate this 50th anniversary, it is easy to cast a cynical eye on the status of school desegregation in America, or the sorry state of race relations—and it's easy to minimize the significance of *Brown.* That would be a grave mistake. Because *Brown,* by destroying segregation's legality, gave the nonviolent army the license to destroy segregation's morality as well. So it's no coincidence that this year we also celebrate the 40th anniversary of the passage of the Civil Rights Act of 1964, the most sweeping civil rights legislation passed before or since, and our democracy's finest hour.

Now, we look back on those ten years between *Brown* and the passage of the Civil Rights Act with some pride. In those years, *Brown's* anniversary became a celebratory signpost, as major events focused on commemorating the date. In Atlanta where I lived it was always an occasion where the NAACP would gather, and speeches would be made, and promises made about great things we'd do in the years ahead. The year after *Brown,* Rosa Parks sat down to stand up for her rights, and the Montgomery bus boycott began. Dr. King's first national address was at a 1957 Prayer Pilgrimage on the third anniversary of *Brown* at the Lincoln Memorial. Later that year the Little Rock Nine successfully integrated Central High School in Little Rock. Sit-ins at segregated lunch counters burst out across the South in 1960, followed by the Freedom Rides in 1961, timed to end in New Orleans on May 17th, 1961. And the forcible integration of Ole Miss in 1962.

In 1963 alone, the year that Dr. King, fresh from the battlefields of Birmingham, told the nation about his dream at the March on Washington, there were more than 10,000 anti-racist demonstrations. Now King of course was the most famous, the best known of the modern movement's personalities, but we ought to remember that this was a people's movement. It produced leaders of its own; and it relied not on the noted but on the nameless, not on the famous but on the faceless. It didn't wait for commands from afar to begin a campaign against injustice. It saw wrong and acted against it; it saw evil and it brought it down. Those were the days when women and men of all races and creeds worked together in the cause of civil rights. Those were the days when good music was popular and popular music was good. [laughter] Those were the days when the President picked the Supreme Court and not the other way around. [applause] Those were the days when we had a war on poverty, not a war on the poor. Those were the days when patriotism was a reason for open-eyed disobedience, and not an excuse for blind allegiance. Those were the days when much of the news media was "fair and balanced" and not just cheerleaders for the powerful. But none of those days were the "the good old days."

Then, the American social order was rigidly stratified and racially codified. Then, to quote John Hope Franklin, "the law, the courts, the schools, every institution . . . favored whites. This was white supremacy." Martin Luther King described those days in 1962. He said, "When you have seen vicious mobs lynch your mothers and fathers at will and drown your sisters and brothers at whim; when you have seen hate-filled policemen curse, kick and even kill your black brothers and sisters; when you see the vast majority of your twenty million Negro brothers smothering in an airtight cage of poverty in the midst of an affluent society; when you suddenly find your tongue twisted and your speech stammering as you seek to explain to your six-year-old daughter why she can't go to the public amusement park that has just been advertised on television, and see tears welling up in her eyes when she is told that Funtown is closed to colored children, and see ominous clouds of inferiority beginning to form in her little mental sky, and see her beginning to distort her personality by developing an unconscious bitterness toward white people; when you have to concoct an answer for a five-year-old son who is asking: 'Daddy, why do white people treat colored people so mean?' . . . when you are harried by day and haunted by night by the fact that you are a Negro, living constantly on tip-toe stance, never quite knowing what to expect next, when you are plagued with inner fears and outer resentments; when you are forever fighting a degenerating sense of 'nobodiness'—then," King concluded, "then you will understand."

And you'll understand then that most Southern Blacks could not vote. Most attended inadequate, segregated schools, if they went at all. Many went to school only a few months each year. Most could not hope to gain an education beyond high school. Most worked as farmers, or semi-skilled laborers. Few of them owned the land they farmed, or even the homes in which they lived.

This was a massive system of racial preferences, a vast affirmative action plan for whites—enforced by law and terror. It had one name and one aim—to crush the human development of a whole population. It began with slave catching in Africa, and it continues on 'til the present day. It's only by acknowledging the name, the nature, and the scope of this problem can we measure the magnitude of our success, or the cost of our failures.

Now the day *Brown* was decided, the NAACP held a news conference to announce an ambitious new agenda. To Thurgood Marshall, *Brown* was the Magna Carta of black America, a declaration of our rights. School segregation, he thought, would be eliminated within five years. He was right about the former, obviously wrong about the latter. Within a year, in *Brown II*, the Supreme Court allowed desegregation to proceed "with all deliberate speed." For the first time, the Court had declared a right and delayed its implementation. Three months after *Brown II*, Emmett Till, nearly my age, was murdered in Money, Mississippi, for whistling at a white woman. His death and the black newspapers that came into my Pennsylvania home created a great vulnerability and fear of all things Southern in my teenage mind. When my parents announced in 1957 we were relocating to Atlanta, I was filled with dread.

Till's death had terrified me. But in the fall of 1957, a group of black teenagers encouraged me to put that fear aside. These young people—the nine young women and men who integrated Central High School in Little Rock—set a high standard of grace and courage under fire as they dared the mobs who surrounded their school.

Here, I thought, is what I hope I can be, if ever the chance comes my way. The chance to test and prove myself did come my way in 1960, as it came to thousands of other black high school and college students across the South. First in the sit-ins, then the Freedom Rides, and then the voter registration and political organizing drives in the rural South, we joined an old movement against white supremacy that had deep, strong roots. For most of us, however, it was the recent *Brown* decision that had created the opportunity for young people to play active roles, to seize and share leadership in the movement for social justice.

Brown was the movement's greatest legal victory. It changed the legal status of black Americans, and ironically made challenges to the established movement's narrow reliance on legal action more possible. Richard Kluger has written: "Not until the Supreme Court acted in 1954 did the nation acknowledge it had been blaming the black man for what it had done to him. His sentence to second-class citizenship had been commuted; the quest for meaningful equality—equality in fact as well as in law—had begun."

No, I believe in an integrated America, in integrated jobs, homes and schools. I believe in it enough to have spent most of my life in its elusive pursuit. I think it is a legal, moral and political imperative for America—a matter of elemental justice, simple right waged against historical wrong. As Jack Greenberg, one of the attorneys in *Brown* (plaintiffs), put it: "The other side's brief talked about federalism, separation of powers, textualism. Our brief talked about right and wrong." And their brief talked about black and white. *Brown* was about black inequality, what Lyndon Johnson called "the one huge wrong of the American nation." The Supreme Court said nothing about Latinos until nineteen years after *Brown* and there never was any significant enforcement of desegregation for Latinos.

Today, "U.S. schools are becoming more segregated in all regions for both African-American and Latino students." By contrast, Asian students are the most integrated. Not only have I spent most of my life in the cause of integration, but in 1947, when I was seven years old, I was a plaintiff in a lawsuit in rural Pennsylvania against segregated schools. This suit never came to trial. The school board had segregated schools by giving students achievement tests, which all blacks failed and all whites passed, but when the two dumb sons of the local white political boss failed the test, they closed the black school, and all of Lincoln University Village's children went to a one-room school together.

Last year I visited Berea College in Kentucky, opened by abolitionists as an integrated school in 1855. It was closed by the Civil War, but opened again in 1866 with 187 students—96 blacks and 91 whites. It dared to provide a rare commodity in the former slave states: an education open to all, to blacks, to whites, to women and men. One of those early students was my grandfather. So like many others, I am the grandson of a slave. He was born in 1863, in Kentucky; freedom didn't come for him until the Thirteenth Amendment was ratified in 1865. He and his mother were property, like a horse or a chair. As a young girl, she had been given away as a wedding present to a new bride, and when that bride became pregnant, her husband, that's my great-grandmother's owner and master, exercised his right to take his wife's slave as his mistress. That union produced two children, one of them my grandfather.

At age 15, barely able to read or write, he hitched his tuition, a steer, to a rope and walked across Kentucky to Berea College and the college took him in. Now he belonged to a transcendent generation of black Americans, a generation born into slavery, a generation freed from servitude by the Civil War, a generation determined to make their way as free women and men. From Berea, he studied for the ministry, married, had six children—one of them my father, Horace Mann Bond.

My father graduated from Pennsylvania's Lincoln University, earned a doctorate in education from the University of Chicago. For him, too, education was a means to a larger end—the uplift of his people and the salvation of his race. How fitting, then, that he would be asked to help the NAACP in its legal campaign against school segregation.

When *Brown* came before the Supreme Court, both its presenters and the Justices who heard it understood clearly its historic potential. In an unusual, but not unheard of procedure, the case, actually four cases combined, from Kansas, South Carolina, Virginia, and Delaware, was argued first in the 1952 term and reargued the next. A fifth case, from Washington, D.C., was argued separately. Among other issues, the Court struggled with the meaning of the Fourteenth Amendment, that portion of the Constitution adopted after the Civil War, guaranteeing equal protection of the laws, as well as due process. In its earliest cases defining the Fourteenth Amendment, the Court had said this: "It ordains that no state shall deprive any person of life, liberty or property without due process of law, or deny to any person within its jurisdiction the equal protection of the laws." And this, "What is this but declaring that the law in the States shall be the same for the black as for the white; that all persons, whether colored or white, shall stand equal before the laws of the States, and, in regard for the colored race, in whose protection the amendment was primarily designed, that no discrimination shall be made against them by law because of their color?"

From this hopeful beginning there emerged, only a few years later, the disgraceful doctrine of "separate but equal" in *Plessy v. Ferguson*. In "laboring with the doctrine for over half a century" before *Brown*, the Supreme Court examined how "separate but equal" applied in a number of contexts, including education. But not until *Brown* was the continuing validity of the doctrine squarely presented. In scheduling *Brown* for re-argument, the Court asked the lawyers to prepare written responses to five questions, two of them dealing with the history of the Fourteenth Amendment and public education. The lawyers turned to historians and constitutional experts, including my father, for assistance.

So while C. Vann Woodward and John Hope Franklin were studying post-Reconstruction policies regarding race relations in the South, and Alfred Kelley and Howard J. Graham were working on the intent of the framers of the Fourteenth Amendment, my father was researching the intentions of the ratifying states with respect to school segregation. Now some scholars, like Henry Steele Commager, declined to help the NAACP in this work; they believed the facts would not support the NAACP's position. But my father knew that both the historical record and the political goals could be pursued without sacrificing either. In the end, the Court regarded the historical evidence as "inconclusive," or a "draw," which may have meant victory for the NAACP. It may have allowed the Court to overcome *Plessy*'s flat statement that the Congress condoned segregation. Free to look for guidance elsewhere, the Court was able to speak for what one historian has called "the American conscience."

And then, perhaps, having done the right thing by denouncing "separate but equal," the Court felt free to delay the implementation of what it had announced. Whatever the reason, the phrase "with all deliberate speed" was added to the lexicon of ignominious judicial pronouncements less than a year after one of the most shameful judicial doctrines had been discarded. The Court, a year after announcing the decision on the merits, ordered the nation to make haste slowly in desegregating the system of separate and unequal schools. The defendants were required, in a masterpiece of ambiguity, "to admit to public schools on a racially nondiscriminatory basis with all deliberate speed the parties in these cases." For the first ten years after *Brown*, the emphasis was more on "deliberate" than on "speed." The focus was on dismantling the dual school systems in the South, the products of *de jure* segregation, and in Southern accents, all deliberate speed meant any conceivable delay.

Actual desegregation was more a legal fiction than fact. President Eisenhower had lobbied Chief Justice Warren to rule for the Southern states for segregated schools; Eisenhower never endorsed the *Brown* decision, and the resistant white South, emboldened by his rectitude, reacted with evasion and delay. Their tactics included violence, expansion of private schools, state support to fleeing white students, proposals to abolish public education, repeal of compulsory attendance laws, and the long discarded theories of interposition and nullification. Prince Edward County, here in Virginia, simply closed its public schools for five years, believing that uneducated children were preferable to integrated ones. Where massive resistance failed, aggressive resistance succeeded. By the end of 1964, ten years after *Brown*, more than 97 percent of all Southern black children still attended segregated schools.

When the '64 Civil Rights Act was being debated and finally passed into law, most in the civil rights community concentrated on the public accommodations sections of the Act, on lunch counters, on restaurants, and on the provisions affecting employment discrimination. Overlooked, for many, were provisions of the Act dealing with education, and overlooked today is how important the Act could have been in making *Brown's* promise a reality.

When Congress was debating the '64 Civil Rights Act, in all of Alabama, only 29 black students attended formerly white schools, only 9 in South Carolina, and none in Mississippi. But the four years following the passage of the '64 Act represent the only period in the 50-year history of *Brown* when there was active support for desegregation from both the executive branch and the courts. For the first time, under a Southern President, Lyndon Johnson, the federal government began to take an active role. This period saw the percentage of black children in school with white ones more than quadruple, rising from 3 to 13 percent but still there were great costs. The integration process became a one-way street, as a few black students, fewer black teachers, and even fewer administrators, were admitted to formerly all-white schools. Thousands of black schoolteachers lost their jobs as black and white schools merged. Lost too was history—revered school names, mottoes, mascots, traditions, plaques, trophy cases, school colors, all of the artifacts that honored black achievement disappeared. Black students found themselves in formerly all-white school buildings that retained the character and identity of the segregated past— Booker T. Washington High School vanished; Robert E. Lee High School persevered.

In President Lyndon Johnson's last year in office, the federal government reviewed 28 communities for compliance with desegregation guidelines; in President Richard Nixon's first year, the figure dropped to 16. By the second year it stood at 15; the third year at 11; the fourth year at 9; the first year of his second term at 1, and by the next year, the number dropped to none. The years 1968 to 1973, however, represent the most active period of Supreme Court intervention on behalf of school desegregation. The court that 13 years earlier had been content to see desegregation proceed "with all deliberate speed" now ordered segregation removed "root and branch" in 1968. And to that end, it permitted busing in 1971.

Johnson's commitment to civil rights had sustained enforcement efforts in the South in the face of widespread white opposition. When Republicans captured the White House, the process was politicized, and the principle sanction available to enforce desegregation, cutting off federal funds, was renounced. Within months of Nixon's election, what was then known as the Department of Health, Education and Welfare (HEW) was under orders to end the threat of funding cut-offs as a prod to integration; enforcement was transferred from HEW to the Department of Justice, which under Attorney General John Mitchell argued in the Supreme Court for less desegregation, not more, establishing a pattern adopted by the Ford, Reagan, and Bush Administrations.

Nixon's HEW secretary took the extraordinary steps of writing to the Fifth Circuit Court of Appeals to say that desegregation plans formulated by his *own* department's experts from Mississippi would cause "chaos, confusion, and catastrophic educational setbacks." The Carter Administration attempted to revive fund cut-off enforcement. Cut-off action was begun in Kansas City. But the *only* limiting amendment adopted by Congress to the '64 Civil Rights Act was pushed and passed by liberal Democrats Thomas Eagleton of Missouri and Joseph Biden of Delaware, when schools in their home states faced desegregation efforts.

The Reagan Administration launched an attack on school desegregation. They invited school districts to reverse existing desegregation orders.

They intervened in court cases even where school boards had not requested it. They asked the Supreme Court to authorize tax exemptions for private segregated schools. They settled cases with remedies that had failed elsewhere. They eliminated the major desegregation aid program.

What distinguishes the administrations of Ronald Reagan and George H. W. Bush was their attacks on virtually all components affecting segregation and discrimination in American education. After passage of the '64 Civil Rights Act, the first President Bush, then a member of the U.S. House, told his fellow Texans, "The new Civil Rights Act was passed to protect 14 percent of the people. I'm worried about the other 86 percent."

The percentage of black students at majority white schools in the South went from zero in 1954 to a peak of 43.5 percent in 1988, proving there is nothing wrong with the premise of *Brown*. It is the promise of *Brown* that has been broken, betrayed by a failure of Presidential leadership, defeated by a lack of Congressional oversight and action, ruined by a retreat by the federal bureaucracy charged with enforcement, and crushed by a series of unfavorable court rulings, ranging from the adverse to the hostile. When William Rehnquist joined the Supreme Court, courtesy of Richard Nixon, all major desegregation cases since *Brown* had been unanimous. Now Rehnquist, as a clerk to Justice Jackson during the *Brown* case, had written a memo for his Justice arguing that the Court should uphold *Plessy v. Ferguson*. Then he lied about it in his confirmation hearing. And as a Justice himself, he cast the first dissenting vote in a post-*Brown* desegregation case in 1973, setting the stage for what would become a new anti-desegregation majority in the 1990s after he became Chief Justice.

So today we have a Chief Justice who has consistently opposed school desegregation and an Attorney General who built his political career on attacking the efforts of the federal courts to desegregate St. Louis and Kansas City schools. As Missouri's Attorney General and then as Governor, John Ashcroft continually attacked the federal courts managing school integration in his state, and when the courts found the state to be "the primary Constitutional violator," he fought to limit the state's contribution to the remedy that the court imposed. It is hardly a surprise, then, that when the current state of school integration is examined, discouraging results abound.

If in the years since *Brown* have not succeeded in dismantling segregated schools, those years have seen American preferences for segregated schools shrink. That constitutes modest achievement for black Americans. For us and for other minorities, separate has never been equal, not then, and not now.

There are few matters on which experts in any given field agree. Educational experts agree that no school district in America has managed to create equal education on a large scale in segregated schools, be they black or Hispanic. This is not to say that one-race schools are never successful. A few are—particularly on the elementary level. But the bottom line is that students who attend schools that are segregated by race and income consistently rank lower in educational achievement, especially at the secondary school level. In short, we can't afford separate schools. The damage done by racial segregation does not grow from the relationship between blacks and whites alone; it grows from the relationship between blacks and whites and green. In America, the education dollar follows the white child. The students most likely to find themselves in schools of concentrated poverty today are not white; they are black and Latino.

Compared with poor whites, poor blacks are more likely to live in neighborhoods where a high percentage of the residents are poor. They interact mainly with others who are poor, who share their disadvantage. They live, squeezed together, in less than standard housing, in neighborhoods denuded of essential services. They shop at stores owned by merchants geared to do business with a poor clientele. Their neighborhoods are economically and racially segregated, bereft of opportunity, out of sight and out of mind. Their children attend schools only with other poor, minority children. As the New Jersey Supreme Court has said, "They face, through no fault of their own, a life of poverty and isolation, most of us cannot begin to understand and appreciate."

Fewer dollars in the parents' pockets mean fewer dollars in the school board's treasury. Children in high-poverty schools read less, get lower grades, miss more days of school. Economic and racial integration are preconditions for equal opportunity. Once they're achieved, they permanently alter the pattern of minority-majority relationships. In cities where school integration does exist, it is not only the most visible form of desegregation, but the *only* one that impacts personally on the lives of millions of whites. That is why many whites have so strongly resisted it; it is also why blacks and other minorities must continue to insist on it.

I recently heard Minnie Jean Brown reflect on her experiences as one of the heroic Little Rock Nine who integrated Central High School in 1957. Someone asked her why she kept coming back to school day after day, despite daily harassment and intimidation that would have driven most people away. From the ferocity of her enemies, she said, "I knew there was something precious inside that school and I was more determined to get it than they were to keep it from my grasp." Now there are those who scoff at *Brown* as if the advantages to black children were simply to be gained by sitting next to white ones in a classroom, as if some kind of skin-to-skin transfer of knowledge and education could take place. These critics miss the point of integrated schools. They are, as one expert said, "truly radical." A public education system that is fully integrated, that treats minorities and whites equally, is the antithesis of the larger society, which is profoundly segregated and unequal. The goals of putting minorities and whites in the same classroom is not only to equalize education, but also to change the formative racial experiences of the next generation.

Today minority children face inequalities in school spending, and even more. They face what Jonathan Kozol calls "punitive testing and accountability agendas" imposed by the No Child Left Behind Act. Schools have adopted a "grill and drill curriculum" that substitutes learning by rote and teaching to the test for the transmission of critical thinking from teacher to pupil.

Our schools present two faces to American society. In one face, they are our most important democratic institution. They're pathways to class mobility and generational progress, and their success or failure impacts the lives and prospects of millions of families and children every day. The other face is an instrument for reproducing the class and race privilege of the larger society, reinforcing the very inequality they are designed to overcome. On our present course, we are formalizing two school systems: one filled with middle-class children, most of them white, and one filled with low-income minorities. For too many, the latter schools have also become a conveyor belt to prison.

Our future as a nation depends on our willingness to continue to reach into the racial cleavage that defines American society and to change the racial contours of our world. In 1954, the federal government's brief in *Brown* argued that school desegregation was a Cold War imperative, a necessary weapon to win America's battles overseas. Current events give us the same imperative, to prove to enemy and to ally alike that our commitment to justice is sincere. Despite progress, school segregation, unequal education are issues everywhere, issues here in the commonwealth of Virginia. African American students are less than a third of the public school population here, but they're half of all students suspended, and one third of those in special education. White students in Virginia are 10 times more likely than their African American counterparts to be placed in gifted and talented programs. White students in Virginia outperform African Americans by 20 percentage points in reading and math. Virginia spends twice as much money to keep her citizens in jail for a year than it costs to send a student to the University of Virginia.

What, then, is to be done? Do we continue to slide backward, back toward *Plessy* and segregation, or can we make *Brown*'s promise at last come true? Those brave Americans who fought and won *Brown* fifty years ago faced obstacles we cannot imagine, and had few resources, little public support with which to do the job. We can do no less.

This fall, we have an opportunity to elect a pro-*Brown* president and a pro-*Brown* Congress that will appoint judges and enforcement officials who understand the Supreme Court was right then and the job is far from over. We can revive the federal aid programs of the Nixon and Carter Administrations. Programs that helped multiracial schools deal positively with issues of race relations, multicultural curricula, more effective classroom operation. We can recruit young people, especially young people of color, into the education profession, ensure they receive full and fair employment opportunities from all school districts, not just minority schools.

We can mount a real fight against housing segregation, ensure minority parents and their children have access to middle-class schools. We can use choice programs, public magnet, public charter schools, if they are enacted in a strict pro-integration mode, forbidding transfers that increase segregation and rewarding those that diminish it. We can amend the No Child Left Behind Act, and provide financial incentives and positive recognition to segregated suburbs that accept significant numbers of minority students from failing schools.

When my grandfather graduated from Berea, he was asked to give the commencement address. He said then: "The pessimist from his corner looks out on the world of wickedness and sin, and blinded to all that is good or hopeful in the condition and progress of the human race, bewails the present state of affairs and predicts woeful things for the future. In every cloud he beholds a destructive storm, in every flash of lightning an omen of evil and in every shadow that falls across his path a lurking foe. But he forgets that the clouds also bring life and hope, that the lightning purifies the atmosphere, that shadow and darkness prepare for sunshine and growth, and that hardships and adversity nerve the race, as the individual, for greater efforts and grander victories."

"Greater efforts, grander victories." That was the promise made by the generation born in slavery a century and a half ago. That was the promise made by the generation that won the great World War for democracy six decades ago. That was the promise made by the generation that brought democracy to America's darkest corners four decades ago, and that is the promise we must all seek to honor today. [applause]

NOTES

PREFACE

1. Andre Millard, *America on Record: A History of Recorded Sound* (New York: Cambridge University Press, 1995), 258–84.
2. David Morton, *Off the Record: The Technology and Culture of Sound Recording in America* (New Brunswick, NJ: Rutgers University Press, 2000), 11–12.

INTRODUCTION

1. Ethel M. Albert, "Rhetoric, Logic, and Poetics in Burundi: Cultural Patterning of Speech Behavior," *American Anthropologist,* pt.2, 66 (December 1964), 35. Quoted in Philip S. Foner and Robert James Branham, *Lift Every Voice: African American Oratory, 1787–1900,* (Tuscaloosa, AL: The University of Alabama Press, 1998), 1.
2. John W. Blassingame, John R. McKivingan, and Peter P. Hinks, eds., *The Frederick Douglass Papers,* series 2, volume 2 (New Haven: Yale University Press, 2003), 91.

3. James Oliver Horton and Lois E. Horton, *Black Bostonians: Family Life and Community Struggle in the Antebellum North* (New York: Homes and Meier Publishers, Inc., 1979, 2nd edition 1999), 32.

1. BOOKER T. WASHINGTON

1. Louis Harlan, *Booker T. Washington, The Making of a Black Leader* (New York: Oxford University Press, 1974), 220.
2. David Levering Lewis, *W.E.B. Du Bois, Biography of a Race* (New York: Henry Holt and Company, 1993), 174.
3. Tim Brooks, *Lost Sounds: Blacks and the Birth of the Recording Industry* (Urbana: University of Illinois Press, 2004), 503.

2. MARCUS GARVEY

1. E. David Cronon, *Black Moses: The Story of Marcus Garvey and the Universal Negro Improvement Association* (Madison: University of Wisconsin Press, 1969), 12.
2. Lawrence W. Levine, "Marcus Garvey and the Politics of Revitalization," in *Black Leaders of the 20th Century,* ed. John Hope Franklin and August Meier (Urbana: University of Illinois Press, 1982), 119.
3. Ibid., 120.
4. UCLA Marcus Garvey papers, http://www.isop.ucla.edu/africa/mgpp/sound.asp.
5. Andre Millard, *America on Record*, 262.
6. Ibid., 193–95; 203.

3. MARY MCLEOD BETHUNE

1. *Mary McLeod Bethune,* interview by Charles S. Johnson, Florida Memory Project, www.floridamemory.com/onlineclassroom/Mary Bethune/interview.cfm, 1.
2. Ibid., 1.
3. Ibid., 1.

4. Blanche Wiesen Cook, *Eleanor Roosevelt: The Defining Years, Volume Two, 1933–1938* (New York: Penguin Books, 1999), 159–61.

5. Ibid., 90. B. Joyce Ross, "Mary McLeod Bethune and the National Youth Administration: A Case Study of Power Relationships in the Black Cabinet of Franklin D. Roosevelt," in *Black Leaders*, 191–219.

4. WALTER WHITE

1. Adam Fairclough, *Better Day Coming: Blacks and Equality, 1890–2000* (New York: Penguin Books, 2001), 85.

2. Kenneth Robert Janken, *White: The Biography of Walter White, Mr. NAACP* (New York: The New Press, 2003), 2.

3. Ibid., xiii–xiv.

4. Blanche Wiesen Cook, *Eleanor Roosevelt: Volume 2*, 181.

5. Fairclough, *Better Day Coming*, 208.

6. Barbara Dianne Savage, *Broadcasting Freedom: Radio, War, and the Politics of Race, 1938–1948* (Chapel Hill: University of North Carolina Press, 1999), 224.

5. CHARLES HAMILTON HOUSTON

1. Genna Rae McNeil, "Charles Hamilton Houston: Social Engineer for Civil Rights," in *Black Leaders*, 222.

2. "The Reminiscences of Thurgood Marshall" (Columbia University Oral History Research Office, 1977), in *Thurgood Marshall: His Speeches, Writings, Arguments, Opinions and Reminiscences*, ed. Mark V. Tushnet (Chicago: Lawrence Hill Books, 2001), 423.

3. McNeil, "Charles Hamilton Houston," 227.

4. Genna Rae McNeil, *Groundwork: Charles Hamilton Houston and the Struggle for Civil Rights* (Philadelphia: University of Pennsylvania Press, 1983).

5. Ibid.

6. Thurgood Marshall

1. "The Reminiscences of Thurgood Marshall," in *Thurgood Marshall*, 413–17.
2. David Wilkins, interview by Kate Ellis and Stephen Smith, April 16, 2004.
3. The NAACP hired Marshall in 1936. In 1940, the organization formed the Legal Defense and Educational Fund to ensure that money donated for legal cases remained tax deductible. Until 1957, the NAACP and LDF shared staff, space, and other resources. That year Thurgood Marshall negotiated the LDF's complete split from the NAACP. The two became entirely separate organizations.

7. Howard Thurman

1. Walter Earl Fluker and Catherine Tumber, *Strange Freedom: The Best of Howard Thurman on Religious Experience and Public Life* (Boston: Beacon Press, 1998), 6.
2. Ibid., 10.
3. Albert J. Raboteau, *Canaan Land: A Religious History of African Americans* (New York: Oxford University Press, 2001), 107.
4. Fluker and Tumber, *Strange Freedom*, 3–4.
5. Ibid., 6.
6. U.S. National Archives and Records Administration, "Shedding Light on Efforts to Promote Religious, Racial, and Class Harmony: The Howard Thurman Papers Project," in *Annotation* 26:2 (June 1998).

8. Dick Gregory

1. Taylor Branch, *Parting the Waters: America in the King Years 1954–63* (New York: Simon and Schuster, 1988), 711; 756–802.
2. Delores Nicholson, *Notable Black American Men* (Farmington Hills, MI: Gale Research, 1999), 1025–27.
3. Branch, *Parting the Waters*, 808–11.

9. Fannie Lou Hamer

1. Sina Dubovoy, *Civil Rights Leaders: American Profiles* (New York: Facts on File Books, 1997), 101.
2. Ibid., 101–12.
3. Jerry DeMuth, "Tired of Being Sick and Tired," *Nation,* 1 June 1964. Reprinted in *Reporting Civil Rights: Part II: American Journalism 1963–1973* (New York: Penguin, 2003), 99–106.
4. Clayborne Carson, *In Struggle: SNCC and the Black Awakening of the 1960s* (Cambridge: Harvard University Press, 1981), 124–25.
5. Dubovoy, *Civil Rights Leaders,* 108.

10. Stokely Carmichael

1. Adam Fairclough, *Better Day Coming,* 311–13; Michael T. Kaufman "Stokely Carmichael, Rights Leader Who Coined 'Black Power' dies at 57," *New York Times,* 16 November 1998.
2. Fairclough, *Better Day Coming,* 312–13.
3. James Oliver Horton and Louise E. Horton, *Hard Road to Freedom: The Story of African America* (New Brunswick, NJ: Rutgers University Press, 2001), 306–7.
4. John Lewis, "Odyssey of a Passionate Radical," *Newsweek,* 30 November 1998.
5. Stokely Carmichael and Charles V. Hamilton, *Black Power: The Politics of Liberation in America* (New York: Vintage, 1967), 50.
6. Kaufman, "Stokely Carmichael"; Lewis, "Odyssey."
7. Patrick Rogers and Ron Arias, "A Panther in Winter," *People,* 22 April 1996.
8. Cicero, Illinois.
9. Grenada, Mississippi.

11. MARTIN LUTHER KING JR.

1. Andrew Young, "Introduction to 'I've Been to the Mountaintop,'" in *A Call to Conscience: The Landmark Speeches of Dr. Martin Luther King, Jr.,* ed. Clayborne Carson and Kris Shepard (New York: Warner Books, 2001), 201–5.
2. David J. Garrow, *Bearing the Cross: Martin Luther King, Jr., and the Southern Christian Leadership Conference* (New York: William Morrow and Co., 1986), 620; Young, "Introduction," 204.
3. Young, "Introduction," 204.
4. Earl Caldwell, "Martin Luther King Is Slain in Memphis," *New York Times,* 5 April 1968, reprinted in *Reporting Civil Rights,* 645–50; Garrow, *Bearing the Cross,* 623.
5. Sina Dubovoy, *Civil Rights Leaders,* 113–29.

12. JOHN HOPE FRANKLIN

1. John Hope Franklin, *A Life of Learning, ACLS Occasional Paper, No. 4* (New York: American Council of Learned Societies, 1988), 14.
2. Ibid., 1–5.
3. *Notable Black American Men,* ed. Jessie Carney Smith (Farmington Hills, MI: Gale Research, 1999), 420–27.
4. Peter T. Applebome, "Keeping Tabs on Jim Crow; John Hope Franklin," *New York Times,* 23 April 1995.

13. SHIRLEY CHISHOLM

1. Shirley Chisholm, *The Good Fight* (New York: Harper and Row, 1973), 162.
2. Ibid., 71.
3. Horton and Horton, *Hard Road to Freedom,* 329–30.
4. Michael C. Dawson, *Black Visions: The Roots of Contemporary African American Political Ideologies* (Chicago: University of Chicago Press, 2001), 146.

14. Barbara Jordan

1. Franics X. Clines, "Barbara Jordan Dies at 59; Her Voice Stirred the Nation," *New York Times*, 18 January 1996; Sandy Grady, "Magnificent Voice Stilled at Last," *Philadelphia Daily News*, 23 January 1996.
2. Molly Ivins, "Barbara Jordan, Closing the Gap in Perception," *Los Angeles Times*, 8 September 1991.
3. Mary Beth Rogers, *Barbara Jordan: American Hero* (New York: Bantam Books, 1998), 68–71.
4. Barbara Jordan and Shelby Hearon, *Barbara Jordan: A Self Portrait* (Garden City, NY: Doubleday, 1979), 184.
5. Ibid., 185–86.
6. Ibid., 193.
7. Grady, "Magnificent Voice Stilled at Last."

15. Benjamin L. Hooks

1. Mark Kram, "Benjamin L. Hooks," *Contemporary Black Biography, V2.* (Detroit: Gale Research 1992), 122.
2. Patricia A. Pearson, "Benjamin L. Hooks," *Notable Black American Men*, 565–68.
3. Peter Applebome, "Spirited Farewell: Benjamin Hooks Chides Bush and Defends N.A.A.C.P.," *New York Times*, 13 July 1992.

16. Joseph Lowery

1. Fran Locher Freiman, "Joseph E. Lowery," *Contemporary Black Biography 2*, 142–44.
2. David J. Garrow, *The FBI and Martin Luther King, Jr.* (New York: W. W. Norton, 1981), 132–34.
3. "Joseph Lowery Consents to Stay On as SCLC President for at Least 90 More Days," *Jet*, 18 August 1997.

17. Louis Farrakhan

1. Henry Louis Gates Jr., "The Charmer," in *The Farrakhan Factor: African-American Writers on Leadership, Nationhood, and Minister Louis Farrakhan,* ed. Amy Alexander. (New York: Grove Press, 1998), 26.
2. Ibid., 28.
3. Simon Glickman, "Louis Farrakhan," *Contemporary Black Biography 2* (1992): 70–74.
4. Phil Gailey, "Farrakhan Is Given a Forum for His Views at Press Club," *New York Times,* 31 July 1984.
5. Fay S. Joyce, "Jackson Criticizes Remarks Made by Farrakhan as 'Reprehensible,' " *New York Times,* 29 June 1984.
6. Drew Von Bergen, United Press International, 31 July 1984.
7. *Washington Post,* editorial, 1 August 1984.
8. Tamar Jacoby, "Day of the Race Men; Crisis in Black Leadership," *Commentary* 103:4 (April 1997): 36.
9. Gates, "The Charmer," 42.
10. Randall Robinson, *Defending the Spirit: A Black Life in America* (New York: Dutton, 1998), 263.

18. Jesse Jackson

1. Joyce Purnick and Michael Oreskes, "Jesse Jackson Aims for the Mainstream," *New York Times,* 29 November 1987.
2. William F. Buckley Jr., "Yale's Capitalist Swine," *National Review,* 29 September 2003.
3. Bryan Ryan and Jennifer M. York, "Jesse Jackson," *Contemporary Black Biography* 27 (2001) 1:90–94.
4. Purnick and Oreskes, "Jesse Jackson."

19. Johnetta B. Cole

1. Allison O. Adams, "Johnetta Cole: Challenging the Status Quo," *Emory Magazine,* Spring 1998.

2. Johnetta B. Cole, *Conversations: Straight Talk with America's Sister President* (New York: Doubleday, 1993), 11.
3. *Tavis Smiley Show,* National Public Radio, 17 September 2003.

20. Lani Guinier

1. Lani Guinier, *Lift Every Voice: Turning a Civil Rights Setback into a New Vision of Social Justice* (New York: Simon & Schuster, 1998), 37.
2. Ibid., 126.
3. Lani Guinier, "Who's Afraid of Lani Guinier?" *New York Times Magazine,* 27 February 1994.
4. Ondine E. Le Blanc, "Lani Guinier," *Contemporary Black Biography* 7:108 (1994):107–12.

21. Clarence Thomas

1. Prepared Statement of Judge Clarence Thomas to the Senate Judiciary Committee, 11 October 1991.
2. Simon Glickman, "Clarence Thomas," *Contemporary Black Biography* 2, 231–37; Scott Douglas Gerber, *First Principles: The Jurisprudence of Clarence Thomas* (New York: New York University Press, 1999), 11–13.
3. Clarence Thomas, "No Room at the Inn," *Policy Review* 58 (1991): 72–79.
4. Kevin Merida and Michael A. Fletcher, "Supreme Discomfort," *Washington Post Magazine,* 4 August 2002.
5. Gerber, *First Principles,* 13.
6. Juan Williams, "EEOC Chairman Blasts Black Leaders," *Washington Post,* 25 October 1984.

22. Randall Robinson

1. Randall Robinson, *The Debt: What America Owes to Blacks* (New York: Dutton, 2000), 9.
2. Glenn C. Loury, "It's Futile to Put a Price on Slavery," *New York Times,* 29 May 2000.
3. Rob Hiaasen, "The Activist with a Passion for Foreign Policy," *Baltimore Sun,* 20 September 1994.
4. Randall Robinson, *Defending the Spirit,* 244.
5. Bob Herbert, "In America; the Spirit of Randall Robinson," *New York Times,* 22 January 1998; Hiaasen, "The Activist."
6. Robinson, *Defending the Spirit,* 223.

23. Julian Bond

1. Megan Rubiner and Candace LaBelle, "Julian Bond," *Contemporary Black Biography* 35 (2002), 12–17.
2. Nagueyalti Warren, *Black Heroes of the 20th Century* (Detroit: Visible Ink Press, 1998), 74.
3. Adam Fairclough, *Better Day Coming,* 314; Clayborne Carson, *In Struggle,* 189–90.
4. Rubiner and LaBelle, "Julian Bond," 12–17.
5. Warren, *Black Heroes,* 78.

PERMISSIONS

Mary McLeod Bethune, "What Does American Democracy Mean to Me?" 1939. Courtesy Bethune-Cookman College, Daytona Beach, FL.

Walter White, Speech at NAACP Convention, 1947. Courtesy Jane White Viazzi.

Charles Hamilton Houston, Personal Recording, 1949. Courtesy Charles Hamilton Houston Jr.

Howard Thurman, "Community and the Self," 1961. Courtesy Olive Wong.

Dick Gregory, Speech at St. John's Baptist Church, 1963. Courtesy Dick Gregory.

Fannie Lou Hamer, Testimony Before the Credentials Committee, Democratic National Convention, 1964. Courtesy Vergie Hamer Faulkner.

Stokely Carmichael, Speech at University of California, Berkeley, 1966. Courtesy Mabel Carmichael.

Martin Luther King Jr., "I've Been to the Mountaintop," speech of April 3, 1968. Used with permission under license granted byb Intellectual Properties Management, Atlanta, Georgia, as Manager of the Estate of Martin Luther King Jr.

John Hope Franklin, Lecture at The New School for Social Research, 1969. Courtesy John Hope Franklin.

Shirley Chisholm, "The Black Woman in Contemporary America," 1974. Courtesy Shirley Chisholm.

Barbara Jordan, Statement at the U.S. House Judiciary Committee Impeachment Hearings, 1974. Courtesy the Estate of Barbara Jordan.

Benjamin L. Hooks, Speech at Gustavus Adolphus College, 1978. Courtesy Benjamin L. Hooks.

Joseph Lowery, "The Black Presence in America," 1980. Courtesy Joseph Lowery.

Louis Farrakhan, Address to the National Press Club, 1984. Courtesy Louis Farrakhan.

Jesse Jackson, "Keep Hope Alive," 1988. Courtesy Jesse Jackson.

Johnetta B. Cole, "Defending Our Name," 1994. Courtesy Johnetta B. Cole.

Lani Guinier, "Different Voices, Common Talk: Why We Need a National Conversation About Race," 1994. Courtesy Lani Guinier.

Randall Robinson, "The Debt and the Reckoning," 2002. Courtesy Randall Robinson.

Julian Bond, "The Broken Promise of *Brown*," 2004. Courtesy Julian Bond.